# THE ETERNAL SELF AND THE CYCLE OF SAṂSĀRA

## INTRODUCTION TO ASIAN MYTHOLOGY AND RELIGION

FOURTH EDITION

**RAJESHWARI VIJAY PANDHARIPANDE**

Cover photo courtesy of www.lotussculpture.com.



Printed in the United States of America

10 9 8 7 6 5 4

ISBN 0-536-95866-1

2005440010

BU/LS

Please visit our web site at *www.pearsoncustom.com*

PEARSON CUSTOM PUBLISHING
75 Arlington Street, Suite 300, Boston, MA 02116
A Pearson Education Company

TO ALL PAST, PRESENT, AND FUTURE STUDENTS OF
"ASIAN MYTHOLOGY"

# CONTENTS

# PREFACE

This book grew out of the course on Asian Mythology which I have been teaching at the campus of the University of Illinois at Urbana-Champaign since 1984. In this book (as well as in the course) the main focus is on Indian mythology and religion and also on Buddhism, which started in India (serving as the bridge between Indian, Chinese, and Japanese mythologies and religions).

I must clarify here that I do not claim or imply that the Chinese and Japanese traditions are secondary to or less important than the Indian—or, for that matter, to any other traditions. The main focus is on Indian mythology and religion because it grew and developed over centuries in almost total isolation. As opposed to this, the Chinese and the Japanese systems (and many other Asian traditions as well) have been so deeply influenced by Buddhism that any serious study of them is bound to be incomplete without knowledge of the mythological, religious and philosophical background of Buddhism in India. Thus, by knowing the Indian system of mythology and religion (which includes Buddhism) thoroughly, one will not find oneself on completely unfamiliar ground while studying the Chinese and the Japanese mythologies and religions; and in the study of the Chinese and the Japanese mythologies and religions one may not be able to go very far without understanding the Indian (i.e., mainly Buddhist) mythology and religion.

One of the main reasons I have written the present book was the lack of any other text which blended together the relevant concepts of religion and philosophy for the study of mythology. In my opinion, without an accompanying discussion of the underlying philosophy, mythology can become trivial—a collection of interesting fairytales, but no more than that. Without discussion of the religious framework, the study of mythology becomes uprooted and unnaturally separated from its context, people, and culture and thereby subject to various kinds of misleading interpretations.

Thus, the present book tries for the first time, to present a comprehensive and systematic overview of the Indian, Chinese, and Japanese mythologies and religions in one place. It is hoped that the readers will be exposed to or make themselves familiar with the oriental thought/world view in general and to the mythologies and religion of these three main traditions in particular. In this book I have selected and discussed representative and salient myths from these three traditions and have tried to show the underlying rationale which not only makes the people of these three countries accept them as their cultural heritage but also unconsciously shapes their conceptualizations of the "self" and the universe in which they live. I have tried my best to keep the level and tone of discussion as clear and rational as possible, at the same time avoiding the danger of either unnecessarily inflating or trivializing the topic at hand. Hence, I hope that this book will be useful not only as an introductory textbook on Asian mythology and religion, but also to anyone who is either about to begin his/her study of Asian mythology or who, having begun his study, feels lost in the forest of apparently unrelated myths and their innumerable conflicting interpretations.

I have included a list of selected readings for each chapter in the book for those who want to pursue further the study of Asian mythology.

Finally, a word about the title of the book. The title "Eternal Self and the Cycle of Saṃsāra" abstracts perhaps the most prominent similarity in the Indian, Chinese and Japanese mythological traditions regarding the notions of human identity. All these traditions believe that there is a non-phenomenal (non-objective) identity on which is superimposed the phenomenal (objective) self (i.e., body and mind)—the latter is transitory and cyclic and everybody is effortlessly and intuitively aware of it, the former is eternal and in most cases, one has to make tremendous efforts to rediscover it. In these traditions this research and rediscovery (of the self) serves as one of the most important fundamental beliefs for organizing, defining, and evaluating human life in this world and at this point in time.

August 2, 1990 Rajeshwari Vijay Pandharipande
*Srāvanī Suklā ekādasī, Śake 1912* Urbana, Illinois

# ACKNOWLEDGEMENTS

Like the River Ganges, this "river" owes its existence in the present form to many of its "tributaries." First of all, I wish to thank all the students of Asian Mythology who were in the course (Religious Studies/Asian Studies 104) in different "cycles," (and to whom I have dedicated this book) for providing me with an opportunity for making concrete the initially nebulous idea of "Asian Mythology." The popularity of the course (each semester about 350 students enroll in the course) at the campus of the University of Illinois at Urbana-Champaign is a tribute to their quest for the unknown, which they, as students, also pursue individually in their various major fields of interest.

I cannot thank enough my teachers, Mr. K. B. Bhave, Prof. B. R. Ashtikar, and Prof. G. T. Deshpande, who initiated me into the study of mythology, religion, and philosophy. It was the training I received from them which enabled me to continue to do research in this field.

I would also like to thank all the Teaching Assistants (Sophia Changjan, Joanne Chou, Jean D'souza, Steve Heinrich, Shamsul Huda, Swati Lal, Wakako Kusumoto, Wen-Ying Lu, Mithilesh Mishra, Sarina Paranjape, Kayla Pennington, Shari Thurow, Tamara Valentine, and Albert Watanabe) who have been involved in teaching the course with me at different times. The effort which they put into teaching this class and the insightful discussions which I had with them have been very helpful in putting together the material for the book. My special thanks are due to Ms. Wen-Ying Lu for helping me render and interpret the myths from the original Chinese texts into English. Similarly I acknowledge with gratitude Ms. Wakako Kusumoto's help with the Japanese material. My sincere thanks are due to Mr. Mithilesh Mishra for his logistic support from proofreading to getting the manuscript mailed to the publisher which involved coordinating numerous aspects of the work, and also for his discussions which forced me to present and describe some of the intuitively understood "mystical concepts" in the mythologies and religions in as much rational light as possible (given the imperfect and imprecise nature of language).

To the editor of this book, Dr. Karen Dudas, I owe a special word of thanks. It was my good fortune to have the manuscript read by such a competent, understanding, and kind editor. If the book reads well, the credit in no small measure is hers.

I am thankful to Ms. Patricia Gallagher for having typed the entire text of this book. I want to specially thank her for putting up with my constant (at times unreasonable) requests to hurry up the process, with affectionate patience and kindness. Her accuracy in typing in the face of so many foreign words in Sanskrit, Chinese and Japanese, with different kinds of diacritics was extremely impressive.

My family—my husband Vijay, my son Rahul, and daughter Pari—deserve special warm thanks for their understanding and continuous emotional and physical support all through the time of writing this book. I would not have been able to complete the book without their support.

I acknowledge with thanks the Vice-Chancellor (at UIUC) for granting me the "Undergraduate Instructional Award" for the project "Developing techniques for teaching Asian mythology," which enabled me to put together the material for the course. Also, thanks are due to the Amoco Foundation for granting me the Award for the Outstanding Project Completed in 1987. I gratefully acknowledge Ms. Tamara Valentine's assistance in collecting material, and typing the preliminary draft of the manuscript for this project.

I wish to express my thanks to Ms. Amy Bridgeman (Senior Editor, Ginn Press) for having constantly and patiently updated the deadline and thus keeping me alive.

I want to express my gratitude to my teachers and colleagues Professors Braj and Yamana Kachru and Professor Hans Hock in the Department of Linguistics and also my colleagues in the Program for the Study of Religion at the University of Illinois for their support at one time or another. The members of the Asian Library, Mr. Narindar Aggarwal, Ms. Shiva Monrad, Mr. Mukesh Kukreti and Mrs. Yasuko Makino, deserve special thanks for their generous help with the books.

Lastly I want to express my sincere thanks to Professor Gary Porton (Director, Program for the Study of Religion) for his unfailing faith in me and his constant encouragement and support. This book would not have been completed without his support.

CHAPTER 1

# Mythology: Its Form and Function

## 1.0 Definition of "myth"

Myths are generally believed to be stories which transcend the limits of time, space, and human existence. They depict an imaginary world of superhuman beings such as gods, demons, etc. It is interesting to note that myths on one hand are believed to present an "unreal," "fictitious" world, and yet they are believed to be sacred and true. This apparent contradiction is resolved if we look at the etymological meaning of the term "myth" which is derived from the Greek word *muthos*. *Muthos* is interpreted variously as a statement, a word, or a decisive, final pronouncement. Myths represent extraordinary events and explanations without trying to justify them by *logos* (logic). Their validity or truth cannot be argued or demonstrated because they are believed to be self-validating. Since they transcend logical verification, they are imaginary and since they are deeply rooted in the faith and traditions of the people and are viewed to be self-validating, they are believed to be true. Mythology is the study of myths.

All societies in all parts of the world have had myths from time immemorial. They are similar to and different from each other; similar because they all deal with human concerns. As Ausband (1983:2) points out, "Myths were created to deal with the questions of what happens to the invisible spark, the mind or soul, that wonders about death while the body is still alive. Observation and reflection tell us that man seeks control and power over certain aspects of the world. Myths tell us how that power and control may be won or lost." Myths depict human concerns about the nature of reality and its relationship with human life. Embedded within those broad concerns are tales of human weakness and suffering, strength and happiness, good and evil. This represents the "universal" dimension of myths.

Myths have a culture-specific dimension as well. The above-mentioned human concerns are expressed, interpreted, and resolved in diverse mythologies within culture-specific frameworks and traditions in different parts of the world. Those frameworks contain different "world views" with various systems of religious beliefs, linguistic symbolism, and sociocultural traditions. A good example of this is the creation-myth across cultures. While the Indian

(Hindu) tradition attributes creation to one abstract principle *Brahman,* the Japanese Shinto myth relates creation to the *Kamis* (the forces of nature), while an old Ainu myth attributes the creation of human beings to the bear.

## 2.0 Function of myths

"What a myth may do is largely the function of what it is taken to mean" (Eliade 1963:70). Scholars from different disciplines attribute different meanings/functions to myths. They are "world-views" and "thought patterns" for philosophers, "literary symbols" for literary critics, expressions of the archetypical shapes of the human mind for psychologists, and for anthropologists, they depict social structures. Despite a predilection to their own approach, all scholars agree that the following functions are commonly shared by most mythologies of the world:

(a) Myths provide explanations for phenomena which are either not directly observable or which cannot be explained on the basis of knowledge of the world. Thus, myths of the ancient mythologies (such as the Egyptian, Greek, Chinese, Indian and Japanese) often deal with the explanation of the creation of the world, life, death, the interrelationship of human beings with the cosmos, etc.

(b) Another function of myths is that they provide sanctions for social, religious and cultural traditions. For example, in India, prayers are offered to the fire god at all major events such as births, marriages, and deaths. This tradition is explained by a Rgvedic myth which treats fire as the priest mediator between gods and human beings. During the time of the sun eclipse certain groups of American Indians throw fire-arrows into the sky. One of their myths says that the sun loses its way and, therefore, people must guide the sun through darkness. A particular line of kings in Athens used snakes for amulets. One Greek myth justifies this custom by attributing the origin of that clan to King Eric Thomos, a man serpent, a foster son of the goddess Athena.

(c) Myths provide culture-independent, as well as culture-specific definitions of good and evil. Gods, light, balance, and order generally depict "good" or positive forces, while demons, darkness, imbalance, and disorder are viewed as "evil" or negative forces. However, cultures and their mythological traditions also differ in their definitions of "good" and "evil." This is expected because the parameters for defining these notions vary from one culture to another. In some cultures and religions, existences are categorized as either exclusively good or evil (e.g. gods are "good," Satan is "evil"). In others, existences are not defined as either good or evil in isolation; rather, they become/or are viewed as good or evil according to their functions. For example, in Hindu and Taoist beliefs, balance of opposite forces is viewed as "good" and imbalance as "evil." Thus those existences which are/become conducive to creating or maintaining the balance of opposites are viewed as good while those which disturb that balance are viewed as evil. Therefore, no existence (whether god, demon, human being, or tree) is viewed as absolutely "good" or "evil." Thus in the former systems, "good" or "evil" is the permanent characteristic of an existence (i.e., Satan is always evil), while in the latter system it is not. For example, in the mythology of Kṛṣṇa (Chapter 7), the cobra Kāliya is viewed as an evil demon only when he threatens the lives of the cowherds by poisoning the water of the river. Once he is chastized by Kṛṣṇa and sent away from the river and the cowherds, he ceases to be viewed as evil.

(d) The literary value of myths is immense. As pieces of literary art they have been a source of entertainment and pleasure for thousands of years. Much like music and dance, myths have been part of the creative heritage of diverse cultures. Moreover, in almost all literatures of the world, both modern and old, myths have been one of the major sources of themes and literary symbols. A large portion of Indian literature in the classical (Sanskrit) and Modern Indian languages has been based on mythological sources. Similarly, a sizable portion of European literature has derived its themes from mythological sources. Specifically, the Indian epic literature (the *Rāmāyaṇa* and the *Mahābhārata*) and the Homeric epics in Greek mythology have been a continuous source of inspiration for other (visual) arts. The separation of the religious and secular which exists in most parts of the modern western world did not exist in the world in earlier periods of time. Myths were viewed as the expression of the sacred, as well as of the human. Musicians, playwrights, architects, and dancers, among others in the European, Indian, Chinese and Japanese traditions, have utilized mythological sources for developing the theory and practice of their arts.

(e) In societies where oral, as opposed to written, tradition has been prevalent (e.g., in countries such as China, Egypt, and India), myths have been used as the means of imparting education—secular as well as religious. For exampl e, *Pañcatantra,* a collection of myths/stories, clearly exemplifies the age-old tradition in India of educating princes through the medium of myths. Each myth in *Pañcatantra* concludes with a moral. Even today, in India, in most villages (and to a large extent in the cities as well), the world view of a child is formulated around the traditional myths (local as well as pan-Indian), which are transmitted from one generation to the next by the older members of the family.

## 3.0 Approaches to the Study of Mythology

Since myths have been viewed differently in different disciplines, there have been different approaches to the study of the mythologies of the world. Two major types may be observed: one which stresses the universal character of mythology and another which focuses on the culture-specific aspect of mythology. While the goal of theologians, anthropologists, and folklorists has primarily been to discover the culture-specific dimension of myths, philosophers, psychologists, and linguists have approached myths from the point of view of tracing their universal characteristics. Philosophers (e.g., David Hume among others) have been interested in discovering the underlying thought patterns (e.g., speculations about the origin of the world, life, and death, etc.) across cultures, which form the basis for the emergence of mythology.

Another influential universalistic approach is observed in the field of psychology in the works of Sigmund Freud and Carl Jung. According to Freud, myths reveal the behavior of the "universal psyche" which has biological rather than historical foundations. Thus, in the symbolic network of myths, according to Freud, we find the working out of human guilt (e.g., the Oedipus complex, related to sexual guilt) and wish-fulfillment of various kinds. According to this approach, the study of myths reveals the "archetypes" or primordial shapes or patterns of thoughts which human beings inherit as part of their disposition through various stages of the development of human societies. These archetypes are expressed in dreams and the myths of the people. According to Jung, the study of myths, like that of dreams, reveals those archetypes which arise from the "collective unconscious" with which human beings deal with the outer world. For example, fear of death and the need to go beyond the fetters of time and space are some of the "archetypes" expressed in myths.

One of the most influential models for the study of mythology has been proposed by Claude Levi-Strauss who through his structural approach within the framework of anthropology provides a foundation for analyzing myths from the different cultures of the world. This approach is intended to uncover the underlying patterns in myths which reveal both culture-specific and culture-independent structures of the societies. According to Levi-Strauss, this structure is "a code which is intended to ensure the reciprocal translatability of several myths." (Levi-Strauss 1969:5).

Another important contribution to the study of myths is James Frazer's (1922) work, *The Golden Bough,* which stresses the relationship of myths to cultural traditions. This social anthropological approach relates the origin of myths to the religious rituals (in particular traditions) by which the gods were propitiated. Later, Bronislaw Malinowski broadened the scope of this approach and treated mythology as a means for introducing and reinforcing the sociocultural parameters. According to Malinowski, its most important functions are "in connection with religious ritual, moral influence, and sociological principle" (Malinowski 1954: 98). A study of myths reveals those sociocultural patterns.

Theologians such as Rudolf Otto (1929) focus on the study of the systems of religious beliefs in the myths and provide a culture-specific dimension to the study of myths. A comparative approach to the study of myths is observed in Eliade (1958) and Campbell (1959), which stresses the significance of commonly shared themes in diverse mythologies of the world. Thus, themes such as the power of the sacred, mythical heroes, spiritual regeneration, mother earth and cosmic regeneration are discussed to uncover universal as well as culture-specific dimensions of mythologies.

## 4.0 Mythology and Religion: An Intimate Connection

It is beyond doubt that there is an intimate connection between mythology and religion. Mythology is one of the major components (in addition to philosophy and ritual) of religion. In mythology, religious concepts are manifested, described, and justified through the medium of stories or narration. In this sense then, mythology is an extension of a religious system. For example, in one of the Chinese (Taoist) myths of *Hun-tun* (chaos), it is said that *Shu* (the northern sea) and *Hu* (the southern sea) carved a human figure out of *Hun-tun.* This was the first creation, from which all further creation of the world took place. This myth elaborates the underlying Taoist religious belief that before the beginning of creation there was "chaos," which was the source of the creation of the phenomenal world, and that the process of creation was the process of ordering "chaos."

Mythology differs from the other components of religion (i.e., rituals and philosophy) in its medium and method respectively. Unlike rituals, which are primarily based on actions (which may or may not use language as their medium), mythology uses the linguistic medium to illustrate religious beliefs. Mythology differs from philosophy in terms of its method of presentation of religious beliefs. Unlike philosophy, mythology uses an allegorical/symbolic framework in which events, characters, and actions function as symbols for underlying religious concepts/beliefs. It is through the dynamics of the network of symbols that mythology presents and justifies religious beliefs. The difference in the three components can be clearly exemplified as follows: the Hindu belief in the *Karma* theory (i.e., actions bring results and the performer of the actions must bear the results in the same birth or in future births) is expressed in the sacrificial rituals of the Hindus by their emphasis on the fact that the good (ritual) actions performed at the sacrificial ritual will bring good results to the sponsorer (*yajamāna*) of the ritual. The same belief in the *Karma* theory is justified in philosophy (e.g., the *Sāṃkhya* system) within the framework of a logical syllogism as follows: There is oil in the sesame seed. If there were no oil in the seed, one could not squeeze it out from the seed. Therefore, one must assume that the oil is in the seed before it is squeezed out of it. Thus one can conclude that the result (such as oil) exists in the cause. In contrast to this, in mythology belief is expressed through the events and the behavior of the characters in a story. In the story of the *Rāmāyaṇa,* Daśaratha the old king suffers the pain of separation from his son. He is reminded of an event in his earlier life when he mistakenly killed the only son of an old couple. It was this *karma* (action) in his past life which is responsible for the grief of separation from his son. (Since he had caused the old couple to suffer the pain of separation from their son, he had to suffer the same pain as well.)

The above discussion may create the impression that religious beliefs can be expressed without mythology and that mythology is not a necessary mode of expression of religious beliefs. However, this is not always true. Religious beliefs about experiences, situations, reality (e.g., the experience of the divine, the nature of god, etc.) which transcend the human realm of experience can only be described through metaphorical/mythological symbolism. For example, symbols for a king or a father are used to describe the nature of god, water is used in the Hindu mythology to describe the one, eternal reality, *Brahman,* etc. If myths are viewed as extended metaphors, one can clearly see the crucial role they play in illustrating religious beliefs. The known and observable is used in mythology as a symbol, a stepping stone, an avenue for revealing the unknown and unobservable. The concept of the cycle of rebirth is described in the *Bhagavadgītā* by use of the metaphor/myth of the *Aśvattha* tree (fig tree). The world is described as the *Aśvattha* tree, the branches of which grow outwards and spread out in the sky (the multiple forms are created in the world). Then the branches turn down toward the ground, and then they dig into the earth (i.e., go back to their original abode) and then burst up out of the ground again in the form of new twigs (*Bhagavadgītā* 15.1). Thus, says the *Bhagavadgītā,* the world is created, it sustains itself in many forms, is dissolved, and is recreated . This example shows that mythology is an essential component of religion. It must be noted here that myths are not restricted to the realm of religion and that they cover other aspects (sociological, psychological, etc.) of human behavior.

## *5.0 Aim of the text*

The myths in this book are collected from three major traditions of Asia—Indian, Chinese and Japanese. Common themes presented here are creation myths, myths about good and evil, myths revealing human concerns about the social and cosmic order, the interrelationship of human beings to the outer world, the meaning or goal of human life, and the concept of order.

The discussion focuses on both the universal and culture-specific aspects of the myths. Myths which are representative of particular religious traditions are chosen to illustrate the foundation of religious beliefs and philosophical systems which often influence the very nature of myths. Religious and sociocultural symbols and images are discussed to illustrate common and diverse patterns in the above mythologies.

The selection and analysis of the myths in this book is not aimed at supporting or arguing against any particular approach, but rather, the emphasis here has been on understanding the "meaning" of the myths within their cultural contexts. Therefore, the analysis of the myths is not restricted by any one approach. Certain obvious similarities across the three mythologies under discussion should be obvious to discerning readers. For example, in all three mythologies, "chaos" (an undifferentiated mass) is viewed as the substantive source of creation, and all levels of existence (i.e. human beings, animals, plants, inanimates) are viewed as interrelated.

The book is not intended to be a theoretical discussion on Asian mythology, but rather a collection and analysis of myths which will provide an avenue to the cultural, religious, and social traditions of the three main traditions of Asia. The material also provides points of comparison at the thematic and formal levels of the three mythologies. Thus, the main aim of this book is to provide an encounter with Asian mythology and thereby enhance understanding of the Asian traditions.

CHAPTER 2

# The Indus Valley Civilization

## 1.0 Introduction

Though myths are considered to be timeless, perhaps the very timelessness of myths is a myth, for the form and the content of myths is always shaped by the time and the locale of their origin, and the characteristic of being timeless is attributed to them by the culture in which they flourish.

It is not an easy task to trace the mythological roots of a country like India which in its breadth, depth, and diversity of cultures and civilizations has often been compared with the whole of Europe put together. However, the first hour of the Indian cultural and religious tradition seems to begin with the Indus Valley civilization which flourished around 3000 B.C. in the north-western parts of the Indian subcontinent. Since much of the mainstream Indian religious and mythological tradition has been of Āryan origin, until the 19th century pre-Āryan civilizations were eschewed as essentially primitive in nature. The discovery of the Indus Valley civilization in the early 20th century by an English archaeologist, Sir John Marshall, clearly revealed that this view of pre-Āryan traditions in India was no more than a myth. Marshall carried out the excavation of the sites of the Indus Valley civilization around two major cities named Harappa and Mohenjo-Daro, both in the valley of the river Indus. This civilization startled the discoverers, since with it was found a city culture, an advanced architecture, an astounding city planning, a well-organized agriculture, a well-developed script, and evidence for the use of metal and beautiful pottery, all of which shattered the hypothesis concerning the "primitive" nature of ancient Indian civilizations.

Much of our knowledge of this civilization is based on brief inscriptions on the seals found in the Indus Valley. Thus information is limited and a lot of it is derived from interpretations of those seals.

## 2.0 Geography

This civilization covered a geographic area of about 950 miles from north to south around the valley of the Indus river. Besides the two major cities, Harappa and Mohenjo-Daro, there are

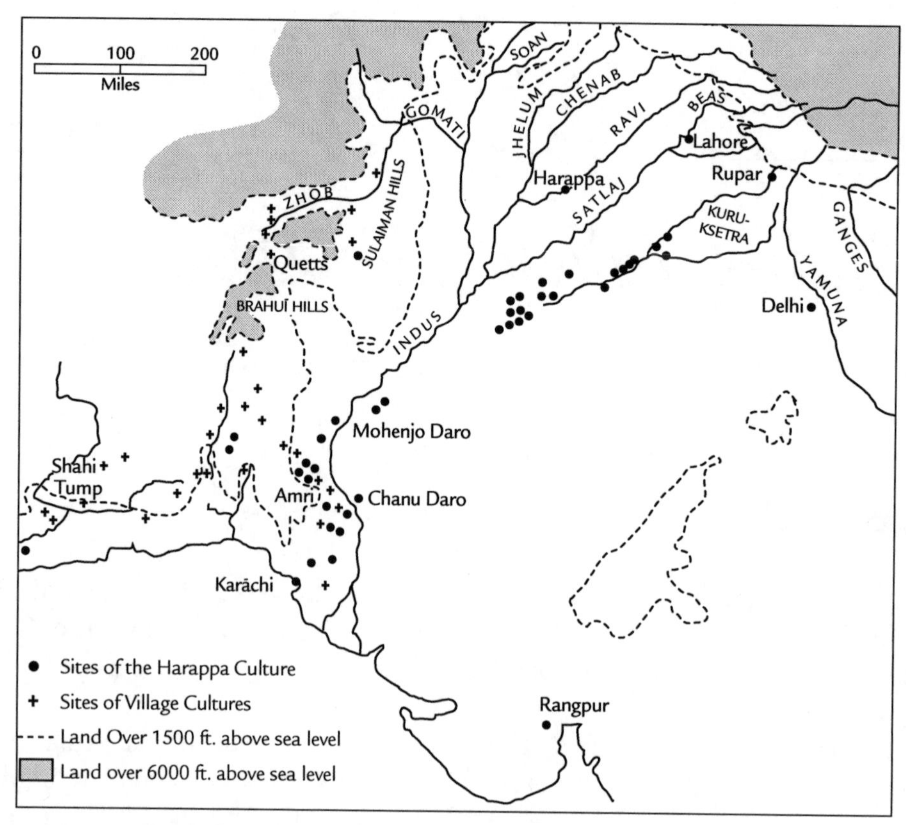


**Figure 1.** Some prehistoric Sites of N.W. India (From Basham, 1959:12)

several other villages which bear the mark of this culture (see map). All in all it covered about 300 miles from east to west in the valleys of the rivers Ravi (left/west) and Indus (right/east).

## *3.0 The City Culture*

Excavations in this area show that the Indus culture was in close contact with the village culture in Baluchistan. However, it was mainly a city culture. The two cities, Harappa, and Mohenjo-Daro, showed similar planning; i.e. they were divided into major square blocks with major streets, which were further divided into small alleys and lanes. In both cities public buildings were built on a large raised brick platform. Those "citadels" were 40 × 20 yards in area and were about 30 to 50 feet high. The houses by the sides of the streets were made of bricks or clay and were of two (or more) stories. There is no evidence of stone buildings. The plan of the houses was similar, with each house having a square yard in the center and rooms constructed around it. The houses had bathrooms, and the drains were connected to sewers which were covered under the main streets.

Some scholars, on the basis of the evidence of three sizes of houses, claim that there were at least three social classes of people: the higher class with more than two storied houses, the middle class with moderately built two storied houses, and the workers class with two-room dwellings, with an area of 20 × 12 feet.

One of the fascinating constructions is a large public bath of 39 × 23 feet in area and 8 feet deep. Scholars believe that this bath, with its well-designed system of drains, might have been used for the ritual religious bath of the priests. In any case, the public bath provides evidence for the importance of purificatory practices (religious or other) in the culture. On either side of the main streets, water-wells built of bricks have been discovered. This clearly indicates that there existed in the culture a system for the supply of water. There were large water reservoirs, again built of bricks, where the water was stored, purified and then distributed to the city. The building of the water-reservoir clearly shows the outlets for incoming as well as outgoing water.

## 4.0 The People and Their Lifestyle

The question of the origin of the Indus Valley people is still shrouded in mystery today. It is not clear whether the Indus Valley people were indigenous or were foreigners who arrived in the subcontinent around 3000 B.C. While the structure of the skeletal remains points to an affinity with the Mediterranean type, some of the pieces of sculpture show similarity with both the Mediterranean as well as the Proto-Australoid people. For example, one statue of a bearded man shows a distinct similarity with the Mediterranean faces of men, while the bronze statue of a "dancing girl" shows a clear similarity with the Proto-Australoid people, with thick lips and flat nose. It has also been proposed that the modern South Indian people of Dravidian origin are a blend of the Proto-Australoid, the Mediterranean , and the indigenous people of India. There are yet other scholars who believe that perhaps there was a widespread local culture which was influenced by the external cultures, leading to the emergence of the Indus Valley culture.

Regardless of its exact origin, there are some characteristics which would make the Indus culture seem to be deeply rooted in the Indian soil. The use of the bullock cart, jewelry, the cultural significance of animals such as the tiger, the elephant and the bull, as well as the male god sitting in the "yogic" posture clearly bear the mark of later Indian culture. The evidence clearly shows that the Indus Valley civilization had a firm agricultural base. The major crops were wheat, barley, peas and sesame. The remains of huge and well-built granaries have been found in both the cities, which show that farming was one of the major occupations outside of the cities. The seals provide evidence for domestic animals such as buffalo, pigs, sheep, dogs, and fowl. Elephants seem to have been prominent animals.

There is clear evidence of the artistic talents of the people. There are dyers' sections, specially built to preserve the dyes, beautiful pieces of jewelry made of copper and bronze, and beautiful sculpture, especially statues made of clay and bronze. Human figurines made of white and red stone depict the style of the sculpture. The most discussed figurine is a bronze statue of a dancing girl with a necklace and metal bangles. According to some scholars, the statue of the dancing girl suggests the existence of a class of "temple-dancers" in the Indus culture. However, there is no other evidence available to support this claim so that it would seem to be mere fanciful speculation.

The beautiful pieces of pottery provide yet another piece of evidence for the artistic talent of the people. The pots were handmade or wheel-turned. A large number of drinking cups have been found which are similar to the ones used in contemporary India. The pots were baked in kilns which looked like the modern fireplaces in American houses, with fire-pits underneath and chimney-like tops for the release of the smoke. The major motifs on the pots were various types of trees (predominantly *Pippal,* and tropical palms) and animals such as deer with long horns, peacocks, etc. Also, oblong-shaped designs and wave-like patterns of curvy lines are observed on the pots. After firing, the pots were painted in three major colors—red, black, and beige. The pottery in general shows the interest of the people in plant and animal life. The presence of beads made of gold, silver, copper, and other stones clearly shows that the people were familiar with the processes of grinding and boring stone, melting metal and sawing. The imaginative mind of the Indus people is amply revealed in toys made of clay in the shape of animals (specially monkeys), birds, whistles, bullock carts, and pawns (which might have been used in the game of chess).

## 5.0 Seals

Over 2000 seals have been discovered in the excavations. These seals are a major source of information about various facets of the culture of the Indus Valley. The seals were square tablets made of a soft stone, steatite.

The seals are believed to have been used by the merchant community for business transactions. They were used as stamps to indicate ownership of property and perhaps served as emblems of families, with each using a particular seal as a family emblem.

On the seals are engraved animals such as bulls, goats, tigers, elephants, and buffalo. Human figures—both male and female—are found as well. Human figures with animal/plant features such as horns and leaves are also found. There are male figures with horns on their heads and female figures with plants, leaves, and flowers growing out of their heads.

## 6.0 Language

The inscriptions on the seals clearly show the use of a well-developed script which contained 270 ideographic characters. The script is not yet fully deciphered. There have been various claims made regarding the origin and nature of the Indus Valley script/language. According to some scholars, it resembles some of the Dravidian scripts used in the southern parts of India. However, no decisive evidence is available to support conclusively this claim. It has also been suggested that the script shows a striking similarity with the symbols used by the natives in the Easterland in the eastern Pacific. Again, due to the lack of any written, engraved, or inscribed data no judgement can be made with absolute certainty.

## 7.0 Religious beliefs

Most of the evidence regarding the religious beliefs of the Indus Valley people comes from the interpretation of the seals. Some of the salient engravings on the seals show the following: (a) a male ithyphallic figure with animal horns, sitting in the yoga-posture, and surrounded by an elephant, a tiger, a rhinoceros, a buffalo, and a deer, (b) a female figure (tree goddess) with plants and flowers growing from her head, (c) plants and flowers growing from the womb of a female figure, and (d) a worship ritual of the tree goddess.

It is reasonably clear from the seals that the people were fascinated by and most probably worshipped as well, the power of fertility seen in all living beings. It appears that plants, animals, and humans were all perceived as the concrete symbols of the power of fertility and, hence, whenever the Indus Valley people wanted to depict or worship fertility, they did not make any clear distinction among the three. This explains why the male "god" had animal horns, and plants and flowers grow from the body of the female "goddess."

Most scholars agree that there existed a strong mother goddess cult in the Indus Valley civilization. This claim is based on the discovery of numerous statuettes of naked women with elaborate hairdresses in practically every house. However, there is a great deal of controversy regarding the nature and importance of the male horned god. The scholars who have described the figure as that of the proto-Śiva, one of the gods of the Hindu Trinity, point to the fact that Śiva, similar to the horned god, is closely connected with the animal world to the extent of being described as *Pashupati* "lord of animals." Scholars who refuse to interpret the horn-god as proto-Śiva mention that the animal which invariably accompanies Śiva, the bull, is conspicuously absent from the group of animals surrounding the horn-god of the Indus Valley. Also, practically every Hindu god and goddess has some connection with some animal(s). Hence the figure of the horn-god surrounded by animals cannot be taken as justification for treating the figure as that of proto-Śiva.

The worship of the power of fertility in the Indus Valley civilization provides us with a fascinating insight into the human psyche. Fertility is an obvious antidote to death—one of the most scary phenomenon for the human mind to accept in all times and in all places. Different cultures in different times have adopted different means of rationalizing death, such as the belief in life after death, reincarnation or rebirth, going to heaven after death or the sheer immortality of some aspect of the human personality. In the Indus Valley civilization, people seem to have believed in countering death by a very simple means—life itself. When seen from this perspective, the prevalent fertility cult in the Indus culture becomes very easy to understand and explain, because no phenomenon other than fertility manifested the power of life (over death) more vividly. The tendency to cling to life (by celebrating fertility) in the face of unavoidable death can be seen in a number of other cultures and civilizations. Consider for example, the mother (an obvious symbol of fertility) goddess cult in the ancient civilizations of Egypt, Mesopotamia, and South America.

A number of cemeteries excavated near Harappa provide information about burials in the Indus Culture. The dead were buried along with personal possessions such as jewelry, pottery, etc. This rite seems to be similar to the old Egyptian burial rite. In a number of cases, pairs of skeletons indicate that a husband and his wife were buried together. This custom of burying the wife with her husband is not unique to the Indus culture; rather, it seems to be commonly shared by the ancient Chinese as well as the Egyptian culture. Although it is difficult to establish a clear connection among apparently similar rites across cultures, one speculation seems plausible; namely that these cultures share the belief in life after death.

## 8.0 Disappearance of the Indus Valley Culture

Like its origin, the end of the Indus Valley culture remains a mystery yet to be solved by scholars. There is no conclusive evidence available to determine the exact factors which were responsible for the disappearance of the Indus Valley civilization. According to one hypothesis, the invasion of the Āryans was responsible for the total annihilation of the Indus culture. Evidence such as (a) the presence of horse-riding invaders (i.e., Āryans) in Baluchistan by 2000 B.C., (b) the arrival of the Kulli (Baluchistani refugees) in Mohenjo-Daro, (c) the attested presence of the more refined weapons of the Āryans in the area around 2000 B.C. and (d) the change in the style of pottery (from the refined Indus style to the coarser Āryan style) has been provided to support the hypothesis concerning the invasion/takeover by the Āryans in the Indus Valley region. In contrast to this, it has been argued variously that some natural disaster such as excessive flooding or famine could have been responsible for the gradual decay of the Indus Valley civilization before the arrival of the Āryans in the area.

Whatever the primary cause of the decay of the Indus civilization, it is certain that the two civilizations—i.e. the Indus Valley and the Āryan—were in contact with each other long enough for the Āryan culture to be influenced by the Indus culture before it was totally lost. This hypothesis of mutual contact between the two civilizations would further explain why certain religious beliefs (e.g. worship of the power of fertility) and certain traditions (e.g. the use of the bullock-cart for ploughing, etc.) typical of the Indus culture found their way into the later predominantly Āryan culture in India.

# CHAPTER 3

# *Mythology of the Vedas*

## 1.0 Introduction

As was mentioned in the last chapter, it is a matter of debate whether it was war or natural calamity which destroyed the Indus Valley Civilization. But, the fact remains that the Indus Civilization did not survive after the arrival of the Āryans in the Indian subcontinent.

The Āryans entered India in about 2000–1500 B.C. through the northwestern region of the country. They were Indo-Europeans who brought with them the Indo-European cultural heritage from Central Europe (though it is to be noted here that the original home of the Indo-European people is a matter of controversy). The Āryans kept coming to India at periodic intervals like waves, one group following another in its wake. Hence, the Āryans continued to spread (from the northwest) northwards and eastwards, displacing and driving the indigenous people into the southern part of India in the process. The existence of small pockets of non-Āryan tribal groups in the mountainous terrain of northern India makes us accept that this process of displacement of the local people was confined mainly to the population living in the plains.

Unlike the well-established city culture of the Indus Valley, the Āryan culture was essentially the nomadic warrior's heritage. They brought with them a new Indo-European language, Sanskrit, and a new world view. The Āryan culture has had an immense impact on the history, religion, and culture of India, to the extent that the entire superstructure of (mainstream) Hindu mythology and religion can be said to have been built on an essentially Āryan infrastructure.

Early Āryan mythology and culture seem to be closely related to the Iranian branch of the Indo-European tribe. The linguistic evidence proves beyond doubt that the language of Avestā (the oldest Iranian religious text) and the *Vedas* (Āryan scriptural texts, see section 2 below) is very similar in terms of vocabulary, sounds, syntax and meter. Similarly, these two scriptural texts share some basic features with regard to the overall structure and functioning of the universe. For example, both texts mention the division of the universe into three realms—heaven, atmosphere, and earth; gods like *Ātar,* (in *Avestā*) and *Agni* (in *Ṛgveda*); and the system of cosmic rules—*aśa* (in *Avestā*), and *ṛta* (in *Ṛgveda*). The central role of fire and water in the Vedic sacrificial ritual (see sections 2 and 5) is also attested in the old Indo-European tradition.

## 2.0 The Vedas

The Vedas were the sacred books of the Āryans, comparable in importance, to the Bible of the Christians and the Qu'ran of the Muslims. The word *veda* is derived from the verbal root *vid* "to know." Thus literally, *veda* means "the book of knowledge." It must be mentioned here though, that the description of the Vedic texts as "books" may not be an appropriate one. This is because the early Āryans did not have a writing system, and therefore the Vedas were transmitted orally from one generation to the other by careful memorization of whole texts. The Āryan priests had developed a complex, elaborate but precise technique of pronunciation and recitation of these texts to keep in tact the "purity" of the Vedas. These priests are rightly described as the first phoneticians of the world. Tradition glorifies the Vedas as being *apauruṣeya* "not created by humans" in nature. The content of the Vedas is believed to be nothing but the "revelations" of the priests (*ṛṣis* "seers") who had the powers to "see" beyond the observable phenomena.

"The Vedas" is a cover term for three different types of "books" (in the sense described above):I. *Saṃhitās,* II. *Brāhmaṇas* and *Āraṇyakas* and III. *Upaniṣads.*

### 2.1 Saṃhitās

The term *Saṃhitā* literally means "put together." There are four *Saṃhitās—Ṛk, Sāma, Yajus,* and *Atharva.* The *Saṃhitā* texts (especially the first three) are the very core of Vedic literature and hence it did not take very long before these four *Saṃhitā* came to be viewed as the *Vedas* "proper," to which are appended the liturgical *Brāhmaṇa* and *Āraṇyakas* texts, and *Upaniṣads,* which explain the underlying philosophy of the Vedas "proper" (i.e., the *Saṃhitās*). Hence the traditionally described four Vedas—*Ṛgveda, Sāmaveda, Yajurveda,* and *Atharvaveda*— are the same as the *Saṃhitā* texts.

(A) *Ṛgveda:* This is the oldest of the *Saṃhitās,* believed to have been "put together" between about 2000–1500 B.C. *Ṛgveda* consists of about 1,028 Sanskrit hymns of various lengths. The whole text is in the metrical style. Most of the hymns are prayers to the various gods. The *Ṛgveda* is divided into ten books (*mandalas*) composed by different priests and in all likelihood at different times. Much of Vedic mythology can be traced from or rooted in the contents of *Ṛgveda,* and hence the study and analysis of this Veda becomes of utmost importance for understanding or describing Vedic mythology. (see section 3.0)

(B) *Sāmaveda:* "Veda of the Sāmas." *Sāmaveda* is a collection of the *mantras* "ritual chants" which were recited by the *Udgātṛ* "priest" at the sacrificial rituals (for a detailed description see sections 5.0 and 9.1). *Sāmaveda* is primarily concerned with the *Soma* sacrifice (see section 3.5). It also discusses the rules and devices for transforming verses (taken mostly from *Ṛgveda*) into *gānas* "chants." The transformation of verses into chants involved changing the linguistic structure of the former (e.g. insertion of an additional vowel, syllable, deletion of a syllable, etc.). *Sāmaveda* is the first document in the Indian literary tradition which deals with the composition of melodies and chants.

(C) *Yajurveda:* "Veda of the rituals." *Yajurveda* is concerned with the practical aspects of the Vedic religion, which was very much centered around the performance of different kinds of sacrificial rituals. These rituals were viewed as the medium through which the Vedic people communicated with the gods residing in the different realms (heaven, atmosphere, and earth) of the cosmos. The Veda also discusses the duties of *adhvaryu,* the "priest" who actually performed the sacrifices, and various sacrificial formulae along with their explanations. The two recensions of this veda are called the *sukla Yajurveda* "white *Yajurveda*" and the kṛṣṇa *Yajurveda* "black *Yajurveda.*" While the former contains only the ritualistic formulae, the latter includes both the formulae and their explanations within the ritualistic context.

While the Ṛgvedic hymns show the power of prayers in persuading the Vedic gods to grant various material gifts to the people, the sacrificial formulae of the *Yajurveda* stress the belief of the Vedic people in ritualistic actions (i.e. sacrifice), which, if performed flawlessly, would induce the gods to bless the sacrificers. The *Yajurveda* thus is the earliest predecessor of the later *Brāhmaṇas,* the entire focus of which is on ritual actions performed for "controlling" rather than pleasing the gods. The *Yajurveda* thus clearly marks the transition from the Vedas (strictly speaking, the *Saṃhitās*) to the *Brāhmaṇas.*

(D) *Atharvaveda:* "Veda of the magical formulae." *Atharvaveda is* distinctly different in its character from the other three Vedas. It represents the concerns, problems, and aspirations of the common people and their belief in the power of the magical formulae. The two types of *atharvan* "magical formulae or charms" discussed here are charms for general well-being, progeny, healing injuries and charms for destroying evil forces such as diseases, evil spirits and enemies. Initially, *Atharvaveda* was not considered by the "elite" faction of the Vedic people to be one of the Vedas on the grounds that it included "black magic" (chanting of the magical formulae to cause destruction of the undesirable forces or persons). Both stylistically and thematically, this Veda is the least homogeneous of all the Vedas.

## 2.2 Brāhmaṇas and Āraṇyakas

(A) The *Brāhmaṇa* texts are one of the richest sources of Indian mythology and religion because these texts describe, explain and justify religious and philosophical concepts mainly through the medium of myths. The *Brāhmaṇas* are the liturgical texts appended to the four *Saṃhitās* and are concerned primarily with sacrificial rituals, emphasizing the discussion of their purposes and the correct technique of their performance. Though the exact period of the "composition" of these earliest Sanskrit prose texts is uncertain, they are generally dated from about the 7th century B.C. These texts have been called *Brāhmaṇas* for the following reasons: (a) they discuss the duties of the *Brāhmaṇas* "priests" in the sacrificial rituals and (b) their main focus is to reveal clearly *Brahman* "the power of the sacrifice." The belief underlying the *Brāhmaṇa* texts is that a sacrifice performed using the "pure" and appropriate language, properly collected ritual materials, and the appropriate method had the power (*Brahman*) to induce the gods to act according to the wishes of the sacrificer. This belief in the mystical power of sacrifice not only provided sanction for the elaborate Vedic rituals but also gave the Vedic Āryans a sense of confidence in the power of their own (ritual) actions. Thus the *Brāhmaṇas* clearly mark the fascinating shift in the Vedic belief system from the stage at which human beings are at the beck and call of the whimsical gods to that at which they actually control the gods through their own actions (i.e., sacrifices). We can safely assume that herein lay the seeds of the theory of *karma* "action leading to result," which was later to become very important.

These texts used both injunctions and explanations to describe rituals. A typical description of a ritual involves injunctions regarding the preparation of the sacred altar, collection and arrangement of ritual-related material (e.g. water, sacred grass, butter, etc.), duties of various priests, and the *yajamāna* "sacrificer," and the performance of the sacrifice. Every ritual action is to be accompanied by the recitation of verses from the *Saṃhitās.* Each of these actions is viewed as absolutely necessary for the overall success of the sacrifice, since it was assumed that *Brahman* (power of sacrifice) resided in every aspect of the sacrifice, including the language, ritual material, and the actual technique used. To illustrate this point, consider the injunction from the *śatapatha* Brāhmaṇa (1.1.1.20): "He (the sacrificer) should not move between them (i.e., the fire and the water)." The rationale given for this injunction is "the fire (*agni*—masculine), and water (*āp*—feminine) form a couple (*mithunam*) and one should not intervene between the two, since together they are responsible for the creation of the universe (i.e., the symbolic "creation" of the universe at the altar).

Some of the most prominent *Brāhmaṇas* are the following: (a) *Aitareya Brāhmaṇa* of the *Ṛgveda.* This is the oldest *Brāhmaṇa* (7th century B.C.) and deals primarily with the duties of the *Hotṛ* (the priest who recites Ṛgvedic verses in the sacrificial rituals). (b) Another important *Brāhmaṇa* of *Ṛgveda* is *Kausitakī.* (c) *Taittirīya Brāhmaṇa* belongs to the (*Tattirīya Saṃhitā* of) *Yajurveda,* while (d) *Śatapatha Brāhmaṇa* belongs to the *Vājasaneyī Saṃhitā* of *Yajurveda. Śatapatha* is of special importance, since it not only describes the duties of the *Adhvaryu* (the priest who actually performs the ritual), but also discusses the magical powers of the ritualistic formulae and actions. (e) Eight *Brāhmaṇas* are appended to the *Sāmaveda,* of which *Tāṇḍya* and *Pañcaviṃśa* are the prominent ones. (f) *Gopatha* is the only major *Brāhmaṇa* attached to the *Atharvaveda.*

(B) *Āraṇyakas:* "pertaining to the forest": Historically, the *Āraṇyaka* texts mark the decline in the concern of the Vedic Āryans for the Brāhmanical sacrificial rituals and an increase in the philosophical and metaphysical speculations which eventually culminated in Upaniṣadic thought. Following the tradition of the *Brāhmaṇa* texts, the *Āraṇyakas* discuss different *vratas* (rites), especially those related to fire (e.g., *pravargya* (milk offering)). Since most of these rites were related to the death-rites in one way or another, their performance within the confines of a village was usually prohibited. Hence going to the forest (*araṇya*) became necessary for the performance of these rites, and hence the name "*Āraṇyaka.*" However, this "going to the forest" gradually began to be viewed as an act of asceticism and the knowledge obtained by these "ascetics" as revelations. It is in this sense, that the *Āraṇyakas* directly anticipate the Upaniṣadic method of pursuing knowledge (i.e., going to the forest to obtain the knowledge).

## 2.3 Upaniṣads "The Philosophical Doctrines"

The Upaniṣads literally mean "to sit close to." The traditional interpretation extends this "sitting close to" to both the guru 'teacher' and the ultimate reality. These texts belong to the third division of the Vedas. They are generally appended to the Brāhmaṇa texts of each Veda. About 150 *Upaniṣads* are available. Belonging to a date later than that of the Vedic *Saṃhitās* and the

*Brāhmaṇas,* the *Upaniṣads* are considered to have been composed in 600 B.C. These texts are composed in diverse forms (i.e., prose, poetry, or a mixture). The most prominent Vedic *Upaniṣads* (i.e., Upaniṣads that are integral to the 4 Vedas) are: (a) *Aitareya Upaniṣad* (of *Ṛgveda* and *Yajurveda*), (b) *Iśa* and *Bṛhadāraṇyaka* (belonging to the Vājasenyī *Saṃhitā* of *Yajurveda*), *(c) Kena* and *Chāndogya* (of *Sāmaveda*), *(d) Kaṭha* and *Muṇḍaka* (of *Atharvaveda).*

The *Upaniṣads* differ from the *Saṃhitās* and the *Brāhmaṇas* in their content. They mainly focus on philosophical questions such as the notions of time, space, matter, the origin of the universe, the world, and humans (and other types of existences), their interrelationship(s), death, life, and immortality. Concepts such as the ultimate reality (the all-pervasive *Brahman*), the individual soul (*Ātman*), immortality (*amṛtatva*), rebirth (*punarjanma*), *Māyā* (phenomenal world) are for the first time discussed in the *Upaniṣads.* Although some of the Upaniaṣadic concepts were analyzed and interpreted differently later on, the fact remains that practically every philosophical concept in the Indian tradition can be traced back to the *Upaniṣads.* In this sense the *Upaniṣads* are the very core of the Indian philosophical tradition.

The *Upaniṣads* are important not only for their philosophical content but also for the methodology they offer for "discovering" knowledge. Emphasis was always placed on testing, analyzing and interpreting the Vedic and the Brāhmaṇical texts from the predominantly rational and empirical point of view. In fact, the overriding creed of the *Upaniṣads* is not to take anything for granted. This basic orientation is exemplified by the practice of exhaustively describing all possible logical answers (often contradictory on the surface) to a question or a problem at hand. The final answer is always to be arrived at by the "seeker of the knowledge." This Upaniṣadic way of discovering knowledge is perhaps one of the most distinctive and unparallelled (in contemporary ancient civilizations) characteristics of the Vedic Āryans.

## *3.0 The Mythology of the Vedas*

The Vedic texts contain the world view of the Āryans and all its diverse facets. These texts present descriptions of the structure of the universe, the interrelationship of each part with the whole structure, and the operation and control of the universe.

Underlying all these Vedic descriptions was the quest for a method, a set of laws, which would explain both the static (structural) and dynamic (operational) aspects of the universe. Such a model would then serve as the basis for understanding the role of the human world in the context of cosmic reality on the one hand and for constructing moral/ethical/social systems on the other.

While Early Vedic mythology stresses the analysis of the cosmos, later developments in the system focus on the interaction of human beings with the world/cosmos around them. Much of Early Vedic mythology revolves around the discussion of the three main concepts: (1) (nature) gods, (2) *Ṛta* "cosmic order," and (3) sacrifice.

Within the Vedic system, the cosmos is divided into three parts: heaven, atmosphere, and earth. Each sphere is viewed as the dwelling place of certain gods. For example, *Varuṇa* "the guardian of *ṛta*" and *Sūrya* "the sun god" are the gods of heaven; *Indra* "the rain god" is the god of the atmosphere, and *Agni* "fire" and *Soma* "the drink of immortality" are viewed as the gods on earth. This distribution of gods is based to some extent on the position they occupy in the cosmos, i.e., the rain in the atmosphere, the fire on earth, etc. Before proceeding further, a brief description of the main Vedic gods is in order.

## 3.1 Agni (the Fire God)

*Agni* in Vedic mythology and religion is the personification of the fire element. Historically, the worship of fire clearly indicates the Indo-European heritage of the Vedic Āryans. Fire-worship was a well-established ritual among old Indo-Iranian and ancient Italian and Greek people. *Agni's* significance was recognized by the Vedic people at the cosmic, ritualistic, and domestic levels. At the cosmic level, *Agni* was viewed as the basic fiery principle which (along with the water) was the major element responsible for all creation. Hence *Agni* is often identified with Sūrya "the sun god," who is bright, shiny, and is responsible for all growth. In this form (as the sun) *Agni* is the "seer of all things" and the "knower of all creation." In the ritual-centered religion of the Vedic Āryans, *Agni,* at the ritual level, was viewed as the priest (*purohita/ṛtvija*)—the spokesman for the sacrificer—and was responsible for conveying the prayers and offerings of the sacrificer to the gods (*havya-vāhana*) and for bringing back the blessings, boons, etc. of the gods to the sacrificer(s).

At the domestic level, *Agni* is viewed as the lord of the house (*gṛhapati*) in the form of the domestic fire, because without *Agni* in the house, no family could survive for long. *Agni* also plays a very important role in the funeral rituals of cremation, because he is the one viewed as the carrier of the dead to heaven. Further, he also conveys offerings to the ancestors. Thus *Agni* establishes a link among three worlds: the heavens, (where the gods lived), the earth (the human world), and the ancestral world. The domestic fire was also often carried to the sacrificial altar where it was then treated as the ritual fire. The ritual fire was important not only for the performance of sacrifices but also in warding off evil spirits.

Since *Agni's* role was viewed as crucial in the cosmic creation, in the proper maintenance of cosmic, social and religious orders through sacrifices, in the life of the individual at home, and in warding off evil spirits (who may cause disturbance in the orders of *Ṛta*), *Agni* too (i.e., along with *Varuṇa*) is at times called the guardian of *Ṛta* (*ṛtasya gopā*).

The abodes of *Agni* are viewed variously as two (heaven and earth) or three (heaven, earth, and water). The celestial fire (including *Sūrya,* the sun god) was viewed to have been kindled by the gods, while the sacrificial and the domestic fire was kindled by human beings (a) by the friction of the wooden sticks (*araṇis*), (b) by sparks from a stone (*aśman*), or (c) borrowed from another hearth. Not surprisingly, the wooden sticks and the stone are regarded as *Agni's* parents. In addition, the disappearance of *Agni* (at the end of the sacrificial rituals, cremation, etc.) is also described in the myths. It is often mentioned that *Agni* hides (i.e., it is in the dormant state) in plants and in water.

The most frequently used metaphors for *Agni* (in addition to the ones already mentioned) are "the banner of the sacrifice" (*yajñasya ketu*), "horse" (who brings the gods), "eater of the butter" (since butter used to be poured into the sacrificial fire), "bird" (who lives on the wood/tree and flies to the sky), "the golden colored," "the one with the golden hair and beard (flames)."

*Agni* has held a prominent place in almost all the religious rituals of the Āryans/Hindus throughout their history, including the present. Rituals related to birth, marriage, and death are inconceivable without *Agni.*

## 3.2 Indra (the Rain God)

*Indra* is the most celebrated deity of *Ṛgveda,* with over 25 hymns addressed to him in the *Ṛgveda.* The existence of *Indra* can be traced back to the Indo-Iranian period, although, the nature and function of the deity is quite uncertain in that period. *Indra* as an anthropomorphic god of rain and thunder is purely a Vedic phenomenon. He is an ambitious, aggresive king and the god of the warriors (hence regarded as a *Kṣatriya* "of warriors caste"). He battles with the demons of drought and darkness and rescues water and light. He is the lord of heaven. *Indra's* strength in his battles, his obsession for *soma,* his thunderbolt (*Vajra*) and his horses are described elaborately in the Vedas.

*Indra* represents the watery element (in the cosmos) which was viewed as essential for the survival of all levels of existence. Therefore *Indra,* who abides in the atmospheric region, is often associated with gods such as *Agni* and *Sūrya* who represent the other important fiery elements in the cosmos.

*Indra's* powerful body is often mentioned, with special reference to his "iron-like" arms with which he wields the *Vajra* "the thunderbolt," (the mythological name for lightning). He has a tawny beard and beautiful lips. He is capable of taking different forms at will. Indra is viewed as the son of *Dyaus* "god of sky" and the twin brother of *Agni.* Two of the major myths are related to his obsession for *Soma* and his killing of *Vṛtra.* He is often offered *Soma* by the sacrificer so that he may gain strength to kill *Vṛtra.*

### 3.2.1 Indra, the Killer of Vṛtra (Vṛtrahan)

*Vṛtra,* literally meaning the "coverer, obstructor" is sometimes called *"ahi"* (the dragon serpent). *Vṛtra* is the personification of the natural phenomenon which obstructs the flow of water and covers the light. Dusty clouds which cover the sun, drought, and ice are all referred to as *Vṛtra.* Thus *Vṛtra* is often referred to as the demon who steals away the cows (the rays of the sun and the springs of water). *Indra* strikes *Vṛtra* with his thunderbolt, and releases the cows—the light and the water are released from *Vṛtra* and there is plenty of light and water for the world again!

This battle between *Vṛtra* and *Indra* signifies the constant conflict between light and darkness, life and death, and the perpetual renewal of life. Thus "the killing of *Vṛtra*" is not one single event, but rather, a continuous struggle, in which *Vṛtra* epitomizes the obstructing force and *Indra* the rescuing force. In a number of *Indra's* daring exploits, the serpent (i.e. *Vṛtra*) coils around the mountain, and Indra strikes him with the thunderbolt.

## 3.3 Varuṇa (the Guardian of Ṛta "Cosmic Order")

*Varuṇa* is the god who holds the highest prestige and respect in *Ṛgveda.* He is the guardian of *ṛta.* In this respect, he presents a Vedic counterpart to the (Indo-Iranian) Avestan god, *Ahura Mazda. Varuṇa* guards both the natural and the moral order. As guardian of the natural order, he regulates the existence as well as the functioning of the natural elements. Thus he is described as the ruler of the three worlds. He keeps heaven and earth apart. He places the sun in the sky, the ocean on the earth. He abides in the wide sky and a small drop of water—he encompasses everything. Similarly, he is described as the regulator of the days and nights; the seasons come and go under his ordinance. The sun shines, the rain falls and the rivers flow according to his governance. In order to guarantee order, *Varuṇa* eternally observes the phenomenal world. He is thus the "divine observer."

He is also the one responsible for the maintenance and supervision of the moral order of *ṛta* among human beings. He observes human beings very closely. Not a single action, not even the blinking of an eye, goes unnoticed by *Varuṇa.* He "measures" (judges) every aspect (ritual as well as secular) of human behavior. Hence, *Varuṇa* is also portrayed as the "punisher" of wrong actions. He has his spies stationed everywhere to keep him informed of every action in the universe. He catches the man who tells a lie or falters in his ritual actions. He has *pāśas* "fetters" with which he binds sinners. He is depicted as an angry *Asura* (the one with demonic revengeful attitudes) who does not tolerate any violation of *ṛta* in natural or moral orders.

There are several hymns which may be offered to him for the forgiveness of sins committed by the worshipper. *Varuṇa* is a gracious judge who, when appeased, forgives sins committed intentionally or unintentionally, grants pardon to his worshippers, and re-establishes ṛta.

The hymns to *Varuṇa* clearly indicate the faith of the Vedic Āryan in both the system of laws which underlie(s) the natural world (of which human beings are an integral part) as well as the system of moral laws which underlies the functioning of human behavior. The concepts of sin and punishment are also mentioned here. A sin is viewed as the violation of ṛta, and punishment is viewed as the "untying of *Varuṇa's* rope," or the retribution of acts. The actions, and not the individuals, are punished or corrected. This justifies *Varuṇa's* gracious behavior toward the worshipper, who, even when held responsible for his sinful deeds, is not condemned to the extent that he cannot be granted *Varuṇa's* forgiveness.

*Varuṇa* is the most powerful god of the Vedic pantheon, since he guards *ṛta* at every level of existence, including the gods, human beings, animals, plants, etc. The whole cosmos must function according to *ṛta;* this is *Varuṇa's* oath. He is the guardian of *ṛta* (*ṛtasya gopā*).

## 3.4 Sūrya (the Sun God)

The affinity of *Sūrya* with the Avestan (Indo-Iranian) god *havare* (sun) is clear. He is the most concrete deity, shining in the sky to bless the world with light. *Sūrya* is viewed as the "all-seer," "expeller of darkness," and thereby "the all-knowing eye of *Varuṇa.*" He measures the days and nights. He is the deity of growth, both physical and intellectual. He induces everybody to perform activities with great zest, vigor and vitality. He drives away sickness.

He is born of *Uṣās* "the dawn," and his father is *Dyaus* "heaven." He is called a bird who flies everywhere. At times he is called a bright shiny horse (since he speedily travels the three worlds). *Sūrya's* close relationship with *Agni* and *Indra* is often discussed in the *Ṛgveda. Sūrya* is worshipped as the god of light, knowledge, growth and life.

## 3.5 Soma "The Drink of Immortality"

*Soma* is the name of the plant as well as the drink made from the plant. *Soma* plays an important role in the Vedic rituals. It is an intoxicating drink, often called *madhu* (sweet drop). It is offered to the gods, who, it is assumed, drink it to gain immortality. It is thus called *amṛta* (the drink of immortality). Its original abode was heaven, but it was brought to earth by the bird (which is one of the symbols of *gāyatrī*, a Vedic meter). Thus *Soma* is the bestower of immortality on both the gods and human beings.

For sacrificial purposes, *Soma* was collected in the forest and then brought to the sacrificial altar where it was pounded on the stone with ritual care; its juice was squeezed out and strained; and then it was offered to the gods, who gained power and encouragement to perform heroic deeds. *Soma* is closely connected with *Indra;* not only does he love to drink it, but it also enables him to kill *Vṛtra.*

There have been several speculations about the origin of the soma plant. According to some, it was a mushroom-like plant called fly agaric; others have identified it with medicinal herbs which had the quality of curing some diseases. In *Ṛgveda,* the medicinal quality of *Soma* is described in the verses in which he is mentioned as the one who makes the blind see, the lame walk, etc.

Whatever its origin, *Soma's* connection with the element water is beyond doubt. *Soma* is viewed as the ruler of water, the son of waters and the one who is intimately connected with *Agni,* the fiery element in the cosmos. This dual connection of *Soma* with both the watery and the fiery elements is not very difficult to explain. At the cosmic level, *Soma,* as the watery element, is essential both for the creation and the sustenance of the cosmos and this is precisely the characteristic that *Soma* has in common with *Agni.* Therefore, its metaphorical description as *amṛta* (the drink of immortality)—the very life-force—seems to be quite appropriate. Similarly, in rituals, its juice (the essence of the soma plant) symbolizes the counterpart of the cosmic drink (*amṛta* "ambrosia") which with its medicinal and intoxicating qualities re-enforces life.

# 4.0 Ṛta "Cosmic Order"

The Vedic Āryans believed that *ṛta* is the cosmic order, according to which everything in the cosmos exists and functions. This abstract cosmic law revealed itself most concretely in the laws of nature which were applicable to every level of existence. Thus the blossoming of a tree, the regular cycle of the seasons, sunrise and sunset, and the cycle of life and death of all living beings were believed to be controlled by *ṛta.* The point to note here is that the power of *ṛta* was belived to be supreme, so much so that not even the gods could go against it. Exclusive responsibility for ensuring the proper functioning of *ṛta* belongs to *Varuṇa.* Hence, *Varuṇa* is called the guardian of *ṛta.* Since *ṛta* holds the cosmos together (in both its static as well as dynamic states), it has also been called *dharman* "the upholder." We will see the later development of this concept as *dharma* "duty" in chapter 4.

The idea of "order" (i.e., proper functioning of system) formed the very core of the concept of *ṛta.* Hence, the laws which upheld the proper functioning of the social order and the ritual order (through the performance of the rituals) were all viewed to be the laws of *ṛta.* In short, it was *ṛta* which as a unifying principle kept the individual, social, ritual and the cosmic orders in harmony.

Since *ṛta* was the eternal law, following *ṛta* was considered to be following the truth (*sat*). All violations of the laws of *ṛta* at any level were viewed as immoral acts or untruth (*anṛta*). For example, cheating a friend was considered to be *anṛta* at the individual level; failure to perform one's social duty and the rituals was *anṛta* at the social and ritual levels respectively, and when the demon *vṛtra* obstructed the flow of water in the universe, he was *anṛta* at the cosmic level.

The concept of punishment, which is elaborated in the later philosophical discussions, is introduced in Vedic mythology within the context of *ṛta.* When Varuṇa inflicts punishment on the gods and on humans, it is assumed that they have deviated from the cosmic law of *ṛta.* There are prayers in the Vedas which express the fear of deviation from *ṛta* and which are offered to *Varuṇa* so that *Varuṇa* will treat the sinners kindly and forgive them.

## 5.0 Sacrifice

Related to the concept of cosmic law is the belief in sacrificial rituals. Fire sacrifices provide a link or connection between human beings, cosmic power and the gods.

Early Vedic records show belief in the control of *ṛta* (and various nature-gods) over human life. It was believed that sacrificial rituals, which were primarily offerings to gods on a fire altar, would please the gods and as a result, the gods would grant the sacrificer's wishes. It was also believed that the sacrificial rituals aided the operation of *ṛta.* The offerings at the sacrifice (*soma,* butter, praises, etc.) were supposed to strengthen the gods who would then carry out their function more effectively. Since each god represented and controlled one aspect of the cosmic order (i.e., *ṛta*), the well-regulated functioning of the gods could automatically guarantee the proper functioning of *ṛta.* Thus sacrifice was viewed as a reciprocal phenomenon which showed to a large extent the interdependency of human beings and gods, even though the gods had an upper hand all the time.

Sacrificial rituals took place around a sacred fire upon an altar where the priest would ritually present offerings to various gods. A whole branch of literature called the *Brāhmaṇas* grew around these sacrificial rituals which, as we have already noted (section 2), stressed the sanctity of ritual action and speech, without which the sacrifice could not be said to be correctly performed, and thus resulting in failure and at times unwarranted, if not tragic, results for the sacrificer.

## 6.0 Monotheism, Polytheism and Henotheism

The real nature of the early Vedic gods has been a matter of much debate and speculation. Early (*Ṛg*) Vedic mythology does not provide a systematic structure in which each god has distinctive form and function; rather, we find here a complex mosaic of various gods with overlapping functions and descriptions. The polytheistic belief clearly suggested by this multiplicity of gods (e.g. *Agni, Indra, Sūrya,* etc.) is further complicated by the multiple identities of each god (e.g. *Agni's* identity with *Sūrya, Soma's* identity with water, etc.). Similarly, many of the gods share similar functions (i.e., *Indra, Agni* and *Varuṇa* are all called *ṛtasya gopā* "guardian of *ṛta*"). This confusing picture becomes clear when we perceive that beneath this apparent indeterminacy and inconsistency lies the search for interconnections among diverse elements in the cosmos. The same or similar attributes have been used in the description of many gods mainly to highlight the interconnections existing among the various facets of the overall cosmic structure. It was this search for and the view of cosmos with interconnected parts that culminated in the concept of *ṛta* which is viewed as a system of abstract rules which determine the nature and operation of all elements in the cosmos. *ṚTA,* the regulating principle in the cosmos, supercedes the powers of all gods, who must abide by the laws of *ṛta.* Thus *ṛta* is perceived as the highest power, and its guardian *Varuṇa* the highest god.

Although *ṛta* is viewed as the controlling power of the cosmos, it is never personified, nor is it viewed as the source—the creator of the universe. Everything might now exist and function according to *ṛta,* but what is the original source, the creator of these multiple existences? In *Ṛgveda,* there are many speculations about the "one" originator of the cosmos, and it is stressed time and again that the many gods must be the expression of one power. Thus in the Ṛgvedic mythology monotheism is also observed. However, the exact nature of the "one" remains obscure and indeterminate. There are two major speculations about the nature of "one" power in the *Ṛgveda;* one is linked to sacrifice, and the other is linked to speculation about the unfathomable *"Eternal Waters"* being the source of the cosmos. Due to belief in the power of sacrifice to bring about (i.e., create) desired results, it was assumed that the cosmic creation took place as a result of the sacrificial offering of the body of *Puruṣa* "the primordial man" (see the myth of *Puruṣa* in section 7 (a)). The origin of each part of the cosmos is ascribed to each part of *Puruṣa's* body. This speculation simultaneously captures the structural interconnectedness of all existences, their underlying unity and their functional diversity. However, the myth of *Puruṣa* does not provide answers to questions such as who performed the sacrifice? and for whom? What kind of existence preceded the performance of the sacrifice remains a major question. The *Nāsadīya* hymn (in *Ṛgveda*) admits the ignorance of the Vedic Āryans regarding the exact origin of the cosmos, although it speculates that the source of cosmic creation must be one (*ekam*). The "one" is described here as the "unfathomable Eternal Waters" which, due to its "inner impulse" (dynamic creative energy) created the universe (see the *Nāsadīya* hymn in section 7 (b)). Because of its emphasis on identifying one-all-powerful force underlying the cosmos, the Vedic mythology is often characterized as monotheistic in nature. Additionally, many scholars have also observed a tendency toward henotheism/kenotheism in Vedic mythology; i.e., each god is described as the supreme power with all the attributes of the all-pervasive supreme divinity. It has been further claimed that this tendency to elevate each god to the level of the supreme divinity marks the intermediate stage in the gradual culmination of polytheism into monotheism.

## 7.0 Myths of Creation in Ṛgveda

### *(a) The myth of Puruṣa "The Primordial Man":*

A thousand are the heads of *Puruṣa,*
a thousand eyes
and a thousand feet.
Encompassing the earth
from all sides,
He exists beyond ten directions.

What has been and what will be—
all is *Puruṣa*
The god of immortality
transcends (all) when nurtured by food.
Such is his greatness but *Puruṣa* is greater than this
All beings are only one fourth of his entire existence,
His three-fourths—immortality exist in heaven
Three-fourths of *Puruṣa.*

The fourth part grew here
over and over again
Then multiplied in His forms,
It traveled to the animate and the inanimate realms.

From Him (from the quarter of the Original *Puruṣa)*
was born *Virāṭ,*
From *Virāṭ, Puruṣa* was born
Soon after His birth,
He transcended the earth
in all directions.
When the gods performed a sacrifice
using *Puruṣa* as the oblation,
the spring was the clarified butter
Summer the fuel and autumn its offering.

On the grass they besprinkled
the first born *Puruṣa* as sacrifice.
The *Devas* sacrificed "with" him
and the *Sādhyās* and the *ṛṣis.*

From that sacrifice
offered in its entirety,
was collected the mixture
of milk and butter.
From that He created
the animals of the air
and the domestic animals

And from that sacrifice
offered in its entirety
were created the hymns and chants,
the meters and the sacrificial formulae.

From that were born the horses,
and those with two rows of teeth
The cows indeed were born from that
and so were the goats and the sheep.

In how many parts did they divide *Puruṣa*?
What became His mouth?
His arms? His thighs?
What were called His feet?
*Brāhmaṇa* was His mouth
His two arms were made the *Kṣatriya;*
His two thighs the *Vaiśya,*
and *Sūdra* arose from His feet.

From His mind was born the moon.
The sun was born from His eyes.
*Indra* and *Agni* were born from His mouth
and *Vāyu* was born from His breath.

From His navel arose the air,
the sky emerged from His head,
from His feet was created the earth,
the directions from His ears.
Thus they created the worlds.
When the gods, performing the sacrifice
tied *Puruṣa* as the (sacrificial) victim,
Seven were the sticks of covering,
and thrice seven were the logs of wood prepared.

The gods performed the sacrifice
for the sacrifice, with the sacrifice of *Puruṣa*

These were the earliest ordinances.
These powers reached the highest heaven,
Where live the *Sādhyas* and the gods.

***(b) The Nāsadīya Hymn:***

At that time, there was neither the non-existent,
nor the existent.
Neither the earth, nor the sky beyond it!
What was hidden? Where?
Who guarded it?
Was there then the water
Unfathomable and deep?

There was no death;
Neither was there immortality
No sign of day or night existed then,
The ONE breathed
by inner power, without the air
Besides that, there was nothing,
absolutely nothing!!

Darkness was engulfed by darkness,
All this, not distinguishable,
was water.
That ONE which was
covered by nothingness,
was born through
the power of *Tapas.*
Then arose desire,
the first impulse of the mind.
The sages exploring their hearts
with wisdom,
found the connection of the
existent in the non-existent.

The dividing line stretched beyond,
What existed below? What existed above?
The bearers of the seed were there,
and there were powers
There was self-existing energy below,
and there was impulse above.

Who really knows?
Who can proclaim it?
Whence was it born?
Whence came this creation?
The *Devas* came after the creation.
Who knows then whence it came into existence?

Whence did this creation
come into being?
Whether He supported it or He did not
The one who dwells in the highest region watches it,
He alone knows it,
or perhaps He knows it not!!

## 8.0 Origin of Society

We have already noted that the *Puruṣa* myth in the *Ṛgveda* depicts the creation of the Universe in general, and of society in particular. This hymn attributes creation to the sacrificial dismemberment of the body of the giant primordial man *Puruṣa.* From *Puruṣa's* head were created *Brāhmaṇas,* from his arms *Kṣatriyas,* from his thighs *Vaiśyas,* and from his feet *Sūdras.* The Āryan society thus was divided into four groups: *Brāhmaṇas,* (the priestly class), *Kṣatriyas* (the class of warriors), *Vaisyas* (the merchant class), and *Sūdras* (the laborer class). The above four were obviously the four major functional pivots of society, i.e., religious and secular education, protection, economic stability, and the smooth operation of the above three functions were assigned to *Brāhmaṇas, Kṣatriyas, Vaiśyas* and *Sūdras,* respectively. The division of society into four groups was thus a functionally based concept. The caste system which to this day is the differentia of the Hindu society in India has its origin in the social structure existing during the Vedic times. The myth of *Puruṣa* shows not only the importance of sacrifice in the lives of Vedic Āryans, but also the phenomenon of a myth sanctioning (in fact here sanctifying as well) an already existing functional division of society. There is much controversy regarding the precise nature of these four social classes; i.e., whether or not interclass mobility was possible, whether or not membership in a class was by birth alone, etc. The main point to note here is that it took quite some time before this social division took on the rigid stratification which led to the emergence of the social castes in India.

## 9.0 Later Developments in Vedic Mythology

The period between the 7th and 1st centuries B.C. marks the crystalization of concepts which were already introduced in the early Vedic texts and also new interpretations of earlier concepts within new ideologies. This period marks the upsurge of the *Purāṇa* "old stories of gods" literature.

## 9.1 Sacrifice

First of all, we will focus on the important changes and developments regarding the concept of sacrifice. Earlier, sacrifice was viewed as a device to please the gods who would then be merciful to the sacrificer. Later on, sacrifice was viewed as the power which would make the gods perform the deeds desired by the sacrificer. The capricious gods thus came under the power of sacrifice. This, however, resulted in a contradiction—that is, how could sacrifice control the gods when ṛta is the most powerful force? A complete answer to this question is extremely involved and would require a lengthy elaboration. But, in a nutshell, the logical explanation of the "control of gods" through sacrifice may be summarized as follows: The sacrificial ritual was believed to be the process of the "re-creation" of the universe at the altar. Each ritual object (water, rice, butter, etc.) signified one aspect of the universe; e.g., water signified the ocean, the wooden sticks signified the plant world and so on. It was a belief in *mimetic* magic (that a symbol is as real as the thing it symbolizes) which underlay this concept of the re-creation of the universe. It was believed that if the whole structure and order of the universe were re-created, the "re-created" universe would automatically generate the power of *ṛta.* The sacrificer, by virtue of his being the source or "creator" of the *ṛta* of this symbolically "re-created" world, arrogated to himself the power to influence *ṛta* and thereby to dictate to the gods the performance of desired actions.

Here lies the important change in the mythological view of the universe. Human beings do not see themselves as helpless creatures at the hands of nature, rather, the center of power has moved closer to the human beings themselves. Their own action—sacrifical re-creation—could control the world around them. Thus sacrifice came to be viewed as the magic wand which gave enormous power to the sacrificer, and, as a result, the whole life of the Āryans in the Vedic and post-Vedic periods revolved around various sacrificial rituals.

Sacrifice had an important social dimension as well. It brought the whole community together to build the altar, collect the ritual material, etc. A flawless performance of every ritual act was essential to guarantee its success. Therefore, the language of the Vedas had to be learned well. Thus sacrifice also provided an opportunity to learn language skills, mathematics, geometry, architecture, religious traditions, etc.

## 9.2 Emergence of one "God"

Various speculations regarding the nature of "one" supreme divinity in early Vedic mythology have already been mentioned. It is observed (though not explicitly mentioned) in early Vedic mythology that the supreme deity must have the power of creation (*Puruṣa* hymn), the power of regulating and controlling the cosmos (*ṛta*), and of sustaining the existence and function of the cosmos (the powers of various individual gods). In the later mythology of the *Purāṇas,* this line of reasoning led to the emergence of a supreme deity as the one God with three heads, symbolizing three powers. The three powers are the power of creation, the power of sustenance, and the power of destruction. In this image of the one supreme god with three faces (*trimūrti*), the "one head" symbolizes the underlying unity of the three faces. The *Eternal Waters* is viewed as the substantive base where the three powers reside. Thus one head is a symbol of the *Eternal Waters.* The three powers are further personified as *Brahmā* "the god of creation," *Viṣṇu* "the god of sustenance," and *Śiva* "the god of destruction." The existence and function of the cosmos is explained as follows: the cosmos is created from the Eternal Waters (by its power of creation—*Brahmā*); it is sustained by the power of sustenance (*Viṣṇu*) and is later destroyed by its power of destruction (*Śiva*).

## 9.3 Purāṇas "Old Stories of The Gods"

*Purāṇas* are texts which primarily incorporate myths about the Vedic gods, as well as some non-Vedic gods. The period of the composition of the *Purāṇas* is generally considered to be the first four or five centuries of the Christian era. Although there is controversy over the exact number of the *Purāṇas,* most scholars believe that there are eighteen major *Purāṇas* (*mahāpurāṇas*) dedicated to the three major gods (i.e., *Brahmā, Viṣṇu,* and *Śiva*) of the Vedic pantheon. The major goal of the *Purāṇas* is to explicate, elaborate and justify the complex philosophical concepts of the Vedic religion and traditions for the common people who could more easily relate to stories than to philosophical expositions.

The *Purāṇas* show a fascinating blending of two layers of meanings—one which relates to the theory or philosophy which underlies the system and the second which relates to the practice of the religion. This explains why each *Purāṇa* is dedicated to the stories (and religious practices) related to one god and yet does not exclude the existence or function of the other gods. At the philosophical level, each *Purāṇa* depicts the belief in the underlying unity of all gods, while at the practical level, they depict the growing sectarian bias of the people which results in the glorification of one god over and above other gods. Each *Purāṇa* is a rich treasure of information about the diverse religious practices (rituals, pilgrimages, etc.) related to the worship of each of the gods.

Additionally, there are several minor *Purāṇas* related to the local Vedic or non-Vedic deities who played a role in the religious life of the people.

One of the major themes of the *Purāṇas* is the conflict between theism and non-theism and the reinforcement of theism. Through the stories of gods and demons, of virtuous and evil human beings, the ultimate victory of the gods is stressed, and thereby gods are depicted as the most powerful forces which control human life. The compassionate dimension of the gods is the theme of many *Purāṇas.* Specifically significant are the *Purāṇas* related to *Viṣṇu* where *Viṣṇu's* primary function of sustaining the cosmos is stressed by depicting him as the most compassionate deity who descends from heaven to the earth to destroy evil and ensure the perpetuation of good.

## 9.4 The Myth of Creation in the Purāṇas

The emergence of the three-faced god was followed by a new myth of the creation of the universe. The myth in a nutshell as described in *Viṣṇu Purāṇa* is as follows: *Viṣṇu,* the god of sustenance lies on a giant many-headed cobra (the symbol of the *Eternal Waters*). When *Viṣṇu* opens his eyes, a multipetal lotus grows from his navel. This multipetal lotus signifies the multifaceted universe which is created by *Brahmā* (the god of creation). *Viṣṇu* sustains this universe (the lotus) for a particular period of time after which *Śiva,* the god of destruction, dances the dance of death (*Tāṇḍava*) and destroys the universe. The lotus flower closes its petals and goes back into *Viṣṇu's* navel. *Viṣṇu* goes back to sleep, only to wake up again, and the whole process of creation, sustenance, and destruction begins again.

The major points in the myth are as follows:

(a) all powers (of creation, sustenance, and destruction) belong to the same source (the *Eternal Waters*). (b) Creation is the separation of "many" from "one" (various petals of one lotus) and destruction is the process of going back from "many" to "one" (i.e., the source). (c) Creation and destruction are two facets of the same phenomenon (i.e., one cannot exist without the other). (d) Destruction does not equal annihilation; rather it is merely the transformation of one form of energy into another. (e) Creation, sustenance, and destruction constitute an unending cycle.

## 10.0 The Notion of Time

Time according to this mythology is measured in terms of the cycle of creation, sustenance, and destruction. Time does not exist independently of this cycle. It is viewed as a dimension of the above process.

The time it takes to complete one cycle is called a *Mahāyuga* "the great age," which consists of 12,000 God years (and 12,000,000 human years). The *Mahāyuga* is further divided into four parts, called the four *yugas* (*yuga* "world age"). The progression of time from *Kṛtayuga* to *Kaliyuga* is believed to be a process of gradual decay of time in its quality as well as in its quantity. The 4 yugas are the following:

| | |
|---|---|
| a. *Kṛtayuga* | 4000 years |
| b. *Tretāyuga* | 3600 years |
| c. *Dvāparayuga* | 2400 years |
| d. *Kaliyuga* | 1200 years |
| | 12,000 years = *Mahāyuga* (the great age) |

The time of 800 years between the end of one cycle and the beginning of the next is included in each *Māhāyuga* (400 years for destruction and 400 years for creation).

Time is thus circular in Hindu mythology. The myth of creation, sustenance, and destruction is basically the myth of eternal return. The destruction of the universe in itself is the cause of re-creation. Thus *pralaya* or the cosmic deluge that occurs after the end of *Kaliyuga* in every cycle is not a negative concept in Hindu mythology, since nothing is permanently destroyed. Death and destruction is only a link between two births or creations. This notion of time is different from the Western notion of time which is unidirectional.

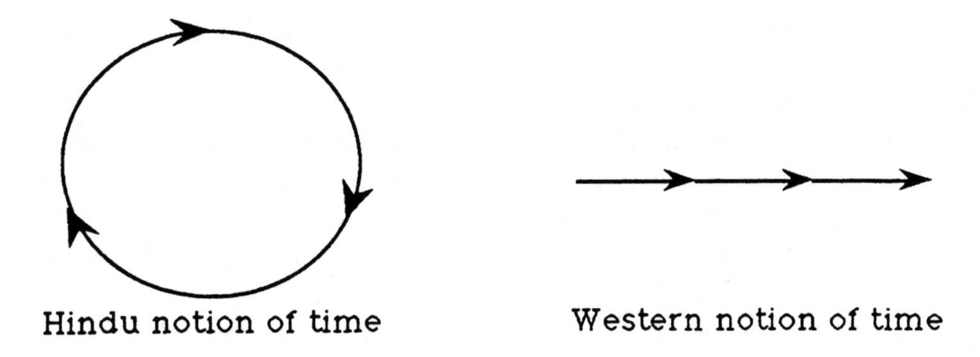


In the Hindu view, both individuals and time are viewed as non-unique entities, since both keep going through the repeated cycles. In the western system, however, the uniqueness of each moment goes hand in hand with the uniqueness of each individual. In the Indian (Hindu) system the only possible uniqueness lies in the relative existence of an individual and the moment in a particular cycle of time.

## 11.0 The Position of Human Beings in the Cosmos

The following diagram may be useful in explaining the Vedic belief regarding the position of human beings in the cosmos.

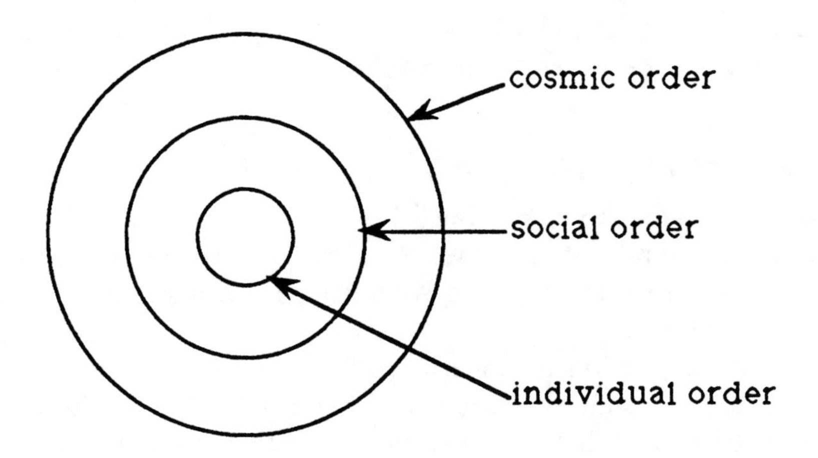


The individual, social and cosmic orders are viewed as interdependent. For each order to function properly, the other two must also properly function. A disturbance at any one order creates a disturbance at the other two orders as well. Thus the gods, society, and individuals must all function in consonance with each other. The duty of a god was to carry out his function according to *ṛta*. The social duty of human beings was considered to be carrying out the different jobs assigned to them by their social class. The social order was to be maintained by following their social (class) duty.

However, it was assumed that the orders could be disturbed by several factors, which could be characterized as deviations from *ṛta.* If people, societies, and cosmic forces failed to perform their duties properly, the orders would be disturbed. It was also believed that such disturbances were to be expected when the universe was going through the last part of the cycle, since those disturbances aided the process of destruction. However, when such disturbances occurred before the final disturbance and disturbed the orders, the god of sustenance, *Viṣṇu,* remedied it by arriving at the scene of the disturbance in a form suitable to fight and overcome the cause of the disturbance.

According to Hindu mythology, in past times many such disturbances have occurred and *Viṣṇu* has appeared in various forms to sustain the cosmos. Those forms of *Viṣṇu* are called the *avatāras* or the incarnations of *Viṣṇu.*

The incarnations (from 1 to 9) follow a chronological order (past to present). Each disturbance was different and needed a different solution and consequently required a different form of *Viṣṇu.* Also, every disturbance was more severe than the previous one, so that, in order to save the universe, *Viṣṇu* had to take increasingly stronger forms. The following are summaries of the myths concerning disturbances and *Viṣṇu's* remedies.

## 12.0 The Avatāras of *Viṣṇu*

The *avatāras* of *Viṣṇu* are numerous, but ten are considered to be the most important. They are: *Matsya* or fish; *Kūrma* or tortoise; *Varāha* or boar; *Narasiṃha* or man-lion, *Vāmana* or dwarf; *Paraśuāma; Rāmacandra; Kṛṣṇa; Buddha;* and *Kālkin.* Of these, the first five are said to have taken place in worlds other than ours; in the next four, *Viṣṇu* lived on earth as a human; and the last is yet to come at the end of the world.

### *12.1 Matsya (the Fish Incarnation)*

"I will take you beyond the shore," said the fish.

At the time of a disruptive storm, when the ocean was just about to swallow the human race, *Viṣṇu* descended on earth in the form of a fish and rescued the human race by saving the ship of Manu, the first man.

Manu, the first man, was once wandering around on the shore. Suddenly, he saw a tiny fish thrown onto the sandy shore by the tide. The tiny creature, flapping its wings and tail, was hovering between life and death. Manu, overwhelmed with pity, saved the little fish by putting it back into the water. Soon the fish began to grow bigger, till it extended over ten million *yojanas* (leagues). Its shiny golden hue radiated a unique charm which barely suggested its divine origin. It had a huge horn on its head. "O, kind Manu, you have saved my life! A kind deed such as this never goes unrewarded. I will save you in the time of disaster. Manu, there is going to be a deluge. The ocean with its millions of waves will rise to the sky. The world will tremble with the roaring sound of the stormy waves. Fear not Manu, I will save you. Build a ship and tie it to my horn and you will be safe. I will sail your ship beyond the stormy ocean . . . to the other shore . . . across the waters . . . to the Himālayan mountains," said the fish.

Thus the first man, and thereby the human race, was saved from the untimely disaster by the fish, who was none other than *Viṣṇu* himself!

## 12.2 Kūrma (the Tortoise Incarnation)

"And with the tortoise as a base, *Mandāra* mountain as a churning stick and *Vāsuki* as a rope, the gods and the demons churned the ocean."

In his second descent, in the form of *Kūrma,* the tortoise, *Viṣṇu* prevented a war between the gods and the demons by providing them both with the opportunity to acquire the drink of immortality (*amṛta*).

*Asuras,* the demons, had once again declared war against the gods, whose king was Indra himself. The victory of the gods was more unlikely than ever, since *Indra* had insulted Durvāsa, the powerful Brāhmaṇa ascetic whose curse had left the gods weak and feeble. The conflict of the opposites—the gods and the demons—was certain and so was the victory of the demons! How could this be prevented? Who would save the gods?

Viṣṇu, the sustainer, came up with a brilliant solution which would ensure the sustenance of both the gods and the demons! "*Kūrma,* the tortoise I will be," said Viṣṇu, "and lay at the bottom of the great ocean. O gods, place the mountain *Mandāra* on my back. Using it as a churning stick and *Vāsuki* the serpent as the rope, churn the ocean, together with the demons. The drink of immortality which lies in the ocean will come out as a result of the churning. Share it with the demons!"

The gods and the demons, equally eager to receive the drink of immortality, agreed. The mountain *Mandāra* was placed on the back of the tortoise, and *Vāsuki* the serpent was twisted around *Mandāra.* The churning of the ocean thus began, with the gods on one side, holding the tail of the serpent, and the demons on the other, holding its mouth.

Out of the cosmic ocean came the fourteen precious *ratnas* (jewels): (1) the moon, (2): the *Pārijāta* tree (which would grant the wishes of its owner), (3) the *Airāvata* (the elephant which became *Indra's* vehicle), (4) *Surabhī* (the cow which would fulfill the desires of its owner), (5) *Vāruni* (the goddess of wine), (6) *Apsaras* (the nymphs of the sky), (7) *Uccaiśrava* (the white horse) (8) *Lakṣmī* (the goddess of wealth), (9) *Śaṇkha* (the conch shell), (10) *gadā* (mace), (11) *Kaustubha* (a precious jewel), (12), *Dhanvantarī* (the doctor, and the author of the Āyurveda system of medicine), (13) *amṛta* (ambrosia—the drink of immortality), and (14) *Hālāhala*—the deadly poison.

There are several versions of this myth. According to some, the gods drank the ambrosia and became immortal. According to another, the battle over ambrosia begins here and continues forever. Neither the gods nor the demons can win. Neither of them can destroy the other, since the existence (i.e., balance) of both is essential for the sustenance of the world.

## 12.3 Varāha (the Boar Incarnation)

"Knowledge was lost to the world and the earth was sinking by the weight of ignorance."

When Hiraṇyākṣa, the demon, had stolen the Vedas, knowledge was lost to the world; the earth was sinking with the burden of ignorance. *Viṣṇu* took the form of a boar and lifted the earth with his tusk and, having killed the demon, brought back the Vedas.

Hiraṇyākṣa, the demon, once performed severe penances and pleased Brahmā, the god of creation. "Enough of these penances Hiraṇyākṣa!" said Brahmā, "Ask a boon, and I will grant it!" Hiraṇyākṣa, delighted to hear those words said, "O powerful one, grant me a boon by which no god, human being, or a beast will be able to kill me!" "So be it" said Brahmā. As Hiraṇyākṣa's misfortune would have it, he forgot to include the boar (*Varāha*) in the list of those that would not be able to kill him.

Now, with the boon bestowed on him, the arrogant Hiraṇyākṣa in his inflated pride stole the Vedas while Brahmā, the custodian of the Vedas, was asleep. Soon Hiraṇyākṣa ran to his abode, the nether world.

With knowledge lost, the earth began to sink into the primordial waters, as the burden of ignorance became impossible for her to bear. Viṣṇu assumed the form of a boar and killed Hiraṇyākṣa. He stabbed his tusk deep into the ocean floor and lifted the earth. The Vedas were brought back and peace and order were again restored in the world!

## *12.4 Narasimha (the Man-Lion Incarnation)*

"Where is your Viṣṇu?" asked Hiraṇyakaśipu.

In the incarnation of *Narasimha,* Viṣṇu assumed the form of a man-lion to kill Hiraṇyakaśipu, who had disturbed the order of *ṛta* by refusing to accept the cosmic power of sustenance (of Viṣṇu), deeming himself to be all-powerful and oppressing the people.

Once Hiraṇyakaśipu, the demon king, performed severe penances. Pleased with him, Brahmā granted him immunity from gods, human beings, and animals. Hiraṇyakaśipu, swollen with pride, said to himself, "I am the most powerful being, for no god, man or animal can kill me, I am the invincible one!" The tyrant Hiraṇyakaśipu then refused to accept the all-pervasive power of Viṣṇu. He killed everyone who refused to accept his superiority over all other powers—including the power of the gods. His own son, Prahlāda, however, was an ardent worshipper of Viṣṇu. Time and again, he tried to convince his father of the omniscience and omnipotence of Viṣṇu. Once, becoming enraged by his son's devotion to *Viṣṇu,* he shouted "Where is your Viṣṇu? Is he in this stone-pillar?" and he kicked the pillar. Out came Viṣṇu in the form of a man-lion. The upper half of his body was a lion and the lower half was a man. "Here I am," said Viṣṇu, who knew that Hiraṇyakaśipu was caught in his own game. Hiraṇyakasipu due to a boon, could not be killed by gods, demons, and humans but he was not granted immunity from a man-lion. Viṣṇu killed Hiraṇyakaśipu and blessed Prahlāda.

## *12.5. Vāmana (the Dwarf Incarnation)*

"The three strides of Viṣṇu."

Viṣṇu took the form of a dwarf to suppress the arrogant demon king Bali, who had conquered the three worlds due to the power he had gained by austerities and penances. This power had corrupted him and made him a tyrant. Viṣṇu taught him a lesson of humility and saved the worlds of the gods and the human beings.

The following myth relates to this incarnation: In the *Tretāyuga,* the second age, a demon king Bali had become the lord of the three worlds—heaven, the earth, and the nether world.

He had acquired this position by means of his penances and austerities. However, once he gained the power, he was no longer a humble virtuous king. He oppressed every being—gods and humans alike. The different orders of *ṛta* were disturbed. Viṣṇu, the god of sustenance, took the form of a dwarf, son of the sage Kaśyapa and Aditi. He went to Bali and said, "Oh, great king, could you grant me a small piece of land?—only as much as three tiny steps of mine can measure?" The king Bali granted him permission to measure and own the three strides of land as he had asked. Little did Bali know that the dwarf was Viṣṇu himself, and his strides were not those of a common dwarf. By only the first two he covered the heaven and the earth, respectively. "Where shall I place this third step?" asked the dwarf, and placed it over Bali's head and pushed him down into the nether world, which truly was the place of demons. Viṣṇu, remembering Bali's earlier virtues, granted him the nether world as his kingdom.

## *12.6 Paraśurāma ("Rāma with the axe"—incarnation)*

The story of this incarnation involves a disruption of the social order caused by a caste-conflict between the *Brāhmaṇas* and the *Kṣatriyas.* Viṣṇu took the form of a *Brāhmaṇa,* who, with an axe in his hand, took an oath to annihilate the *Kṣatriyas* who were oppressing the *Brāhmaṇas.*

The myth of this incarnation is as follows: Once, when the powerful *Kṣatriya* king Kārtavīrya was wandering around in the forest, he happened to notice *Kāmadhenu* (the cow who had the power of fulfiling every wish of her owner). The "wish-granting" cow belonged to a learned *Brāhmaṇa* of great repute called Jamadagni. "What is the use of such a cow to an ascetic like Jamadagni, who has transcended all worldly desires and who lives in the forest? It is a powerful king like me who deserves a cow like this." And the arrogant king abducted the cow for himself and returned to his capital. At this time the only person at home was Jamadagni's wife who was not strong enough to stop the king.

When Jamadagni and his five sons returned to their hermitage, they found the cow missing. When the youngest son Paraśurāma heard the story of the king's arrogance, he immediately left to wage a battle against the king and consequently killed him. In order to avenge the death of his father, Kārtavīrya's son killed Jamadagni, when he was alone in the forest.

Seeing all this, Paraśurāma picked up an axe and declared, "The world will soon be without a single *Kṣatriya,*" and took an oath to annihilate the whole *Kṣatriya* race from the face of the earth. According to the myth, Paraśurāma destroyed the whole *Kṣatriya* race from the earth twenty-one times.

## *12.7 Rāma (the Hero of the Epic Rāmāyaṇa)*

The earth was being oppressed by Rāvaṇa, the demon king. At the request of Brahmā and Śiva, Viṣṇu decided to "descend" to the earth in the form of the son of Daśaratha to kill Rāvaṇa and to establish order. The story of Rāma is elaborately narrated in the epic "*Rāmāyaṇa*" composed by Vālmiki (for further discussion see chapter 4).

## 12.8 Kṛṣṇa (the Incarnation of the "Blue God")

In his incarnation as Kṛṣṇa "the blue god" of the cowherds (of the north-western part of India), Viṣṇu killed the demon king Kaṃsa who oppressed the common people in his country. In the story of this descent, the conflict between the powerful (the king) and the powerless (the common people) is depicted, and in the form of Kṛṣṇa, Viṣṇu represents the identity, survival, and victory of the common people over the oppressive king (for further discussion see chapter 7).

## 12.9 Buddha ("The Enlightened One")

Viṣṇu's ninth descent is very interesting. According to the *Bhāgavata Purāṇa, Buddha,* the founder of Buddhism was in fact the ninth descent of *Viṣṇu,* whose mission was to distract those people who did not believe in the system of Hinduism and divert them from the "right" path, thereby bringing about their destruction. This myth treats the Buddhist rejection of caste, the Vedas and the Hindu gods as the path toward destruction.

## 12.10 Kālkin ("The Warrior Riding the White Horse"—Incarnation)

According to Hindu mythology, this descent of Viṣṇu is yet to occur. In *Kaliyuga* (the last age), Viṣṇu will descend upon the earth in the form of Kālkin, a man mounted on a white horse, with a shining sword in his hand. Before the destruction of the universe, Kālkin will descend (for the last time in this cycle) to abolish the disturbances caused by the evil actions of people.

Viṣṇu Purāṇa describes the situation on the earth very vividly. In *Kaliyuga,* according to *Viṣṇu Purāṇa,* there will be disturbance at every level—cosmic, social, political, and moral. Society will be unstable; kings will be oppressive. Falsehood and wickedness will be the legitimate means to succeed in life. Possession of property and expensive clothes will be signs of dignity and high rank. Piety and devotion to god will rapidly decrease. People will pay tribute to wealth. Passion will rule in every walk of life, with marriages based on passion alone. Women will be considered as objects of sensual pleasure. Dishonesty will be the way of life. There will be no place regarded as sacred. People will treat the earth merely as the source of material wealth. The production of wealth will decrease. The world will run short of resources to sustain its people. People from different countries will intermingle. The powerful will oppress the powerless.

In general, the world will show the signs of readiness for total chaos and destruction. But since the universe will still be a little away from the final point of destruction, Viṣṇu will descend as Kālkin to save the world for the last time before *Śiva* dances his dance of death and destruction (*Tāṇḍava*).

# CHAPTER 4

# *Mythology of the Epics: The Rāmāyaṇa*

## 1.0 From Vedic to Epic mythology

Epic mythology is separated from Vedic mythology by more than half a millennium, during which time Indian philosophical, religious, and mythological systems underwent several changes due to turmoils and upheavals caused by the unstable socio-political and religious situation in the country. In order to understand Epic mythology, it is important to take a look at the sociopolitical context which prevailed in India during the period between 500 B.C. and 200 A.D. The Āryan culture gradually permeated throughout the land and exerted its influence on the indigenous cultures (i.e., Indus, Dravidian, Munda, etc.), and in turn, was also influenced by them.

Āryan religious and social systems were challenged and rejected by two religions in the 5$^{th}$ to the 4$^{th}$ century B.C.: Buddhism (founded by the Buddha), and Jainism (founded by Mahāvīra). In the 3$^{rd}$ century B.C. Asoka, a king of the Maurya dynasty who himself became a Buddhist, actively patronized and propagated Buddhism, not only in India but also in such neighboring countries as Ceylon, Burma, Thailand, etc. The expansionist attitude of the Gupta and the Maurya kings whose power was centered in Magadha (presently the state of Bihar), created turmoil within the country. The political instability in India was enhanced by constant invasions of the Greeks, Śakas, and Hūṇas from across the northwestern border of India.

In this context, the Vedic religious and social systems had to be clearly defined and defended both at the levels of theory and practice to cope with the needs of the time. A group of texts, *Dharmaśāstra* "code of behavior," interpreted the Vedas and Vedic injunctions in the context of contemporary society and, moreover, codified the laws which were introduced as guidelines of social and religious behaviors in Vedic literature. *Manusmṛti* "the laws of Manu" (3rd century B.C.) marks the origin of what is viewed today as Hindu Law. However, *Manusmṛti* incorporated the current customs and traditions of non-Vedic people as well which facilitated acceptance of the Vedic principles by the non-Āryan population as well.

A prominent feature of the religious system during the post-Vedic period is the emergence of the doctrine of *Bhakti* "devotion" to a personal god. The abstract philosophical notions of *Brahman,* (ultimate reality) and *Ātman* (the embodied soul) were not denied; neither were the Vedic gods rejected. But choosing one of the gods (generally *Śiva* or *Viṣṇu*) and elevating him to the level of *Brahman,* and then worshipping his idols/icons/images with religious ritual to the exclusion of other gods is a major development in the religious system. This idol-worship provided a concrete manifestation of the formerly abstract notions of the "almighty" and also provided the sanction for the worship of local gods (Āryan and non-Āryan) who were treated on a par with the Vedic gods. The religious system thus included some variation in the paths prescribed to establish identity with *Brahman,* the ultimate reality (i.e., the path of intellectual rationalization and realization of one's identity with *Brahman,* and the emotionally satisfying path of identifying with the ultimate reality through worshiping of a personal god).

This variation in the Vedic belief system needed to be justified and questions regarding the relative superiority of the particular gods and paths had to be discussed. The epics, particularly the *Bhagavadgītā* (part of the epic *Mahābhārata,* see chapters 4 and 5), present an integrative approach to religion, justifying it on the basis of the re-interpretation of the system. "All paths" says the *Bhagavadgītā* "are the right paths"; they each lead to *Brahman;* worship of any god is essentially the worship of one god (since all gods are but the manifestations of one god).

In general, by the time of the Epic mythology, the Vedic religion had become crystalized enough to be identified as a well-defined system of theory and practice and had become flexible enough to incorporate the diverse strands of social and religious traditions which existed and emerged during that period.

The concepts which provided the basis for the codification, justification, and flexibility of the Vedic systems are *karma, dharma,* and *Māyā.*

## 2.0 Karma

The Sanskrit noun *karma* is etymologically derived from the verb root *kṛ* "to act, to do" and literally means "action." The term acquired various additional meanings in different contexts at different periods of time, although its original meaning has been consistently preserved. In Indian mythology, the term *karma* was first used in the Vedic *Brāhmaṇas* (900 B.C.), where it refers to "ritual actions" of performing sacrifices, offering gifts to gods, chanting Vedic mantras, etc. Due to belief in the efficacy of ritual action, the meaning of the term *karma* was further extended to "action which causes the intended result." This relationship between ritual action and the intended result did not admit the intervention of any divine will and was viewed as a chain of cause (i.e., action) and effect (i.e., result). In this context, then, the term *karma* referred to both the actions and their intended results. It was also believed that in order for the intended results to occur, the "correct" ritual actions had to be performed and failure to perform "right" actions would bring about undesirable results. It was also observed (in *Pūrva-Mīmāṃsā* philosophy) that the result of the actions (*karma*) could remain unmanifested (*apūrva*) until the proper conditions arose (i.e., the intended result of a ritual may not be experienced immediately).

This view of *karma* had an enormous impact on the worldview of the people. This "cause and effect" theory was later on extended to all actions (ritual/nonritual). It was assumed that all actions bring results and that one's situation in the present is the result (*phala*) of actions performed in the past. Similarly, the totality of actions performed in the present will determine the situation in the future. Since the intended results of the action do not necessarily occur immediately, one lifetime may not be enough for the agent of the action to experience results. In such a case, in order to experience the results one needs to be reborn. Thus the original theory of cause and effect gave rise to the theory of rebirth, i.e., it is desire which induces action, action brings about result, and therefore, in order to experience the results one has to be reborn.

This theory of *karma* provided explanations not only for the differences in the dispositions of the individuals but also for the differences in their life-experiences. Moreover, it provided an ethical dimension to the theory of causality; i.e., "good" actions bring "good" results, while "bad" actions bring "bad" results, just as a good seed produces a good plant, while a bad seed produces a bad plant. Accordingly, the consequence of right or wrong actions will have to be borne by human beings in the next or some other life, if not in this life.

The *karma* theory in general stressed human control over the kind of rebirth and life-experiences. The *karma* theory thus also justified the four-fold division of the society. By the time of the epics this four-fold division of society had become quite rigid. Membership in a particular class was determined by birth. According to the *karma* theory, birth was determined by the *karma* of the last birth. Therefore, the very fact that one has been born in a particular class is a proof of his/her eligibility to be born in that class. *Chāndogya Upaniṣad* (5:10:7) clearly points out that the one who performs "right" actions is born in the *Brāhmaṇa, Kṣatriya,* or *Vaiśya* class. On the other hand, the one who fails to perform the "right" actions is born as a *Śudra,* a dog or a pig. The *karma* theory, in addition to justifying the social class-system, provided a definite hope for improving the quality and nature of one's life—if not in this birth, over different births. From the above perspective, one must accept one's position in life and treat the present station as an opportunity to improve one's future situation. Human beings themselves must take responsibility for their actions in the past as well as the present.

## 3.0 Dharma

The question as to what is a right or meritorious action is answered by the dictates of *dharma* "duty." Each action which is in consonance with one's duty is a meritorious action and amounts to following one's *dharma. Dharma* "duty" thus has a two-fold character: it refers to duty according to one's social class and also according to one's stage in life.

Etymologically speaking, *dharma* refers to the law which sustains everything. Within the context of human behavior, *dharma* is the law which sustains human beings as members of society. Thus the word *dharma* refers to the duties of a human being toward society and toward himself. As a member of society, one's duty is determined by his social class *(Brāhmaṇa, Kṣatriya, Vaiśya, Śudra,* cf. Chapter 3). For example, because such acts would be contrary to his *dharma,* a learned *Brāhmaṇa* could not refuse to teach; nor could an able warrior refuse a war.

*Dharma* also requires that as an individual, one has duties to perform at different stages in life. It is believed that the life cycle is divided into four phases (periods) and each phase requires an individual to perform particular duties. The stages are called *āśramas* or stations. These are stations through which every human passes. They are as follows:

(a) *Brahmacaryāśrama*—"student's stage." The major duty of the individual is to educate himself under the guidance of a teacher with whom the student would live for 12 years after initiation into this phase. At the age of 12, boys of the first three social classes would be initiated into education and this phase would last until the age of 24. During this stage, the student would wear a sacred thread around his chest and would not marry. The student-teacher relationship was close, similar to that between son and father. The student was expected to learn the Vedic texts, the science of medicine, astrology, weaponry, music, etc.

(b) *Gṛhasthāśrama*—"householder's stage." This stage would begin after the education was complete. The individual then would be expected to marry and produce children. This stage was considered to be the most important one. It focused on marital love, (i.e., its importance and role), the centrality of family life in the life cycle, and, finally, the expansion of one's own identity (i.e., by raising a family and identifying oneself with all the members within the family). This stage was also important for religious reasons. The funeral rites had to be performed only by the son of the deceased, in the absence of which, it was believed that the deceased could not be saved from hell. Interestingly, the very meaning of the word *putra* "son" is "the one who saves his parents from the hell named *pu.*"

(c) *Vānaprasthāśrama*—"forest dweller stage." After enjoying the sensual pleasures of life, in this stage the person is expected to mentally withdraw from worldly attachments and concentrate on spiritual development by reading the Vedas and *Upaniṣads,* meditating on one's true self, etc. The main idea was to become an ascetic—one without attachment. (Earlier on, people would actually go into the forest to be away from the world of senses and attachment to family in order to concentrate on their spiritual development.) This stage was considered to be preparation for the next stage. Gradual withdrawal from the material world was encouraged and was built into the system of duties.

(d) *Sanyāsāśrama*—"hermit's stage." In the third stage the person would not actually leave home, but rather would perform his duties with an attitude of detachment towards the worldly life. In the fourth stage, one was expected to break all ties with the world of the senses—including one's family—and become a forest-dweller who was fully prepared for death. The forest-dweller did not own any property at this stage and withdrew physically and mentally from everything related to this world.

Another important point to note about *dharma* here is that a conflict was likely to arise between one's individual and social duty, in which case one's social duty had to take precedence over one's individual duty.

## 4.0 Brahman and Māyā

The term *Māyā* is defined in several ways. However, two of its characteristics are clearly evident in the mythology. One is its creative power "*Śakti*" the other is its opposition to the ultimate reality *Brahman.*

*Māyā* is the creative power inherent in *Brahman* (as an intrinsic attribute) which causes the one indivisible ultimate reality (i.e., *Brahman)* to be manifested as the entire phenomenal world of endlessly diverse forms, including gods, nature, and human beings. It is the causal link between the ultimate, abstract reality *Brahman* and its physical manifestation—the multidimensional universe. The term *Māyā is* used to denote the creation, i.e., the manifested world. In this sense *Māyā* refers to all existence.

The second important aspect of *Māyā is* its functional opposition to *Brahman.* Hindu mythology presents a definition of what is viewed as "real." Within this mythology "real" equals permanent. Therefore, *Māyā,* the world of senses, is not real. And accordingly, the term *Māyā is* interpreted as "illusion" (i.e., not real, or that which creates the illusion of reality). *Māyā,* the world of existences, although created from *Brahman* is transitory; it is eternally changing—passing through the cycle of creation, sustenance, and destruction, while *Brahman* is eternal. This is the opposition between *Māyā* and *Brahman: Māyā* is transitory, changing, and therefore unreal. *Brahman* is eternal, unchanging, and therefore real.

Because of its transitory nature, *Māyā* is viewed as the source of human suffering. It is viewed as a feminine principle which creates this transitory world of attractive forms and lures human beings into believing that it is real (permanent), and thereby causes utter grief to human beings who suffer due to the loss of everything they cherish throughout their lives. *Māyā* is viewed as a temptress who creates a veil between human beings and the eternal *Brahman.*

Human beings get attached to *Māyā* and forget their real self (*Ātman* 'soul'), and consequently, by identifying themselves with their bodies get caught in the cycle of rebirth. (See also chapter 6.) The goal of life, according to Hindu mythology, is to transcend *Māyā,* to go beyond transitoriness and to attain what is "real." This quest for reality is well described in the Upanisad in the following passage

tamaso ma jyotirgamaya
asato mā sad gamaya.

(lead me) from the darkness to the light
from the unreal to the real.
*(Bṛhadāraṇyakopaniṣad 1.3.28)*

### 4.1 *Viṣṇu's Māyā!*

What is *Māyā?* How is it related to *Brahman? Is Māyā* real or unreal? If it is the power of *Brahman,* it must be real (like *Brahman* itself), if it is creation, it must be unreal. How does one understand the mysterious nature of *Māyā?* These are questions which are often raised in philosophical speculations as well as in the myths in various *Purāṇas,* and in folk tales. The myths are generally presented in the form of a dialogue between *Viṣṇu* 'the sustainer of the creation and destruction' and his disciples, who wish to comprehend the nature of *Māyā.*

For example, one of the myths in the *Bhāgavata Purāṇa* tells us about Mārkandeya, the great *rsi* 'sage' who was granted a boon by *Viṣṇu,* the latter being highly pleased with Mārkanḍeya's extraordinary austerity and devotion. "Choose any wish and I will grant it to you," said Viṣṇu. "I want to know the secret of your *Māyā,*" said Mārkanḍeya. "It is due to the power of *Māyā* that you, the indivisible one are perceived as manifold." "So be it," said Viṣṇu. Thereafter Viṣṇu reveals to him the powerful, enchanting, and yet illusive nature of *Māyā* in the following manner.

One day Mārkanḍeya was sitting on the bank of the river Puṣpabhadrā when he had the following vision: a violent storm arose; dark fierce clouds showered torrential rains; the loud noise of thunder and lightning shook the world. The four oceans overflowed and flooded the whole earth. Mārkanḍeya saw himself witnessing the whole world, sky, heaven, the galaxies being submerged into the rising waves of the ocean. It seemed that these were the waters of deluge. Mārkanḍeya, like a blind man, hungry and thirsty, tortured by the alligators, kept wandering in the darkness. At times he was sucked into whirlpools; he was beaten by the stormy waves. He experienced pleasure and pain alternately, wandering through the Māyā of the deluge. All of this appeared to Mārkanḍeya to last a long, long period of thousands of years.

Suddenly he saw a Banayan tree. On a small leaf of the Banayan tree there lay a beautiful little baby, who appeared to radiate light. He lay contentedly, sucking on his little toes. There was an inexplicable, irresistable charm in the innocent smile on the coral-like lips of the infant. As he approached closer to the infant, he was suddenly sucked inside the baby's stomach, and to his surprise he saw an infinite multitude of forms inside the baby—the sky, heaven, galaxies, earth, mountains, oceans, time past and present, the Himalaya mountain, everything was exactly as it was before the deluge. While he was lost in this vision of the universe, he was suddenly expelled with the exhalation of the infant's breath and once again he found himself in the deluge—and there was the huge Banayan tree standing tall, with the infant of inexhaustible charm, lying on its leaf, as green as the leaf itself. Filled with an uncontrollable longing to embrace the child, he approached. At that very moment, the child disappeared like the hopes of an unlucky man. So also disasppeared the waters of the deluge and the Banayan tree. Mārkanḍeya once again found himself in his hermitage. This was the vision of *Māyā* that Mārkandeya had.

Another myth of the vision of *Māyā* is the following popular tale. (There are different versions of this tale in different parts of India.)

Nārada, a devoted disciple of Viṣṇu, insists on experiencing the true nature of *Māyā.* Viṣṇu explains the two-fold nature of *Māyā* —one as creative power *(śakti)* and the second, the creation of manifold forms itself. "However, the real/unreal nature of *Māyā* is inexplicable," says Viṣṇu. "But I want to know it" insists Nārada. Since a good teacher must never refuse knowledge to a student, Viṣṇu grants Nārada his wish, and sends him to a nearby village to fetch some drinking water for him.

There Nārada was greeted by a beautiful girl named Rati (which is also the name of the wife of Kama—the god of love and desire) who offered him a pail of water. As Nārada was about to leave, Rati's father pointed out to him that evening was setting in and soon it would be dark, so he should stay over with them for the night and leave the next morning.

Nārada agreed. The next morning Rati's mother asked Nārada if he would be gracious enough to help them out in the Pūjā (worship) to be performed to *Lakṣmi*, the goddess of prosperity which Rati's father had planned for the sake of the well being of the entire village. Rati's father was a headman of the village and therefore it was his responsibility to carry out the ritual successfully. A learned Brāhmaṇa like Nārada could not refuse this request. Nārada stayed in the village the next day, followed by many more days and nights—until neither Nārada nor the villagers could remember when Nārada had first come to the village. It seemed like Nārada was always there in the village.

Nārada became as much part of Rati's family as of the village. Gradually and willingly, he took over several of the responsibilities of Rati's father, who was getting old. No one was surprised when Nārada married Rati and formally entered the family. Nārada's involvement in the family and the village increased as he became the father of three beautiful children and succeeded Rati's father, after his death, as the headman of the village. With Nārada's hard work, loving care and proper organization, the village flourished with bountiful crops and prosperity.

By now Nārada was totally immersed in *Māyā*. The more he gave himself to the family and village, the more he got entangled in the wells of *Māyā*. The joys and pains of his life looked very "real" to him. Nārada had forgotten the original purpose of his arrival in the village and it did not seem to matter to him anymore.

But Nārada's bliss did not last forever. One rainy day in the monsoon season, Nārada's village was struck with torrential rains; the river, unable to contain the enormous flood of water, overflowed the village. Nārada, his wife and children were caught in the deluge-like waters. Nārada desperately tried to save his wife and children but had no success. His wife and three children were drowned right in front of his eyes, and he could not do anything to save them. The blow of losing his family benumbed Nārada. The whole family which had appeared to be so "real" vanished in a trifle like a beautiful dream—and so did the village which he had cared for like his own child. The floods destroyed in a moment's time what he had taken a lifetime to create and nourish.

While he was swimming through the waters, Nārada's own words echoed in his ears "There is only one thing I want to know *Bhagavan* (Viṣṇu)—Your *Māyā*. How do people get caught in the illusion of *Māyā?*" Nārada found that his question had been satisfactorily answered. His revelation of the powerful, enchanting and illusive nature of *Māyā* was very vivid and intimate. He needed no further explanations or expositions about the "real" nature of the world—bewitching *Māyā*.

## 5.0 The Rāmāyaṇa: 'Story of Rāma'

The *Rāmāyaṇa* was composed by Vālmīki some time during the period 400–200 B.C. in about 24,000 verses. No other work of literature has had such an enormous and all-pervasive impact on the lives of the people in India. Around the story of Rāma, the hero of the epic, is interwoven a network of complex philosophical issues such as disturbance in the cosmic order *(ṛta),* the role of the gods in its re-establishment, and the role of *karma* in human destiny as well as in cosmic justice and rebirth, etc. The *Rāmāyaṇa* is also a mirror of the spiritual and ethical values of the people—especially with respect to questions of good and evil, conflicts of individual vs. society, parameters for judging right action, and the role of destiny in human life. The answers that the *Rāmāyaṇa* provides to these questions are believed by tradition to be essentially valid for all times and in all ages. Even today *Rāmāyaṇa* is considered in India to be the epic of "ideals." For example, *Rāmrājya* 'Rāma's rule' is a synonym for an ideal society. Also, each of the major characters has been viewed as the "ideal" (Rāma as the ideal king, Sītā as the ideal wife, Bharata as the ideal brother and so on). It is interesting to note here that even in the present changed times, although emulating the ideals of the *Rāmāyaṇa* has become increasingly difficult for people, nevertheless these ideals have not been discarded and have been found by tradition to be perpetually relevant.

The *Rāmāyaṇa* portrays the development of Hinduism from Upanisadic abstract philosophy to the devotion of the gods (Viṣṇu and Śiva) of the Hindu trinity. Viṣṇu's role as the god of sustenance is more directly depicted in the *Rāmāyaṇa,* where Rāma is the 7th descent of Viṣṇu who "comes down" to earth to destroy Rāvaṇa, a demon who was disturbing the cosmic order. Thus the Rāmāyaṇa stresses the inseparability of the human and the divine realms and reinforces the Upanisadic view of the interrelatedness of all phenomena.

The historical dimension of the *Rāmāyaṇa* is of enormous value. It is generally believed that it presents a picture of the Indian social and political situation which existed around 200 B.C., when the Āryans had conquered almost the entire northern subcontinent and were proceeding towards the South. The central theme of the epic is the conflict between Rāma, the Āryan king, and Rāvaṇa, the non-Āryan king of Lankā. Hence, it appears that the *Rāmāyaṇa* is perhaps the only historical document which describes the territories occupied by the Āryans and the non-Āryans respectively, and the differences in the cultural and sociopolitical systems of these two. However, the *Rāmāyaṇa* remains essentially a magnificent epic of human emotions and dilemmas, actions and destiny, notwithstanding the loud religious and historical overtones echoing all through the epic.

The *Rāmāyaṇa* is considered to be the oldest classical epic in Sanskrit literature. Numerous later epics, plays and poems, including the well known *Raghuvaṃśa* by Kālidāsa, and *Rāmcaritmānas* by Tulsīdās, have been based on the *Rāmāyaṇa.* The thematic and formal structure of the *Rāmāyaṇa* has been consciously used as a model for epic poetry in later Sanskrit literature in particular, and Indian literature in general.

## *6.0 The Mythical Origin of the Rāmāyaṇa: The Birth of a Poem*

Indian tradition ascribes the following mythical origin to this epic poem. Human creativity (i.e., the creation of a poem by a poet) is equated in the tradition with cosmic creation by Brahmā.

The *ṛṣi* (the 'seer', the ascetic) Vālmīki once went to the Tamasā river for a bath. While he was wandering on the banks of the river, his attention was captured by a pair of beautiful *kraunca* birds who were singing songs of love, completely oblivious to the world around them. Suddenly the male bird was struck by a hunter's arrow and fell off the tree and died. The melody of love was suddenly transformed into a melody of pathos. So touching and moving was the cry of the female bird, separated from her loved one, that Vālmīki's heart could not contain the agony caused by it and his pain found expression in the following words: (as the tradition says *śokah* 'pain' was transformed into *ślokaḥ* 'poetry,' verse).

*mā niṣāda pratīṣṭhāṃ tvamagamaḥ śāśvatiḥ samāḥ*
*Yatkrauñcamithunādekamavadhīḥ kāmamohitaṃ* //
'O hunter, you will never attain eternal peace, since you have killed
one of the *kraunca* birds who was lost in the ecstasy of love.'

Such was the spontaneous creation of the poem! Brahmā, the god of creation, appeared before Vālmīki and called him the creator of the world of words *(śabdasrsti)* and commissioned him to compose the story of Rāma. Brahmā blessed Vālmīki with a boon. "As long as there exist mountains and rivers on this earth, the story of Rāma will be cherished by the people of the world."

This myth not only provides a divine sanction for the story of Rāma, but also metaphorically symbolizes the central theme of the Rāmāyaṇa—the unexpected separation of the lovebirds, Rāma and Sītā, caused by the "evil" demon Rāvaṇa, and the final destruction of Rāvaṇa by Rāma (which in the tradition is interpreted as the final outcome of Rāvaṇa 's own evil karma, similar to the hunter's action).

## 7.0 *The Story of the Rāmāyaṇa*

The story in the Rāmāyaṇa is divided into seven chapters entitled: *(1)* Bālakānda, *(2)* Ayodhyākānda, *(3)* Aranyakāṇḍa, *(4) Kiskindhākāṇḍa, (5) Sundarakāṇḍa,* (*6*) Yuddhakānda, and *(7) Uttarakāṇḍa.* The entire story can be presented in the following four major parts for ease of exposition.

### *Part I: Life in Ayodhyā*

### *7.1 Viṣṇu's Descent: The Birth of Rāma*

Once in the city of Ayodhyā, the 'unsurpassed one' in its wealth of royal treasures and virtuous people, there ruled a king named Daśaratha (the one who could single-handedly fight ten chariots in the war). With able counsellors such as Mārkaṇḍeya and Kashyapa and royal priests such as Vaśiṣṭha and Vāmadeva, Daśaratha was able to rule the country justly and wisely. His three beautiful wives, Kausalyā, Sumitrā, and Kaikeyī, lived happily together with royal decorum and dignity. However, like the speck on the moon this picture of peace and joy was touched with a misfortune. The king had no son! There was no son to perform the funeral rites, to continue the name of *Raghuvaṃśa* 'the clan of Raghu', to take over the reins of the sovereign king. After all human attempts failed, Daśaratha decided to perform the

Aśvamedha 'horse sacrifice,' which involved the offering of the royal horse. The successful performance of this sacrifice would guarantee the birth of progeny to the sacrifier. All the arrangements for the sacrifice were made. The whole atmosphere in Ayodhyā, once again, breathed the joy of the anticipated result—the birth of the royal progeny! The good karma of performing the *Aśvamedha* had to occur.

Meanwhile, all was not well in heaven. The gods were very perturbed because of the situation on earth. Rāvaṇa, the demon (rākṣasa) king of Lankā had become oppressive and arrogant, for the power of invincibility had corrupted him. He had acquired this power (of invincibility) by the performance of sacrifices. Brahmā, pleased with him, had asked him to wish for a boon. Rāvaṇa had asked for immunity from the gods, demons, and demigods (yakṣas). Thus it was the divine grace of Brahmā which was at the root of the power and corruption of the demon king. The gods, *Gandharvas* and *ṛṣis* went to Brahmā and said, "The demon named Rāvaṇa is torturing all three worlds and wants to transcend everybody—*Indra,* other gods, *Gandharvas,* and the Brāhmaṇas. It is your boon which is responsible for his arrogance. The whole world is frightened. The sun does not shine, nor does the wind blow. Even the ocean with multiple waves is totally motionless in his presence. Do something about it!"

Brahmā suddenly remembered that the demon had not asked for immunity from human beings. Thus he could be killed by a human being! While Brahmā was telling this to the gods, there arrived *Viṣṇu* seated on *Garuḍa* 'the eagle'. "O! Viṣṇu," said the gods, "you are the sustainer of the universe. You can descend to earth in the form of Daśaratha's sons and destroy this evil Rāvaṇa." Thereafter, *Viṣṇu,* determined to divide himself into four parts to be born as Daśaratha's sons, descended to earth where Daśaratha was performing the *Aśvamedha* sacrifice. He had a bowlful of *pāyasaṃ* 'a mixture of rice and milk' in his hand. Daśaratha, pleased with his arrival said, "Welcome *Bhagavan* (god)! What may I do to propitiate you?" Viṣṇu, of infinite prowess, advised Daśaratha to distribute the *pāyasam* among his wives, who upon eating the mixture would bear sons for him. Having gained this assurance from Viṣṇu, Daśaratha's joy knew no bounds. He gave half of the portion to Kausalyā, the eldest queen, and the remaining half was equally divided between Sumitrā and Kaikeyī, the other two queens. Thus, as a consequence of Viṣṇu's boon, four sons were born to Daśaratha—Rāma was born to Kausalyā, Lakṣamaṇa and Śatrughna to Sumitrā, and Bharata to Kaikeyī.

This was the beginning of the story of Rāma.

## *7.2 The duty in the forest*

The four children were growing up in the royal palace of Ayodhyā, becoming more and more accomplished in the art of weaponry and the knowledge of the Vedas and thus fulfilling the wishes of their parents. Sixteen years had passed when Viśvāmitra, the Brahmarsi, a sage of well-known prowess, came to Daśaratha's court and informed him of the disturbances in the forest where he used to perform sacrificial rituals for the well being of the people. Two demons called Mārica and Subāhu, at the instigation of Rāvaṇa, the demon king, were bent on destroying the religious sacrifices by sprinkling blood and flesh on the holy altar. Viśvāmitra reminded the king of his *dharma* of protecting the religious activities of the Brāhamanas and asked him to send Rāma with him to the forest to destroy the demons.

The king, although unwilling to send young Rāma to confront a disaster like this (of facing the mighty *rāksasas* 'demons'), abided by Viśvāmitra's request, since a king, he thought, was *dharmabhṛt* 'upholder of *dharma.*' However, he sent Lakṣmaṇa with Rāma to help him in his adventure. Rāma and Lakṣmaṇa, with their enormous strength, fought the demon away and established peace in the forest. The whole world of animate and inanimate beings rejoiced. The trees showered the princes with a rain of flowers to express their delight.

## 7.3 The wedding

Years had passed. Janaka, the king of Mithilā, was planning to perform a sacrifice and Viśvāmitra had promised him that he, with the two princes (Rāma and Lakṣmaṇa) would protect the sacrifice. Viśvāmitra asked the two princes to join him on his journey to Mithilā. He aroused their warriors' curiosity about a bow of Śiva's which Janaka had inherited from his ancestors. "No one has ever been able to bend this bow" said Viśvāmitra in a provocative manner and he suggested a challenge for the princes. As they reached Mithilā, Janaka welcomed them and told them the story of his daughter Sītā's birth and of his intentions of getting her married to a worthy man. "Sītā is not born of any human parents. I found her in a furrow (which translates as *Sītā* in Sanskrit) while I was ploughing a piece of land. She is indeed a *bhūmi-kanyā* 'daughter of earth', whom I have raised as my own daughter. She is as beautiful as she is virtuous. I intend to offer her hand to the prince who proves himself worthy of her by bending this bow of Śiva's. So far, hundreds of princes of great valour have come and gone without success. I am a disappointed father as they are disappointed suitors! If Rāma succeeds in bending the bow, I will offer Sītā to him." Rāma of course accepted the challenge and with his divine power broke the bow as soon as he pulled the string. The twang echoed happiness in the world as in the hearts of the beholders. On being informed of Rāma's marriage, Daśaratha arrived with his other two sons, Bhārata and Śatrughna. Following the advice of Viśvāmitra and Vaśiṣṭha, Janaka offered Sītā to Rāma, his younger daughter Urmilā to Lakṣmaṇa, and the two daughters of his younger brother Kuśadhvaja—Māṇḍāvya and Śrutakīrti—to Bharata and Śatrughna, respectively. The four well-matched couples took their marriage vows in the presence of the fire-god Agni; they walked around the fire altars announcing their commitment to each other and asking for divine blessings.

Heaven showered them with blessings, for it was certain now that the destruction of the demon Rāvaṇa was imminent.

## 7.4 Kaikeyī's wrath and the power of karma

The four couples were enjoying their married life when Daśaratha declared his wish to enter the *Vānaprasthāśrama* (the third stage in life) when he should renounce his throne and retire in a forest to concentrate on his spiritual life. Rāma, his dearest and eldest son, was ready as well as worthy to become king. Rāma's selection as a future king was immediately accepted with great enthusiasm for he was loved by all—never did he hurt anyone! The family, the courtiers and the citizens were all delighted and preparations were made for the coronation of Rāma. The auspicious day was only a night away when the lightning of misfortune struck the city of Ayodhyā. Mantharā, the maidservant of Kaikeyī, was not happy with Rāma's selection as the future king. Mantharā poisoned Kaikeyī's ears against Rāma by portraying the glories of the queen-mother (Rāma's 'mother Kausalyā was going to be conferred this title) and the perils of the one who is not a queen-mother (who would be Kaikeyī). "Rāma and Kausalyā will be held high in your husband's esteem and they will treat you and your son as nobodies! Do something about this!"

Kaikeyī, who had always loved Rāma dearly, thus changed her mind toward him and angrily announced to Daśaratha her disapproval of Rāma's coronation. Daśaratha was shocked and he could no longer bear the pain of disapproval by his most beloved wife, Kaikeyī. "What can I do to appease you?" asked Daśaratha. And Kaikeyī's reply was no less than a call of destiny, which had chosen Kaikeyī to move the "right pawn" in the game of royal affairs.

Kaikeyī knew how to control the situation for in the past she had saved Daśaratha's life in a war, and in gratitude he had promised her two wishes which he would grant anytime during his life. And the time had come! Kaikeyī said, "Oh, King, grant me two wishes. First, I would like Rāma to be banished to the forest for fourteen years and second, my son Bharata should be made king instead!" Daśaratha had to keep his promise. 'Do not grieve," Rāma, the ideal son told his father and mother. "I will carry out the desire of Kaikeyī, and all will be well!" Leaving the grieving city Ayodhyā and all his loved ones behind, Rāma set out for the forest. Lakṣmaṇa, who always followed Rāma as his shadow, could not stay behind. Similarly, Sītā, the ideal wife , could not stay behind to enjoy the luxuries of the royal palace while her husband lived in the midst of the miseries of the forestlife.

The three then went to the forest to spend the next fourteen years of their lives. Events were unfolding in such a way that the divine plan (i.e. Rāvaṇa 's destruction) was bound to succeed!

### *7.5 Daśaratha's death*

As Rāma left Ayodhyā, Daśaratha could not bear the pangs of separation on top of his own sense of guilt—for he had sent his son away. There was no solace for him. He was reminded of the power of *karma.* In his earlier life he had been very fond of hunting. Once while wandering in the forest he had mistaken the sound of the pitcher (being filled with water) for the sound of the elephant and had shot an arrow in that direction with the intention of killing the elephant. Instead, he found to his dismay that he had killed the only son of the blind parents for whom the son was fetching the pitcher of water! The blind parents had put a curse on him: "You in your old age will die of the anguish caused by separation from your son!" The effects of *karma* could not be averted; king Daśaratha died desparately calling, "Rāma, where are you gone, my son?"

## *Part II: The life in the forest*

### *7.6 Bharata's decision*

When Bharata, who was at his uncle's at the time of Rāma's banishment and Daśaratha's death, found out about all these events, he rushed back to Ayodhyā and blamed his mother

Kaikeyī for causing these disasters. He had never wanted to be the king—only a good brother to the king. He disregarded his mother's wishes and set out for the forest to convince Rāma of his mother's folly and bring him back to accept the kingdom again.

Rāma grieved at the news of his father's death, but he refused to accept the crown. For he was the *dharmavid* 'one who knew his duty' and would not ever turn from it. Bharata declared to Rāma that in that case he would only be the caretaker of the kingdom (which rightly belonged to Rāma) until Rāma's return. Thus Bharata placed Rāma's sandals on the throne, signifying Rāma's presence on the throne and began to look after the affairs of the kingdom.

## 7.7 Śūrpaṇakhā's story

The royal couple and Lakṣmaṇa were living very contently and happily in the forest. One day Rāvaṇa 's sister, Śūrpaṇakhā 'the one with big nails' appeared in their hut and beseeched Rāma to marry her, since, she argued, she was a powerful demoness and would take any form to make Rāma happy—for she had the magic power to change her form as she wished. Rāma, because of his total loyalty to his wife, rejected her and instructed his brother to send her away. When the demoness made advances toward Lakṣmaṇa as well, the latter, in a state of anger, cut off her nose and ears! Her anger knew no bounds. She informed her brothers Khara and Rāvaṇa of these insults! Khara in turn tried to take a revenge on Rāma, but Rāma succeeded in killing him. Thus, Śūrpaṇakhā's insult and Khara's death planted the seed of conflict between Rāma and Rāvaṇa.

## 7.8 The golden deer

Now Rāvaṇa could not just sit tight! He had to avenge his sister's insult and brother's death. He sent Mārica in the form of a golden deer which roamed around Rāma's dwelling. Sītā was immediately struck by its unusual beauty and longed for its skin for her garment. "Go Rāma, fetch the deer," said she who was inviting her own disaster! Rāma, in order to fulfill her desire, went away and shot the deer. At the time of death, Mārica (in the form of the deer) changed his voice like Rāma and then he deceitfully cried "Oh Lakṣmaṇa come, save me!" This was merely a trick to get Lakṣmaṇa away from Sītā, who then would be left unprotected. Sītā, mistaking those words for Rāma's, forced Lakṣmaṇa to go to help Rāma. And that was the destined moment for Rāvaṇa to arrive at Sita's door in the form of an ascetic begging for food. The compassionate woman offered him food, but the beggar turned into a giant demon who asked her to marry him, claiming he was the king and would provide all the luxuries she could ever dream of.

Sītā, the most honest, loyal, and devoted wife of Rāma, refused him and as a consequence was forcibly abducted by Rāvaṇa, who flew with her through the sky to his capital city, Lankā. Jatāyu 'the old wise vulture' unsuccessfully fought Rāvaṇa, and could not stop him from abducting Sītā. Sītā, crying helplessly, dropped her ornaments one by one, leaving a trail to help Rāma to locate her later on. Rāma and Lakṣmaṇa returned and were shocked and angry to find Sītā missing! And the search for Sītā began.

## *7.9 Rāma helps Sugrīva and sends Hanumāna to Lankā*

Rāma, desparately trying to find any lead to Sītā's whereabouts could only rely on Jatāyu's account of the incident, which revealed Sītā's abduction by Rāvaṇa, the king of Lankā. Lankā was across the ocean, how could it be reached? In the meantime, Rāma had helped a monkey king, Sugrīva, to rescue his wife, Tārā, who had been abducted by his brother Vāli. Rāma killed Vāli in order to return Sugrīva's wife and kingdom to him. The grateful Sugrīva could easily identify with Rāma's plight and thus promised to help Rāma.

Sugrīva's friend Hanumāna was a giant monkey, the son of the wind god and swift as the wind itself, Hanumāna agreed to fly over the southern ocean to locate Sītā and collect the necessary information for her rescue.

## *7.10 Hanumāna's adventures*

Hanumāna, with a mace in his hand, flew over the ocean and reached Lankā, the beautiful golden city of the demon king Rāvaṇa. There he found Sītā, lonely and desolate, sitting in a grove of *Asoka* trees, like a pale crescent moon covered with the clouds. She had rejected Rāvaṇa 's proposition of marriage and had thus been subjected to this peril! She was surrounded and guarded by demonesses. Hanumāna, the tricky one, found an opportune moment to talk to her. He showed her Rāma's ring and assured her that he was a messenger from Rāma and therefore, a friend, not an enemy. Sītā told her story to him and said that she would patiently wait for Rāma to come and rescue her. Hanumāna, successful in his venture, returned to Rāma with the news from Sītā.

## *Part III: The end of evil*

## *7.11 The bridge from "good" to "evil"*

Rāma was left with no choice but to wage war against Rāvaṇa, who with his ten heads was as arrogant as ever and would never return Sītā on his own. Sugrīva and Hanumāna, with the help of the monkeys, decided to build a bridge over the ocean between the southern tip of *Bhārata bhūmi* 'India' and Lankā. The bridge was the product of destiny—stone by stone it was built like the grand plan of destiny. Preparations for war were made on both sides of the bridge.

## *7.12 The war*

The appointed moment had arrived when "good" and "evil" must meet—direct conflict was the only solution, for neither side would give up. Finally, after a long dreadful war between Rāma's and Rāvaṇa 's armies; after the deaths of Rāvaṇa 's brother Kumbhakarṇa 'pot ear' and son Indrajit the 'one who conquers Indra'; and after the death of Rāvaṇa himself, the war came to an end.

Rāma had defeated Rāvaṇa; evil had finally been destroyed and Viṣṇu's mission was successful. Interestingly, after his death, Rāvaṇa 's soul merged into Rāma. The evil merged into the good! For there exists no evil in the absolute sense; it was only Rāvaṇa 's desire to overpower Rāma and the others which made him evil and hastened his death. But after his death, balance and peace were restored in the world.

### 7.13 Sītā's fire trial

Sītā's joy knew no bounds when Rāma welcomed her with the ardent love which only she knew. But the ordeal was not yet over for the beautiful wife of Rāma. She had to prove to the world, though not to Rāma, that she was still the same chaste woman—that Rāvaṇa had not even touched her; that her body as was her mind, was pure. Rāma, against his wishes, asked her to go through a fire-trial, in which she had to walk through the fire (Agni) who would then declare his judgement regarding her purity.

As pure gold shines all the more in the fire, Sītā's purity glittered in the fire. Agni 'the fire-god' himself declared her chastity. Rāma and the whole world praised Sītā, who had just passed the most difficult of the tests.

## Part IV: The aftermath of the war

### 7.14 Sītā's banishment

As Rāma and Sītā returned to Ayodhyā, Bharata welcomed them with renewed joy. Rāma became the king at last. However, as life always plays unexpected tricks (like the hunter's arrow falling on the love-birds), Rāma's life was once again stricken with the arrow of destiny. The citizens of Ayodhyā had rejoiced in Rāma's return but were skeptical about Sītā's chastity—how could a demon king allow her to survive without satisfying his wishes? Was Sītā really pure? The people also felt that, as a king, Rāma was setting a bad example by accepting a wife who had lived in another man's house.

Rāma was deeply hurt when informed by his counsellors that his citizens doubted Sītā's purity. For there are no bounds to *dharma* (duty), he thought, and a king must always follow it at all cost. He felt himself duty bound to respect his people's opinion regarding his wife's chastity.

Thus Rāma, the *dharma* incarnate, decided to abandon Sītā, who was pregnant at the time. Sītā's second trial began when Lakṣmaṇa, instructed by Rāma, abandoned her in the forest in the hermitage of Vālmīki, the most compassionate ascetic. When Sītā was informed by Lakṣmaṇa of the cause of her banishment, she told him, "Tell your brother Rāma, I am pure and chaste, but I must have committed some sin in the last birth and so I must suffer. Rāma must follow his duty. A king must abide by the wishes of his countrymen and I must follow my duty. I will not let the family of Rāma be terminated! I wish to die of this disgrace, but I will not!"

Overwhelmed with pain, Lakṣmaṇa returned to Rāma, for whom the world held no joy anymore.

## *7.15 Sītā's return to her abode*

Sītā gave birth to twin sons, Lava and Kuśa, in Vālmīki's hermitage. With the passing of time they grew to be handsome young boys, perfectly instructed by Vālmīki in art and music. Time passed. Rāma was performing a sacrifice to which Vālmīki was invited. Vālmīki arrived at the palace with the twins, who recited the story of Rāma as taught to them by Vālmīki. The court was delighted to hear the story, beautifully sung in a melody which touched the hearts of everyone. When asked, the twins told Rāma of their teacher, Vālmīki, who then came forward and revealed to Rāma the real identity of the boys. Vālmīki spoke before the court and vouched for Sītā's purity and instructed Rāma to accept her. Rāma asked Sītā to vouch for her own chastity before the assembly again!

Sītā, the innocent and yet the accused one, declared her innocence, but she could tolerate the burden of shame no more. "O Mother Earth, if I am pure, if I have never, in body and mind allowed anyone else beside Rāma to be my husband, then take me in! Let this be proof of my chastity!"

Those words bore the power of truth and chastity. While the court watched in silence, mother earth *pṛthvi* 'stretched out one' (to embrace existence), appeared before the assembly and embraced her daughter. Thus Sītā disappeared into the bosom of the earth from which she had appeared, for her mission was over, she had been the instrument used in bringing about the destruction of evil.

For Rāma there was no joy left in the world. Time himself arrived in the form of a sage, reminding Rāma of his divine origin and asking him to return to his abode in *Vaikuṇṭha* 'heaven', since his mission on earth had been accomplished. "The world is *Māyā*—a transient dream of yours! You must transcend it!"

And Rāma returned to heaven again.

## ***8.0 The role of the supernatural and karma in human destiny***

The story of Rāma is also a story of human life which in the religious–philosophical Indian (Hindu) tradition is viewed as part of cosmic reality. According to this view, human life is essentially embedded in and is influenced by the dynamics of cosmic operations. The plan of an individual human life thus must fit into the larger plan of cosmic operation, which is variously described as *niyati* 'destiny' (literally 'predetermined') or *daiva* 'divine law' (literally, pertaining to gods). This belief stresses the limitations of human beings' power/control over their own lives and the supremacy of divine power. The *Rāmāyaṇa is* full of events which are constant reminders of this underlying belief. The major events, such as the birth of Rāma, Rāma's exile to the forest, Rāma's refusal to return to Ayodhyā, the abduction of Sītā by Rāvaṇa, and the war between Rāma and Rāvaṇa are nothing but milestones in the "divine plan" which led to the destruction of Rāvaṇa. Belief in the "divine plan" also provides the rationale for the sequence of the events. Moreover, it resolves not only the apparent contradictions in the behavior of the characters, but also the anomalous and illogical nature of the events. For example, why should Rāma and Sītā, paragons of virtue, be banished to the forest? Why should Kaikeyī, the sensitive and loving mother, send Rāma away? Why did Sītā, after having denounced all luxuries of the royal life for the sake of Rāma be obsessed with the golden deer? Why did Rāma, the acclaimed intelligent king, not realize that there could not possibly exist a golden deer? These questions are answered on the basis of belief in the predeterministic nature of human life, which is guided and controlled by supernatural/divine powers.

It is important to note here that the above discussion covers only one side of the whole story. Blended with the above belief (in the power of the supernatural) is also belief in the *karma* theory, which stresses the power of humans' actions and their control over their own lives. Actions bring results, according to the *karma* theory, and the actor must bear the consequences of his/her acts. These two beliefs—belief in the divine plan and belief in human action—are not presented as conflicting or mutually exclusive beliefs. They are, on the other hand, functioning together in the *Rāmāyaṇa.* The divine plan is realized mainly through human actions. The divine plan may be the goal but the medium of its realization is viewed as human *karma.* In fact, the *Rāmāyaṇa* stresses belief in the natural connection between human actions *(karma)* and the divine plan *(niyati).* The events and the characters in the epic are presented as *naturally disposed* to abide by the divine plan.

For example, was it not Daśaratha's own *karma* (of killing the only child of blind parents) in earlier life which caused his death by grief for his son, Rāma? Was it not Kaikeyī's own good deed of saving her husband's life which enabled her to acquire the status of the queen mother? Was not Sītā's own action of sending Rāma away to kill the golden deer responsible for her abduction by Rāvaṇa? The *Rāmāyaṇa* in general presents the story of Rāma as a tale of human weaknesses and strengths, which are the immediate cause for behavior; and yet it stresses belief in the dominance of higher (divine) powers over the lives of human beings.

## 9.0 "Good" and "Evil" in the Rāmāyaṇa

The Indian tradition views the story of Rāma as a conflict between "good" and evil" and the ultimate conquest of "good" over "evil." While Rāma is the symbol of good, Rāvaṇa is the symbol of evil. However, a critical analysis of the *Rāmāyaṇa* points out the difficulty involved in defining the parameters for judging "good" and " evil." Consider for example the following questions, which cannot be answered in a straightforward fashion: Why was Rāma viewed as *purusottama 'the best of men'*? Was it simply because he was *avatāra* (descent) of Viṣṇu and killed Rāvaṇa to establish the order of *ṛta?* What about his behavior toward his wife? Did he not betray the innocent Sītā who had even walked willingly through the fire for the sake of her love and loyalty toward him? Hence, was he not an "evil" husband and an irresponsible, if not nasty, father? Also, was Rāvaṇa all evil? Was he not a responsible king who always protected his citizens? And finally, if he was "evil," why does his soul merge with Rāma after his (i.e. Rāvaṇa 's) death?

The apparent contradictions and discrepancies presented by these questions can be explained if we take into account the definitions of "good" and "evil" in the traditional system of beliefs of Hinduism. In Upaniṣadic philosophy, no existence (inanimate, human, or divine) is viewed as good or evil in the absolute sense of the term. That is so because everything emerges from one *(Brahman) who* transcends both "good" and "evil."

However, the question that still remains to be answered is this: even if nothing is "good" or "evil" according to this mythology, how do people still perceive and treat some things as "good" and some other things as "evil"? For an adequate answer to this question, we will have to discuss the nature of the creation of the universe in this mythology.

In the phenomenal world of *Māyā,* creation means only the creation of opposite forces—life and death, man and woman, light and darkness, etc. Consequently, no existence or phenomenon can be labelled as "good" or "evil." For the sustenance of the universe, all opposite forces have to exist, but in a state of balance. It is this state of balance of different opposite forces at different levels that is viewed as " good" in this mythology. Recall here, the concept and laws of *ṛta,* which signified ' order' (i.e., harmony or balance), and by which everything had to function in the universe. This way of defining "good" very logically entailed that everything that threatened or destroyed the balance (of opposite forces) had to be viewed as "evil."

When there is a perfect balance of opposites, all orders of *ṛta,* cosmic, social, individual—function properly. When one existence tries to overpower other(s), the balance and, thereby, the order, is disturbed. However, once the imbalance is removed, and the balance is restored, that particular form (which had created imbalance) is no longer viewed as evil. Thus evil is merely *temporary* evil in Hindu mythology. Accordingly, Rāvaṇa is viewed as evil because he oppresses other existences and creates a disturbance in the order of ṛta. After death, however, his soul (which like *Brahman* is beyond all dualities including "good" and "evil") merges back into Rāma, who as *Viṣṇu* is the very manifestation of *Brahman.*

The concepts "good" and "evil" are viewed as relative and not absolute in another respect, i.e., they are viewed as *temporarily* good or evil relative to a particular order. For example, Kaikeyī may be evil within the social or individual order but is not viewed as evil within the cosmic order for her sending of Rāma to the forest (since without her decision to send Rāma to the forest, Rāvaṇa would not have been killed). Similarly, Rāma was good (as a king) at the social order. He always abided by his *dharma* and valued his citizens' opinion much more than his own happiness. He followed his social duty even when it meant putting his wife through the fire-trial. One can argue for Rāma being evil within the individual order (for being very unjust to Sītā), but then *dharma* clearly dictated abiding by one's social duty over and above one's individual duty, even when it made one negligent regarding individual duty.

CHAPTER 5

# *Mythology of the Epics: The Mahābhārata*

## 1.0 Introduction

The *Mahābhārata*, similar to the *Rāmāyaṇa*, is an epic which presents another magnificent view of the ancient people of India. In a number of ways this epic is closer to the life of the people than the *Rāmāyaṇa*. While the *Rāmāyaṇa* depicts society and individuals as they ought to be (ideal), the *Mahābhārata* portrays society and individuals as they were at that time. While both epics deal with the conflicts between *karma* and *dharma,* they differ from each other in terms of the solutions which they advocate. The most pertinent question to be raised here is: What is more important: individual happiness or the survival of the larger (i.e., social and cosmic) orders? This question crosses the barriers of cultures and societies. Diverse cultures have provided diverse answers to the question. The answers are the avenues to the world views of different cultures which are beautifully presented in the classics of the world. While the *Rāmāyaṇa* advocates the supremacy of *dharma* over individual happiness, the *Mahābhārata* shows the power of individual passions which overshadow one's commitment to *dharma. As* a consequence, the major characters of the *Rāmāyaṇa* are willing to yield their personal/individual duty and happiness in favor of their *dharma* 'social duty'. The major characters in the *Mahābhārata* are willing to fight for their individual gains as opposed to their *dharma—their* social duty.

Both *Rāmāyaṇa* and the *Mahābhārata* deal with the same theme of human life. While the one shows how life can be sustained by adhering to the laws and orders of *ṛta,* the other shows how it is destroyed by violating the laws and orders of *ṛta.* The concept of *dharma* is the key to the understanding of both epics. *Dharma* when observed, preserves order; when violated it brings about destruction.

## 2.0 Date of the Mahābhārata

The *Mahābhārata* was composed during the period of 200 B.C. to 400 A.D. and was orally transmitted through generations of bards who would add their own interpretations and even content to what they had received. Thus we find several extrapolated passages in the *Mahābhārata.* There is a great deal of variation at both thematic and structural levels. The chronology of the interpolated passages can be determined by linguistic evidence. The original composer of the epic is considered to be Vyāsa, who plays a major role in the epic. The *Mahābhārata is* divided into 18 chapters; the 18th chapter is the *Bhagavadgītā* which outlines the philosophical foundation of the epic. The fact that the Mahābhārata includes the story of the *Rāmāyaṇa* indicates that the *Mahābhārata* succeeded the composition of the *Rāmāyaṇa.*

## 3.0 The Story of the Mahābhārata

### 3.1 Satyavatī's story

The story of the epic begins with a romantic tale of the fishermaid Satyavatī and the king Śantanu. Once Śantanu, while wandering in the forest met a fishermaid named Satyavatī whose unique beauty and charm captivated Śantanu's heart. When Śantanu proposed to Satyavatī with a promise of making her the chief queen, the fishermaid stated her conditions for the marriage: "I will marry you, o king, if you promise me that my son (as opposed to any of your other queen's son) will have the honor of becoming your successor to the royal throne." Śantanu was caught between love for his oldest son Bhīṣma (who according to tradition would be the king after Śantanu) and his passionate attraction to Satyavatī. However, Bhīṣma resolved the dilemma by denouncing his right to the kingdom and, moreover, by taking an oath of celibacy which would guarantee no threat from him to the family of Satyavatī's sons. Thus, Bhīṣma's great sacrifice made possible the marriage of the king and Satyavatī. Satyavatī's children (from Śantanu), Chitrāngada and Vicitravīrya, succeeded Śantanu. But as fate would have it, Chitrāngada died young in a battle with a *Gandharva.* Bhīṣma, with the intention of winning three brides for his half-brother Vicitravīrya, went according to the Kṣatriya practice to Kashī to abduct the three princesses, Ambā, Ambikā and Ambālikā. While Ambikā and Ambālikā readily married Vicitravīrya, Ambā, the oldest of the three, refused to do so. She declared her love for the king of Śālva, to whom she was secretly engaged. Bhīṣma allowed her to go to Śālva, who to Ambā's dismay insulted her and rejected her, saying she had been won over by Bhīṣma and was no longer worthy of his (Śālva's) love.

Ambā, angry and disgusted, held Bhīṣma responsible for her misfortune and decided to perform *tapas* (penances) in order to take revenge against Bhīṣma. Śiva, pleased with her *tapas,* granted a boon to her, according to which she would be reborn as a man and kill Bhīṣma. Satisfied with the boon, Ambā immolated herself only to be born again so that she might kill Bhīṣma.

In the meantime Vicitravīrya died childless. Satyavatī, ambitious woman that she was, invited her son Vyāsa by Parāśara (before her marriage with Śantanu) to produce progeny through Ambikā and Ambālikā. Vyāsa agreed and Dhṛtarāṣṭra was born of Ambikā, and Paṇḍu was born of Ambālikā. Since Dhṛtarāṣṭra was born blind, the kingdom was entrusted to Paṇḍu. Dhṛtarāṣṭra and his wife Gāndhārī gave birth to one hundred sons who later came to be known as Kauravas, and five sons of Paṇḍu were called the Pāṇḍavas.

Duryodhana, and Duśśāsana were the most prominent of the Kauravas, while Yudhiṣṭhira, Bhīma, Arjuna, Nakula and Sahadeva were recognized as the five Pāṇḍavas: the first three were born of Paṇḍu's first wife Kuntī, and the last two were born of his second wife, Mādrī.

## *3.2 Kuntī, the queen mother*

The five Pāṇḍavas were not actually Paṇḍu's sons, since Paṇḍu, due to a curse, was forbidden to have any marital relations with his wives. Kuntī had received a magic spell *(mantra)* from Durvāsa, a sage. This spell, when used by her, had the power to bring to her any male she wished; he would then be obliged to create progeny through her. Kuntī had summoned Sūrya, 'the Sun god', through this spell while she was still an unmarried girl. As a result, a son named Karṇa was born to her. Kuntī, out of fear of social criticism, abandoned her child and left him floating in the river. Karṇa was later rescued by the royal charioteer of Duryodhana, Adhiratha, who raised the boy with love and care. After marriage, when Kuntī discovered her husband's inability to produce children, she used the spell and called Yama (who fathered Yudhiṣṭhira), Indra (who fathered Arjuna) and Vāyu (who fathered Bhīma). She then gave the spell over to Mādrī, who summoned the twin gods of medicine *(Aśvinau)* and gave birth to twins, Nakula and Sahadeva. Since Karṇa was raised by the charioteer of the Kauravas, the Pāṇḍavas were always counted only as five.

## *3.3 The conflict between the Kauravas and the Pāṇḍavas: the question of sovereignty*

Paṇḍu, the king, died young, as he committed the "forbidden" act—he made love to his wife Mādrī. With Paṇḍu dead and Dhṛtarāṣṭra being blind, responsibility for the kingdom and the princes was once again placed on Bhīṣma. All of the princes were being trained in the *Kṣatriya* tradition by the same teacher, Droṇa. Karṇa, though recognized as a charioteer's son, was being trained by Droṇa as well. It was very clear however that the two sets of cousins saw and treated one another more as competitors /opponents than as relations. Both wanted to inherit the royal throne. Kama and Arjuna even as young children developed a strong hatred toward each other, since they each thought the other was inferior in valor and skill. Once in a public event, when Karṇa expressed his wish to engage in combat with Arjuna, Arjuna declined the challenge, complaining that he would fight with his equal—a king and not a charioteer's son! Karṇa was enraged by this comment but was quite helpless. Duryodhana could not contain his wrath and said, "Does anybody ask the source of a river or the lineage of a brave hero? The question is irrelevant. However, I declare Karṇa to be the King of Anga. This new position of Karṇa should satisfy the desire of the Pāṇḍavas to fight their equals." Karṇa was touched by Duryodhana's love; Kuntī, though she recognized her son Karṇa, did not openly admit it, and the rest of the people realized that this event marked the first sign of the hatred the two sets of cousins had been nurturing in their hearts.

## 3.4 *Lākṣāgṛhā—'the house of lac'*

Yudhiṣṭhira, the oldest of the Pāṇḍavas, was deemed to be the most eligible king by both the citizens and by the old king Dhṛtarāṣṭra whose blindness had disqualified him from kingship, making his brother Paṇḍu and his family the legitimate successors to the royal throne. Yudhiṣṭhira was a just, truthful, strong, generous, and loyal king to his citizens and so were his brothers.

Duryodhana and his brothers became jealous as the popularity of the Pāṇḍavas increased. Duryodhana begged his father Dhṛtarāṣṭra to send the Pāṇḍavas away to Banaras to enjoy the festival being celebrated to worship the god Śiva. This would give Duryodhana an opportunity to win over the citizens by offering generous gifts to them. Moreover, Duryodhana had an evil plan to kill the Pāṇḍavas while they were in Banaras in the house of lac. Purocana, a friend and courtier of Duryodhana, was instructed to build a mansion of lac, an inflammable material which at the proper occasion would be set on fire, killing the Pāṇḍavas inside. Vidura, the Pāṇḍavas' uncle and advisor, warned them of the danger awaiting in Banaras. He had also sent a man to dig a tunnel under the house of lac so that the Pāṇḍavas might secretly escape from it. Both parties were thus ready to play their cards. The Pāṇḍavas, with their mother Kuntī, went to Banaras to enjoy the festivities. A year passed uneventfully. The Pāṇḍavas finally decided to take matters into their own hands and execute their plan of escape. One day Kuntī invited the whole town for a feast. At the end of the party, the Pāṇḍavas themselves set the house on fire and escaped through the tunnel. Bhīma, the strongest of the Pāṇḍavas, carried his mother and his brothers through the tunnel. Vidura's messenger was waiting for them at the end of the tunnel, and he took them beyond the river Ganges in a boat. Destiny had played a trick on the Kauravas. A poor woman who had come for the feast, along with her five children, was burnt in the house of lac. It was believed by the people and the Kauravas that the Pāṇḍavas were killed in the fire.

## 3.5 *The Svayaṃvara*

After emerging from the tunnel, the Pāṇḍavas lived in the city of Ekacakra in disguise as Brāhmaṇas. It was there that they heard the news of the Svayaṃvara 'bride choosing her groom' of the princess of Pancāla, called Draupadī. Draupadī, the beautiful daughter of Drupada, the king of Pancāla, was ready to marry. The Pāṇḍavas decided to attend the ceremony. Having taken an auspicious bath, decked with beautiful diamonds and silk attire, Draupadī arrived at the assembly of the prospective grooms mounted on an elephant with her brother Dhṛṣṭadyumna. The condition of the *Svayaṃvara* was announced by Dhṛṣṭadyumna, "O princes, look at the target placed very high near the ceiling of the palace. Here is the bow and here are the arrows. The one who strings the bow and shoots five arrows through the aperture of the revolving disc and hits the target and is of good birth will win my sister."

Hundreds of princes tried and failed, including Duryodhana and others. Karṇa arose with great confidence and pride. But before trying his skills he was insulted by Draupadī who announced, "I will not marry a charioteer's son!" Karṇa looked up at the sun once and put down the bow and left in agony and anger.

Arjuna was the only successful contender at the *Svayaṃvara*. However, the other princes questioned Arjuna's eligibility to marry a *Kṣatriya* princess, since Arjuna (along with his brothers) was disguised as a *Brāhmaṇa*. It was declared by Kṛṣṇa, Pāṇḍavas' cousin, that Arjuna and Bhīma, who were fighting the other princes, were none other than the *Kṣatriya* princes—the Pāṇḍavas.

In the meantime, Kuntī was waiting for Bhīma and Arjuna to come home, since the other three had returned home early fearing that they would be recognized as the Pāṇḍavas. As Bhīma and Arjuna returned home with Draupadī they teasingly said, " Mother, look what we brought today!" Thinking of her son's regular custom of bringing home the food they had collected in town as begging ascetic, Kuntī replied, "Share it equally among the five of you, whatever you have brought." Thus Draupadī became the wife of the five brothers.

Later on at the formal wedding, Yudhiṣṭhira revealed his and his brothers' true identity.

## *3.6 Indraprastha—the capitol city of the Pāṇḍavas*

The news of the Pāṇḍavas' survival and wedding soon reached Hastināpura, the capitol of Duryodhana. The old king Dhṛtarāṣṭra decided it would be fair to grant the Pāṇḍavas half of the kingdom and allowed them to establish a new capital, Indraprastha. Little did he suspect the events which were to follow!

## *3.7 The game of dice*

Duryodhana was not satisfied with the partition of the kingdom, for he wanted it all to himself. Driven by his ever-growing ambition, he devised another plan to displace the Pāṇḍavas. Śakuni, Duryodhana's deceitful uncle and advisor, came up with a plan which could not fail, since it was based on Yudhiṣṭhira's well-known weakness for gambling and his acute sense of responsibility toward the kingdom. Śakuni and Duryodhana decided to challenge Yudhiṣṭhira in a game of dice. They knew he could not refuse the invitation, since it was a matter of pride for the king and moreover it was his (perhaps the only) weakness. The plan was to play a game full of deceitful moves advised by Śakuni.

And so did it happen. Yudhiṣṭhira, calling the invitation "the call of fate," enthusiastically accepted it and lost at every single move he made. The more he lost, the more he wanted to play to prove his superiority. He lost his treasures, his kingdom, his brothers, himself and, finally, he staked his wife Draupadī and lost her!

This was the moment of triumph for Duryodhana and the rest of the Kauravas who had been outwitted and outpowered by the Pāṇḍavas over and over again in the past. "Bring the glorious queen of the Pāṇḍavas here," ordered Duryodhana. Draupadī, helpless, trembling with anger and sorrow, was dragged to the court by Duśśāsana, Duryodhana's brother, who insulted her by trying to disrobe her in the assembly. Draupadī beseeched her husbands to protect her but did not get any help from them. She then prayed to the "lord of the world" Kṛṣṇa to protect her and, lo and behold, she was protected! As Duśśāsana pulled off each of her garments, ever fresh new garments clothed her body, until he gave up. Draupadī then bravely questioned the transaction in the game of dice. "How could Yudhiṣṭhira, who had lost himself to Śakuni (and had become a slave), use a free woman like her as a stake?" asked Draupadī. The whole assembly was taken aback by her sound reasoning and courage.

Dhṛtarāṣṭra suddenly shuddered at her words. "Perhaps she is right! Something is wrong!" he thought. Moreover, he had noticed evil omens, such as the wailing of a jackal and the braying of an ass. Dhṛtarāṣṭra felt that he had to do something or otherwise face disaster. He said to Draupadī, "My daughter, ask for a wish and I will grant it." "Free my husbands with all their weapons and chariots," Draupadī answered. "Granted," said Dhṛtarāṣṭra. "Anything else?" "Nothing is necessary" said Draupadī, "for, once freed, the Pāṇḍavas can conquer the whole world."

Thus the five Pāṇḍavas became free again by virtue of their wife and they started their journey back to Indraprastha. However, before long, Yudhiṣṭhira was invited again by Duryodhana and Śakuni to play the game of dice. Yudhiṣṭhira, quite aware of the deceitful game which Śakuni had played earlier and would play again, still accepted the invitation. Perhaps, his obsession for the game of dice had clouded his intellect. The condition of the game this time was that the loser(s) would spend twelve years in the forest and the thirteenth year incognito. If recognized, the loser would have to spend another twelve years in the forest.

Luck was not in favor of the Pāṇḍavas. They lost the game of dice again due to the deceit of the Kauravas and Śakuni.

## *3.8 Arjuna's tapas*

As the Pāṇḍavas were passing their time in the forest while Duryodhana was ruling the country, a holy man visited them. He advised Arjuna to undertake the vow of austerities (*tapas,* see section *5)* in the Himālayas. This *tapas,* he claimed, would please Śiva, which could enable Arjuna to destroy the Kauravas. Arjuna, clothed in deer-skin, lived on withered leaves and fallen fruit and at times without any food or water. Constant *tapas* and the worship of Śiva generated enormous power in Arjuna. The whole world began to tremble with the heat of his tapas. Śiva, satisfied with Arjuna's effort, decided to test Arjuna's power before granting him a boon.

Śiva himself purposely shot an arrow at the same boar at which Arjuna had just shot his arrow. "This is the victim of my arrow" both Arjuna and Śiva claimed. The disagreement could only be solved by combat. Śiva, pleased with Arjuna's valor, granted him a divine bow named *Gāndīva* the unfailing weapon and several other weapons, on the condition that they should not be used against weak enemies. Thus the ultimate victory of the Pāṇḍavas was guaranteed.

## 3.9 Kurukṣetra and the Mahābhārata

At the end of the thirteenth year, the Pāṇḍavas demanded their kingdom back. "We want our kingdom back or we will wage a war," was the ultimatum which they gave to the Kauravas. Duryodhana, waiting for this opportunity, declared war against the Pāṇḍavas. Kaurava's army was commanded by Bhīṣma and Droṇa, while the Pāṇḍavas's army was under the supervision of Draupadī's brother Dhṛṣṭadyumna. The game of dice was going to be played on the battlefield at Kurukṣetra and men were using their own lives as stakes.

## 3.10 Droṇa's death and Bhīma's deceit

The war was a fierce one. Each group was anxious to destroy the other. The Pāṇḍavas soon realized that as long as Droṇa was alive victory over the Kauravas was not possible. Bhīma thus devised a master plan. Knowing that Droṇa would become very weak if his beloved son was killed, Bhīma killed an elephant which had the same name as that of Droṇa's son Aśvatthāmā and went around shouting, " Aśvatthāmā is dead! Aśvatthāmā is dead!." Droṇa suddenly became motionless. He felt he had no strength left to fight anymore. However, he wanted to confirm the news with Yudhiṣṭhira, for he knew Yudhiṣṭhira would never lie. Droṇa asked Yudhiṣṭhira "Has Aśvatthāmā really been killed?" "Yes," said Yudhiṣṭhira, Aśvatthāmā is dead." However, Yudhiṣṭhira very softly uttered the words "the elephant" after "Aśvatthāmā," but Droṇa did not hear. Filled with despair Droṇa lay down his weapons. At that moment, Draupadī's brother Dhṛṣṭadyumna killed Droṇa, and the Pāṇḍavas felt more assured of victory in the war.

## 3.11 Bhīṣma

Bhīṣma, the greatest warrior on the Kaurava's side, was endowed with a special power which had been granted to him by his father after Bhīṣma took the oath of lifelong celibacy. This power made it impossible for him to be killed against his wishes. Thus, with Bhīṣma on the Kauravas' side, the Pāṇḍavas could not win the war. Yudhiṣṭhira decided to ask the grandfather Bhīṣma how he wished to die. "Who would be the honored warrior by whose arrow you wish to die pitamaha (grandfather)?" asked Yudhiṣṭhira. Bhīṣma answered, "I do not fight with the unarmed or with women. But I wish to die only by arrows shot by either Arjuna or Kṛṣṇa." Arjuna, who was reluctant to kill Bhīṣma, was reminded by Kṛṣṇa that it was his duty as a warrior to kill him. However, there was another warrior who was anxious to kill Bhīṣma. It was Śikhaṇḍin, who was Ambā reborn as a woman *Śikhaṇḍinī* and later changed into a man (Śikhaṇḍin). It was Ambā's mission (and Śikhaṇḍinī's/Sikhndin's in the present birth) to kill Bhīṣma. But how could this happen, since Bhīṣma would neither fight with her nor did he want to be killed by anyone besides Arjuna or Kṛṣṇa.

Both Śikhaṇḍin and Arjuna shot arrows at Bhīṣma. The latter did not launch a counterattack against Śikhaṇḍin (since he was originally born as a woman) but fought back Arjuna's weapons. Finally, although wounded by Śikhaṇḍin's arrows, Bhīṣma was killed by arrows shot from Arjuna's Gāndīva. Both were satisfied—Śikhaṇḍin for having accomplished the desired goal of killing Bhīṣma and Bhīṣma for attaining the desired death by Arjuna's arrows.

## 3.12 Karṇa—the son of Kunti

Kuntī, the queen mother was extremely anxious about the safety of her children. Kuntī knew that Karṇa had been born with a natural coat of mail and earrings which made him virtually invincible against all weapons. At the same time Indra, Arjuna's father, was worried about Arjuna's safety. Indra thought of a solution for his problem. Karṇa was known for his generosity. After his morning bath, Karṇa used to perform his morning worship and, if asked at that moment, Karṇa would not refuse anyone's request. Therefore, Indra managed to appear before Karṇa at that moment and asked Karṇa to give him his coat of mail and earrings. "Here, I give you my mail and earrings, but I ask you to give me one invincible arrow in exchange for my gift." "So be it," said Indra and gave Karṇa an arrow called *Vāsava.*

Now Kuntī could not contain her anxiety and went to meet Karṇa with the hope of persuading him to join the Pāṇḍavas—for was he not their brother? As Kuntī approached Karṇa, he said very respectfully, "What can this son of a charioteer do for you, o respectable lady?" "You are my son and not of a charioteer! Karṇa, you are a *kaunteya* (son of Kuntī) just like your brothers the Pāṇḍavas. Do not fight with them; join them."

"How can you claim any right to me now when you yourself abandoned me when I was a helpless baby? Duryodhana is my friend, I will not betray him for anyone's sake! However, I can promise you that I will not fight with anyone else besides Arjuna (among the Pāṇḍavas). The number of your children will remain five, since either Arjuna or I will be alive after the fight."

Thus Karṇa, the proud, insulted son of Kuntī, did not lose his dignity; neither did he lose his generosity. The fight between Karṇa and Arjuna was fierce. Both were strong, skillful and well trained, and both had divine prowess. Their fight looked like the age-old struggle between Sūrya (the Sun god) and Indra (the rain god). Vāsava (Indra's weapon) and Gāndīva (Śiva's weapon) were used and their might was tested. Finally, after long attacks and counterattacks, Karṇa died and Arjuna won.

The Pāṇḍavas were ultimately declared to be victorious. However the long–awaited victory did not bring joy to the survivors.

## 3.13 The vision of the dead

Yudhiṣṭhira was made king, but the aftermath of the war was beyond imagination. The loss of their loved ones was too deeply felt by the survivors for them to be able to enjoy the victory. The old king Dhṛtarāṣṭra, his wife Gāndhārī, and Kuntī were sitting together and talking about the happy days when the children were alive, when life was full of excitement and joy. Then Vyāsa, the son of Satyavatī, the old sage with the supernatural powers, arrived. He promised the king and the queens that he would let them see their dead children and relatives once more by using his supernatural powers.

Eagerly the king and the queens waited for the opportune moment at the banks of the river Ganges. The expectation of seeing their people again was too much to contain within their hearts. As night came, Vyāsa called the dead from the Kauravas and the Pāṇḍavas' sides. Suddenly there were tremors in the water of the Ganges. Through the waves emerged the kings and other warriors. Duryodhana and his brothers, with Bhīṣma, Karṇa and Droṇa, arose in royal attire and so did Śikhaṇḍin, Drupada, and others. And the king and the queens could see them with the special vision granted to them by Vyāsa.

There was a unique gathering of the living and the dead. But the atmosphere was very different from the atmosphere on the battlefield. The emotions of hatred, revenge, pride, anger, jealousy and passion had vanished. Everyone was serene and peaceful. Karṇa and Arjuna embraced each other as long-lost friends and so did Droṇa and Drupada. Karṇa was united with his brothers and had no ill-feelings for Kuntī, who was overwhelmed when Karṇa accepted her as his mother. The Pāṇḍavas and the Kauravas were united——as closely as if, they were twigs on the same tree!

This celebration of the merging of 'opposites' seemed real enough to make the whole terrible war seem like a dream—an illusion, a fleeting scene in eternity. And with the first rays of the dawn, the dead and living were separated again, their hearts soothed by the peaceful reunion.

### *3.14 The journey to heaven: Yudhiṣṭhira's test*

The Pāṇḍavas, having ruled the country for thirty-six years, decided to retire. They planned to go on the pilgrimage of death—the journey to heaven. It was believed that heaven existed beyond the high peaks of the Himalayas. The Heaven was viewed as a blessing, a reward which one would receive as a result of one's meritorious acts on earth. Although heaven was believed to be the abode which could be obtained only after death, a person with certain special qualifications could reach it while alive *(sadeha* 'with body'). The condition for this was very difficult to fulfill and only a few could qualify for this honor. It was believed that only one who had never committed a "wrong deed" in his life could receive this honor. The Pāṇḍavas, with their devoted wife Draupadī, set forth on their journey to heaven with Yudhiṣṭhira's loyal dog who would not leave them.

This pilgrimage in itself was a test, a parameter for judging whether there really lived a man who led a flawless life. If a person died on the way, this was an indication that he/she must have committed transgressions during his/her life, and therefore could not go to heaven alive.

As the Pāṇḍavas proceeded on their way, first Draupadī, Arjuna, Bhīma, Nakula and then Sahadeva fell dead one by one, leaving Yudhiṣṭhira alone with his dog. What were the transgressions of those Pāṇḍavas? What had Draupadī done which caused her death on the way? The epic Provides the following reasons: Draupadī died because she did not love all her husbands alike—she loved Arjuna the most. Arjuna could not complete the journey since he was excessively proud of his valor. Bhīma's fault was that he was too much attached to worldly enjoyments such as good food and drink. Nakula's arrogance concerning his own beauty and Sahadeva's excessive pride in his intelligence were responsible for their downfall on the pilgrimage to heaven. The unseen power of *karma* had declared them unworthy to proceed to heaven while they were alive. Yudhiṣṭhira, who never acted in his own selfish interest and who spent his life seeking the wellbeing of others, was the "chosen one."

Yudhiṣṭhira saw the god of the gods, Indra, waiting to greet him in the royal chariot at the doors of heaven. "Welcome, o king, to the realm of happiness," said Indra. But Yudhiṣṭhira refused the invitation, for how could he enjoy the pleasures of heaven without his brothers and his wife? Indra assured him that they would later join him in heaven. Yudhiṣṭhira then agreed to enter heaven with the dog. However, Indra objected to receiving the dog in heaven, for how could Indra allow a lowly, defiled animal like a dog to enter heaven? Yudhisthra could not be persuaded by Indra to enter the gates of heaven without the dog. "This dog has been a loyal friend of mine," said Yudhiṣṭhira. "I cannot leave him. If he is not allowed in heaven, I will not enter it either." At that moment, *Dharma,* the god of justice (who was an incarnation of the god of death himself) appeared before Yudhiṣṭhira and said, "You passed the test. The dog truly was none other than an incarnation of me. I was testing you. You have proved yourself to be an unselfish and caring person who is ready to decline even the pleasures of heaven for the sake of a loyal friend—dog."

## 4.0 The motif of war in the Mahābhārata

The term *Mahābhārata,* which etymologically means 'the great *Bhārata*' (the name of the war which took place between two royal families of cousins), symbolizes the motif of "war and conflict" in the epic.

The *Mahābhārata* is a tale of war at various levels; i.e., individual, social, and cosmic. War or conflict (in the general sense of the term) is not presented here as a solution to problems, but as an outcome of the imbalance of opposite forces at different levels. The motif of war thus emphasizes the recognition of opposite forces and the necessity of their balance for the smooth functioning of society and the cosmos.

### 4.1 War at the cosmic level

The *Mahābhārata* emphasizes the Hindu belief, that wars/conflicts exist only at the level of *Māyā* in the phenomenal world of opposite forces. At the level of ultimate reality *(Brahman),* there exists no conflict, since *Brahman is* viewed as the one, eternal, all pervasive. The world of *Māyā is* rooted in *Brahman* like the waves in the ocean, it emerges from *Brahman,* it sustains itself and it returns to *Brahman* again.

The story of the *Mahābhārata* can be viewed as a metaphorical illustration of the above concepts. *Satyavatī* (literally, the one who holds the truth) is a symbol of *Māyā* and is responsible for the creation of the two familes of the Kauravas and the Pāṇḍavas, who are viewed as opposite forces in the "great war." Thus, *Satyavatī,* like *Māyā,* creates opposite forces, (i.e., the Kauravas and the Pāṇḍavas) which are at war only while they are part of this phenomenal transitory world. Once they merge back into the *Eternal Waters,* (or *Brahman)* all conflicts cease to exist. This is illustrated by the myth of the 'Vision of the Dead' in the Mahābhārata story.

According to that myth, Vyāsa gives "special vision" to the old king Dhṛtarāṣṭra and the queens, so that they see their dead relatives. Their jealousy and hatred mattered only in this world. The epic symbolically describes this, depicting the protagonists and antagonists in the war as part of the *Eternal* Waters, symbolically the Ganges, where all opposites merge. Satyavatī's world is the world of *Māyā* which transforms the one *(Brahman or* one family) into many multiple forms. The war between the two families is as transitory as the world itself. They are the indistinguishable waves in the *Eternal waters.*

Another dimension of war at the cosmic level is the opposition that exists between two major personalities in the Mahābhārata story, i.e., Satyavatī and Kṛṣṇa. While Satyavatī symbolized *Māyā* (which we have already noted), Kṛṣṇa symbolized *Brahman,* the ultimate reality. Satyavatī besides being the direct cause of the creation of the opposite forces (i.e., the Pāṇḍavas and the Kauravas), was also the principal motivating force responsible for dragging and yoking to this world even the characters who had nothing to gain by their actions in this world—notably, Vyāsa and Bhīṣma. It was Vyāsa who was summoned by Satyavatī to produce children through the two wives (Ambikā, and Ambālikā) of his half-brother Vicitravīrya. It was Bhīṣma who was manipulated by Satyavatī to forcibly abduct the three princesses, Ambā, Ambikā, and Ambālikā, for his half brother Vicitravīrya. Vyāsa was a born ascetic and Bhīṣma a self-declared celibate. But both of them became willing tools in the hands of Satyavatī who had her own plans for ensuring the continuation of the royal line she had started.

On the other hand, Kṛṣṇa as a symbol of *Brahman,* asks people to mentally withdraw and detach themselves from the pleasures of this transitory world in all situations and circumstances. That is why it was no contradiction for Kṛṣṇa to make Arjuna fight in the war, because Kṛṣṇa incessantly kept reminding Arjuna that actions (including a war) were inescapable in this world. It was the fruit of one's actions that one must transcend (see chapter 6 for detailed description).

## *4.2 War at the social level*

The *Mahābhārata* depicts the turmoil which occurs at the social level as a result of individuals' revolts against the social order. In the *Mahābhārata,* the four-fold division of society is shown to be very rigid; it did not freely allow interclass mobility, since membership in a class was determined by birth and not by a person's qualifications. Similarly, the social structure had become quite hierarchical in nature in terms of prestige and respect, the lower classes were not given the same privileges as the higher classes. Unlike the characters in the *Rāmāyaṇa,* the characters in the *Mahābhārata* challenged the system and revolted against it. Satyavatī, although a fishermaid, was ambitious enough to marry Śantanu, a king; Karṇa, who was recognized as a charioteers's son, wanted to be evaluated by his own qualifications and not by his birth.

The story of Ekalavya, a hunter's son, clearly reveals the rigidity of this system, which punished anyone attempting to transcend the social structure. Ekalavya, skilled in wielding bow and arrows, wanted to learn the art of weaponry from Droṇa, the royal teacher of the Kaurava and the Pandava princes. He was denied that privilege by Droṇa since he belonged to a low caste. Nevertheless, Ekalavya was determined to pursue his goal. He made a clay-idol of Droṇa, worshipping it everyday as his teacher and pursuing and practicing his self-training in weaponry in front of it. By great effort and perseverance, Ekalavya became a very skilled archer. One day, annoyed by the barking of a dog belonging to the princes, he shot seven arrows in the dog's mouth in such a way that it could not bark anymore although it was totally unhurt. When the dog ran back to the princes, Droṇa and the others were amazed at the skill of the archer. Droṇa searched for him and found out that a low-caste prince of Nisadha, Ekalavya, was the person responsible for this astonishing feat. Ekalavya claimed that he owed his skill to Droṇa, whom he honored as his teacher. Drona, although full of admiration for Ekalavya, could not tolerate the violation of the social system. How could he allow a low-caste person to be skilled in the art of weaponry like the Kṣatriya princes? Droṇa said to Ekalavya, "If you indeed consider me to be your teacher, then you must pay me the teacher's fee that you owe me." "Anything you ask, sir; I am ready to offer to you," said Ekalavya. Droṇa replied, "I would like for you to cut off your right thumb and present it to me as the fee." Ekalavya kept his promise, and consequently lost his thumb and the skill of archery to the social system which he had tried to overcome.

There are other events in which the individuals in the *Mahābhārata* fight social laws. For example, Ambā, who was expected to marry Vicitravīrya, refuses to do so. Similarly, Kuntī does not hesitate to use a magic spell to conceive children through persons other than her husband. Draupadī, instead of abiding by her husband's wish to use her as a stake at the game of dice, challenges Dhṛtarāṣṭra's justice and Yudhiṣṭhira's right to use her as a stake.

## 4.3 War at the individual level

At the individual level, the motif of war is observed in the conflicts between Droṇa and Drupada, Ambā and Bhīṣma, Karṇa and Arjuna, Duryodhana and Bhīma, etc. Those conflicts are guided mainly by the individual's passion for power, wealth and glory. These individual conflicts indicate that the individuals in the *Mahābhārata* in general place more emphasis on self-interest (as opposed to society's interests).

At the individual level, war has yet another dimension: the conflict between the different identities and roles of an individual. For example, consider Karṇa's dilemma regarding his true identity; i.e. whether he was one of the Pāndava princes or a charioteer's son. Kunti's dilemma was between her roles as a mother and the queen mother (i.e. whether or not she should publicly own Karṇa as her son). Dhṛtarāṣṭra's conflict was between two roles—one as a just king and the other as the father of the Kauravas.

Arjuna's conflict regarding his individual and social duty stemmed primarily from the indecision he was faced with; that is, whether he was an individual first or a warrior first. In the 18th chapter of the *Mahābhārata* (i.e., *the Bhagavadgītā),* Arjuna, who was ready to fight on the battlefield, was suddenly confronted with the question, "Why am I fighting this war? For whose sake? Fathers, brothers, and relatives are going to be killed in the war. What is the value of a victory which is defiled by the blood of loved ones?" Arjuna was fighting a war between his two identities—one the warrior who must fight for society and one the individual who must protect himself and his family.

Kṛṣṇa, Arjuna's charioteer, who is *Brahman* incarnate, resolves Arjuna's dilemma and provides a unified explanation for all conflicts and wars in the world. In his advice to Arjuna, Kṛṣṇa, in a nutshell, focuses on the real nature of human identity (i.e. a combination of perishable and imperishable dimensions, a combination of body and soul) and the ultimate goal of life, which is to escape the cycle of rebirth. (see chapter 6 for more discussion)

## 5.0 Tapas and the notion of power

The epic poetry of both the *Rāmāyaṇa* and the *Mahābhārata* marks an important development in the history of religion related to the notion of power. The locus of power had been gradually turning toward human beings. In the beginning, the power to control the operations of different orders of *ṛta* was believed to belong to natural phenomena (recall Chapter 3) and then to sacrifice (in the Brahmanic literature). Now the center of power that controlled the functioning of the whole universe was believed to be in human beings themselves. It was believed that cosmic energy or power abided in everything in the universe, including human beings. This power was dormant and was not realized as a result of non-use. It was believed that mental and physical exercises *(yoga)* and austerities and penances, etc., were some of the devices which could revive that inherent cosmic power in the individual.

The belief was that this power is generally suppressed, since human beings often try to find the locus of power in the outer world and do not pay any attention to the source of power within themselves. Mental and physical exercises are a means of cleansing the mind and body of the impurities which keep the power suppressed.

*Tapas* literally means "heat, energy." The term is used to denote both the processes of mental and physical exercises as well as their result, i.e., the power, energy generated by this process.

It was believed that if one does *tapas,* one can acquire cosmic energy and thereby control the universe. The intensity of this energy is often compared to that of the sun. Doing *tapas* was considered to be the process of creating the sun within oneself, which would give one enormous control over the world. This notion of *tapas* placed human beings at the top of the hierarchy of power. The individual emerges as the ultimate force in Hindu mythology and religion. The story of Agastya nicely illustrates the power of *tapas.* Agastya, by doing *tapas,* had acquired the ability to drink the whole ocean, and as a result, the gods had to stop him.

*Tapas* gave individuals a magic wand which enabled them to go beyond the limits of class in society. Also, it gave full control of cosmic and other affairs to human beings. In the *Mahābhārata,* characters such as Ambā, Arjuna, and Drupada do *tapas* to fulfill their wishes.

## 6.0 Inevitability of destruction

The *Mahābhārata* is unique in one more respect, i.e., it conveys a violent message—namely that destruction is inevitable when the time is ripe for it.

The point that can be raised here is: When there was a disturbance in the cosmic order in the *Rāmāyaṇa,* Viṣṇu the god of sustenance took responsiblity for reestablishing order. However, no such effort is visible in the *Mahābhārata.* Kṛṣṇa, who is another incarnation of Viṣṇu, does not stop destruction; rather, he seems to be the main catalyst that hastens the process.

The *Mahābhārata,* as the author suggests, takes place at the end of the third *yuga (dvāpara yuga)* and at the beginning of the fourth *yuga (kali yuga).* The end of the cycle is imminent. The world is aging, it is losing its vitality both at the physical as well as ethical levels, since these levels are never separated in Hindu mythology. The *Mahābhārata* shows that every aspect of the world is breaking down and it is evident that no one can prevent the impending catastrophe.

# CHAPTER 6

# *The Bhagavadgītā: "The Divine Song"*

## *1.0 Introduction*

The Bhagavadgītā 'divine song', though a small (only 700 verses) part (18th chapter) of the voluminous epic, the *Mahābhārata,* has become the rallying point of Hindu religious and philosophical traditions for the last 1600–1900 years. The reason for the total acceptance of the teachings of the *Bhagavadgītā* by one and all in the Hindu tradition lies in the fact that it not only boldly reaffirmed the inseparability of the spiritual and the worldly life but it also provided a clear and well-formulated guideline for any person to realize his/her true identity *(Ātman)* through *any* path or method which suited or helped that person. This lack of dogma is the natural outcome of the essentially eclectic approach of the *Bhagavadgītā.* Perhaps this is the only 'book' in the Hindu tradition which incorporated every major philosophical and religious doctrine (e.g., Vedic rituals, Upanisadic abstractions, *Sāṃkhya, Yoga,* etc.) and integrated them all to define the central tenet of Hinduism namely that religion is a way of life

## *2.0 The context of the Bhagavadgītā*

The Bhagavadgītā begins in the context of the war fought between the Pāṇḍavas and the Kauravas. Arjuna, accompanied by his charioteer Kṛṣṇa, was getting ready to fight the war. He wanted to observe both sides (i.e., the Kauravas and the Pāṇḍavas) on the battlefield to prepare himself psychologically and physically to fight the war. However, as he looked at both sides, he saw his own relatives—grandfathers, cousins, uncles, and teachers—standing in front of him as his enemies. Suddenly he was overcome by an acute feeling of depression, for he thought "Why am I fighting this war? for whom? All my loved ones are assembled here on both sides. Are they not the people for whose sake I desire victory? What good is victory when one has to kill one's own people?"

Arjuna was confronted with the dilemma: Should I or shouldn't I fight? Should I follow my *dharma* toward my relatives or should I follow my *dharma* toward society? Which *dharma is* more important? At this moment of conflict, Arjuna got so confused that he declared he would not fight the war.

Kṛṣṇa, Arjuna's charioteer and *Brahman* incarnate, pointed out to Arjuna that (i.e., the conflict of *dharmas is* faced by everyone in life, and that inaction i.e., withdrawal from the war), which is what Arjuna had opted for in the situation, was not the right response. The answer to the question whether or not one should perform a particular action depends on who the person is (the identity of the person), what his/her goal is in life, and how he/she achieves it. Only when one is clear about the answers to the above questions one can decide whether an action is right or not. Whichever action is conducive to the achievement of the goal is the right action (and therefore should be performed), whereas an action which is not conducive to the goal is not the right action (and therefore, should not be performed).

Although the questions mentioned above in the *Bhagavadgītā* are context–specific (the war in the *Mahābhārata),* they are presented as universal questions which must be answered in any conflict in human life. The answers to these questions are provided within the framework of the Hindu tradition and worldview.

Three of the major concepts in the *Bhagavadgītā* can be discussed in the context of the following three questions: (a) The question of identity, (b) The goal of life, and (c) the methods/paths of achieving the goal of life.

## 3.0 The question of identity

According to the *Bhagavadgītā,* each individual has two dimensions of his identity—one physical *(deha* 'body') and the other spiritual *(Ātman* 'embodied soul'). While the body is transitory, the *Ātman is* permanent. While the body belongs to the realm of Māyā, the *Ātman* is *Brahman* (i.e., ultimate reality) wrapped in a body. The body is like a pitcher full of water floating in the ocean. *Brahman* is like the ocean and *Ātman* is the water inside the pitcher; the only barrier between the water inside *(Ātman)* and outside *(Brahman)* is the pitcher; i.e., body itself. The body is transitory and compositional in nature, and therefore it dies and is reborn. *Ātman* is non-compositional and eternal in nature; hence "it is never born, it never dies; it cannot be said of him that he came into being and he will be no more." *(Bhagavadgītā 2.20)* Also, "The weapons do not kill him, the fire does not burn him. The water does not drench him; the wind does not dry him." *(Bhagavadgita 2.2 3).* These two quotes emphasize the indestructibility of *Ātman.* It is also claimed here that suffering, pain, and death are applicable only to the transitory body. There can not be any suffering or pain at the level of *Ātman,* since it is one all-pervasive reality, *Brahman,* which simply witnesses the various changes (physical, mental and emotional) affecting the body and yet is never affected by any of these. Human beings identify themselves with this temporary aspect of their personality (body). Therefore, they say they love, hate, they grow, they suffer, and they die. They forget that *Ātman,* the eternal self in them, is untouched by those changes. Kṛṣṇa points out to Arjuna that Arjuna is concentrating only on this fragile dimension of his own and his relatives' personality. Therefore he thinks that he could kill them and they would die. In fact, neither can he kill the "eternal" in them nor can the "eternal" die. "Like a man changes his old clothes and puts on new, so does *Ātman* change the old body and enter into a new one. Therefore do not grieve, (*Bhagavadgītā* 2.2 2)," Kṛṣṇa advises Arjuna.

The Bhagavadgītā thus traces the two-fold dimensions of human personality or self-one transitory and the other permanent. Because of his identification with the transitory dimension (body), an individual feels separated or isolated from everyone /everything else, as well as from Brahman. Ātman is the permanent dimension which connects an individual with Brahman (which is identical to Ātman in reality) and with all other existences (since everything is rooted in Brahman). The *Bhagavadgītā* emphasizes that, as long as human beings identify themselves with the body, they are bound to suffer. They can be completely and permanently free only when they identify themselves with *Ātman* (and thereby with *Brahman).*

## 4.0 The goal of life

The goal of life, according to the Upanisadic Hindu tradition in general and the *Bhagavadgītā* in particular, is to identify oneself with Brahman—the ultimate reality. The *Bhagavadgītā* presents very strong justifications for this goal of life: (a) If one wants to be permanently free from the sufferings of life, this freedom (*moksa*) is possible only if one identifies oneself with *Brahman,* which is permanent. When one realizes *aham Brahmasmi* 'I am *Brahman,* all suffering vanishes. (b) This knowledge of one's identity with Brahman, is also the knowledge of the essential identity of all existences and their interconnectedness. In short, the *Bhagavadgītā* says that the "true" or "real" identity is the global identity which is permanent, while the narrow, individual identity is unreal and transitory. The goal is to transcend this individual, separate identity and realize the global identity; i.e. "I am *Brahman*"; to get away from an isolated self to a (globally) connected self.

How does one transcend the body—the transitory existence? This is a question which is discussed at great length in the *Bhagavadgītā. If* the theory of *karma is* accepted, one is permanently trapped in the transitory existence of the body. According to the theory of karma, actions must bring results, and, in order to experience the results, one is born again. Thus the cycle of rebirth continues (*lokaḥ ayaṃ karmabandhanaḥ* the world is tied by the chain of *karma' (3.9)),* and so does the suffering. The *Bhagavadgītā* argues that it is not action per se, but rather the attachment to the results of actions which "binds" human beings to the cycle of births. If one performs an action out of the desire for its results for oneself, only then is one held responsible for it and thereby is born again to bear the consequences of that action. If one performs actions for the sake of one's duty (i.e., without any attachment to their 'fruits'), then one is not responsible for the results and thereby is not born again. Desireless action cuts the roots of the tree of *karma* and thereby stops the cycle of rebirth. According to the *Bhagavadgītā, the* one who has achieved the goal (i.e., the one who has identified oneself with *Brahman*) never performs actions for the sake of the enjoyment of their fruits, but, rather, only for 'for the sustenance of humanity'. (See also the discussion on the path of action in section 8.)

## 5.0 Is Heaven the ultimate goal?

Another related question discussed in this context is that of the desirability of heaven. If attachment to anything (e.g., heaven) is the cause of rebirth and, thereby, suffering; then to what extent is it desirable to perform meritorious acts for the sake of attaining heaven after death? According to the *Bhagavadgītā,* heaven is not the ultimate goal of life, since it is not considered to be a permanent abode in the Hindu system of beliefs. One goes to heaven to experience the results of one's meritorious actions. However, when the *punya* 'merit' of the righteous actions is used up, one has to return to earth and the cycle of rebirth continues. The length of time in heaven is determined by the amount of merit acquired by an individual during her/his span of life. Heaven is only a temporary reward for righteous actions. However, for the one who wants to escape the cycle of rebirth altogether, heaven is not desirable. However, it is claimed in the *Bhagavadgītā* that the desire for heaven is better than other selfish desires, since in order to achieve heaven one performs righteous acts. Moreover, after the stay in heaven, when one returns to earth, one is expected to be born in a form (human) in which one can attain *moksa* 'liberation from the cycle of rebirth.'

## 6.0 The paths or methods for achieving the goal of life

The question, "How does one accomplish the goal of life?" receives a long discussion in the *Bhagavadgītā.* The *Bhagavadgītā,* which is dogmatic about the goal of life (i.e. release from the cycle of rebirth and identity with *Brahman),* is very liberal about the paths to be taken. Any path which leads one to the realization of identity with *Brahman is* the right path. In fact, it is claimed in the *Bhagavadgītā* that people differ in their dispositions and therefore they will always be inclined to follow different paths suitable to their dispositions. Although, in principle, the *Bhagavadgītā* approves of any path, it outlines three major paths for people of different dispositions *(sāttvika* 'pure/lucid', *rājasī* 'passionate', and *tāmasī* 'inert'). The three paths are: (a) *jñāna yoga* 'the path of knowledge', (b) *karma yoga* 'the path of action', and (c) *bhakti yoga* 'the path of devotion'. These paths are called *yogas.*

The term *yoga* literally means 'union' (i.e., with *Brahman).* The way, method, device which leads to union with *Brahman* is also called *yoga* 'path'. The three paths are three different ways of reaching the same goal, no one path is preferred over others.

## 7.0 Jñana yoga 'the path of knowledge'

This path of knowledge emphasizes realization of identity with *Brahman* within oneself. Thus the term *jñāna* 'knowledge' does not refer only to the intellectual or objective knowledge of oneness with *Brahman,* but rather it denotes the personal and intuitive experience of oneness with *Brahman.* This yoga can be divided into two parts for the sake of exposition: (a) *āsana yoga* (physical exercises), and (b) *dhyāna yoga* (meditation). One can experience oneness with *Brahman* by first withdrawing from one's narrow identity with the body and then concentrating on the larger global identity. However, since body and mind are generally engrossed in the material objects of the five senses (tasting, seeing, hearing, touching, and smelling), a person must make the body go through a number of steps (i.e. physical exercises, etc.) which bring the body and mind under his control. Then he must concentrate all his physical and mental energies on meditating upon *Brahman.*

Meditation helps the mind to withdraw from the attachments to the material world. As the intensity of concentration grows, the person's mind becomes fully absorbed in meditation, and the distinction between the object of meditation and the meditator vanishes; they become one. Similarly, the distinction between the object of meditation and the external phenomenal world also vanishes. The meditator becomes one with everything within and without. He realizes his identity with *Brahman.* The *Bhagavadgītā* incorporates concepts from Patanjali's *Yoga-Sūtra* (2nd century B.C.) to emphasize the freeing of the body and mind from the world of the senses as a prerequisite to the realization of the self *(Ātman).*

## 8.0 Karma Yoga 'the path of action'

Another path for release from the cycle of rebirth is *karma yoga* 'the path of action'. Kṛṣṇa advises Arjuna that actions performed without any attachment to their result or "fruits" do not bind the performer of the actions to the cycle of rebirth. It is the intent (selfish motive) behind actions which binds human beings to the cycle of rebirth. Thus social duty, when performed without any attachment to its results, does not bind the performer to his actions. Hence Arjuna is advised by Kṛṣṇa to perform his duty as a *Kṣatriya* 'warrior' (to fight the war) for the sake of duty and not for its fruit (i.e., winning the war).

The *Bhagavadgītā* explains why the path of desireless action is better than the path of inaction (although it seems more logical to renounce all actions in order to escape their results) as follows: as long as the body is sustained, it is extremely difficult if not impossible, to not perform any action, since the body is naturally geared toward action. Moreover, there is no guarantee that inaction would result in detachment from the world of the senses. One may not perform any action but may keep thinking about sense-pleasures. Since it is the intent behind the actions that cause rebirth, it is crucial to have an attitude of detachment from sense-pleasures. Finally, desireless action (i.e., duty performed for the sake of duty) helps one to grow out of one's narrow identity and attain the larger identity (i.e., identity with society and so on), which is a step toward the ultimate goal, identity with all–pervasive *Brahman.* In fact, the *Bhagavadgītā* points out that one who has achieved that goal should also perform action (without any attachment to the results) simply for *lokasaṃgraha* 'for the sake of the sustenance of the cosmos society, and people'. It is important to note here that the Bhagavadgītā prescribes desireless action for the spiritual goal of individuals but does not ignore the need to maintain social structure. Both the spiritual goal and social needs are fulfilled by following the path of action.

## 9.0 Bhakti yoga 'the path of devotion'

The *Bhagavadgītā* suggests the path of devotion for those who are of an emotional temperament. The follower of this path worships a personal god (i.e., an idol, or any concrete symbol such as tree, rock, etc.) of his/her choice. The devotee offers all his/her possessions, actions, and emotions to a personal god. Everything he/she does, or thinks, is done for the personal god and never for the self. The bond between the god and the devotee grows stronger and the attachment to the rest of the world weakens. Like the person who follows the path of knowledge *(Jñānayogī)* and the person who follows the path of desireless actions *(karmayogī) the devotee* (Bhaktiyogī) also develops an attitude of detachment from the world. The intense attachment to a personal god results in a total merger of the devotee's identity with that of the personal god. This attachment of the devotee to a personal god is different from the attachment which an individual has to anything in the material world, since the attachment to another individual or an object (e.g. house) makes the individual perform actions generally for fulfilling selfish desires. Thus, the individual is never able to free himself from the clutches of *karma* or from the bonds of *Māyā* (i.e. the escape from the cycle of rebirth becomes impossible).

In contrast to this, attachment to a personal god does not separate the devotee from the rest of the world, since for him the personal god is in fact the symbol of Brahman, the all-pervasive reality. By identifying with the personal god, the devotee identifies with the entire cosmos. Secondly, the attachment to the personal god and any actions performed for the personal god are not for any selfish gain. This belief in a personal god as the very symbol of *Brahman* causes a devotee to easily accept other persons' personal gods or various symbols thereof. This in fact explains the phenomenon of a Hindu devotee accepting and worshipping the personal gods of other sects besides his own.

CHAPTER 7

# The Mythology of Kṛṣṇa: The Divine As Human

## 1.0 Introduction

The myths of Kṛṣṇa are perhaps the most popular and most cherished myths in India. Their wide appeal is due to the fact that they depict the human dimension of the divine. The identity of particular and universal, many and one, human and divine, *Ātman* and *Brahman,* is the overwhelming theme of the Kṛṣṇa mythology. The themes are exploited in numerous ways.

While the *Rāmāyaṇa* and the *Mahābhārata* focus mainly on the divine aspect of the human personality and the presence of the universal in the particular, the Kṛṣṇa myths present the human dimension of the divine. Kṛṣṇa is the embodiment of the divine, who laughs and cries, enjoys and suffers, loves and hates, promises and deceive—like a common human being. To be human is to be divine is the message of the myths!

This human dimension is seen in the myths at the spiritual (religious), social, and individual levels, as will be seen in the following discussion.

## 2.0 Dates and sources of the Kṛṣṇa myths

The biography of Kṛṣṇa was elaborated for the first time in the *Harivaṃśa* (the geneology of Hari-Kṛṣṇa) around 400 A.D. Although the *Mahābhārata* depicts Kṛṣṇa as an old man, the advisor friend of Arjuna, it does not include stories of Kṛṣṇa's birth, childhood, and youth. It is the *Harivaṃśa,* which was originally supposed to be an appendix to the *Mahābhārata,* which focuses on Kṛṣṇa's personal life story.

The *Bhāgavata Purāṇa* elaborates Kṛṣṇa's story at greater length. Similarly, the Viṣṇu and *Padma Purāṇas* deal with several aspects of Kṛṣṇa's life. After the eleventh century A.D., Kṛṣṇa played a major role in devotional literature in the modern Indian languages in medieval India. Kṛṣṇa's appeal as a common person has made him a hero of all time. Kṛṣṇa's stories are sung, enacted, and painted in almost all corners of India. The legend of Kṛṣṇa continues to live in India even today.

## 3.0 Various dimensions of the Kṛṣṇa myths

The Kṛṣṇa myths stand out in Hindu mythology for several reasons. One of the major features of the Kṛṣṇa myths is that they represent the religious as well as social traditions of the common people. Epic mythology is the mythology of the elite in society. The epics deal with the religious, social, and individual problems of the Brāhmaṇa and Kṣatriya classes (the priests and warriors, respectively). In contrast to this, the Kṛṣṇa myths deal with the problems, conflicts, and life in general of the cowherds in the Northwestern part of India. Their "world view" and their ways of grappling with the problems created by humankind and nature form the major themes of the Kṛṣṇa myths. Kṛṣṇa is the god of the cowherds who are being constantly suppressed by King Kaṃsa, whose oppression is only intensified by natural disasters such as forest fires, floods, droughts, torrential rains, and so on.

These common people, who live by selling milk and butter, depend on their cattle for a living. Their struggle for survival, metaphorically describes the survival of the "little man," the common people who have to survive suppression of every kind. Kṛṣṇa is their god and himself is a cowherd. He represents their only power—he who defends them from all attackers, natural and human. Since Kṛṣṇa's complexion and function resemble the clouds and water (water being a life-giving force), he is aptly called Kṛṣṇa, literally "blue"—the blue god of the cowherds. The myths depict this dimension of Kṛṣṇa's personalitly—the protector of the common people.

## 4.0 Divine in the concrete form

Another dimension of the Kṛṣṇa myths is that they illustrate the common people's view of the divine. The divine is not abstract *Brahman;* rather, it is concrete and human. Kṛṣṇa is *Brahman.* Kṛṣṇa can be seen, touched, befriended, hated, and passionately loved. The Kṛṣṇa myths convincingly argue in their presentation that the ultimate and formless *Brahman* can be envisioned through the particular, restricted form of Kṛṣṇa. The myths point out a crucial point in Hindu philosophy; namely, that it is through the world of forms, particulars, many, and the transitory that the formless, general, one and eternal *Brahman* can be realized. It is only by living through *Māyā* that one can transcend *Māyā.* The Kṛṣṇa myths emphasize the greatness of the "little," "particular," and concrete "form."

## 5.0 Bhakti—the religion of love

As opposed to the path of knowledge *(jñāna mārga),* the Kṛṣṇa myths focus on the path of love. The major argument is that human beings can become one with the ultimate, not by getting rid of human emotions but rather by focusing those emotions toward Kṛṣṇa. It is the object of love which makes the difference, say the myths. As long as the object of love is the transitory world, there is no hope for permanent happiness. However, by loving Kṛṣṇa, the permanent, the ultimate reality, with all the passions with which one loves this world of *Māyā,* human beings can reach their goal and identify with the ultimate. Thus the Kṛṣṇa myths in the religious traditions are interpreted as advocating the path of love for god, which is called devotion or *bhakti.* The myths are interpreted as a metaphor for life. The handsome *gopas,* cowherd boys and beautiful *gopīs,* cowherd girls are *Ātmans—individual* souls madly in love with Kṛṣṇa the supreme soul, *Brahman.*

The tie of love binds both Kṛṣṇa and the cowherds. Both are anxious to be united. There exists the intense attachment of erotic love between the individual souls trapped in their bodies and *Brahman.* Kṛṣṇa plays his flute, which signifies the call of the divine. As soon as the cowherds hear this call, they run away from their homes and the village, which represent the material world of mundane duties, attachments, and relationships. The call of Kṛṣṇa is irresistible! The cowherds, both males and females, go to the forest when Kṛṣṇa plays his flute. The full moon gradually works its spell and the cowherds are completely under Kṛṣṇa's charm. The forest symbolizes the "twilight zone"—the area between "this world" and the "other world." Once in the forest, the cowherds forget their attachment to the mundane world. The village is left behind and with it all other relationships. The only relationship they care for is the relationship with Kṛṣṇa.

The *gopīs* hold hands and form a circle around Kṛṣṇa and dance and sing to the rhythm of the universe. This dance plays an important role in the myths. This is the "dance of souls." Each individual represents *Ātman,* which, while dancing with Kṛṣṇa, becomes one with him. Each *gopi* thinks she has her own Kṛṣṇa. Kṛṣṇa duplicates himself as many times as the *gopīs* need him to. Thus the dance signifies the ultimate unification of an individual and *Brahman.* Everyone steps out of his own individual form and becomes one with Kṛṣṇa.

The Kṛṣṇa myths have been a major source of love-poetry in medieval India. The mysticism in the myths of love has elevated human emotion or love to the divine level.

## 6.0 Superiority of the folk god

It is the opinion of a number of scholars that the Kṛṣṇa myths depict "folk mythology." The Kṛṣṇa myths mark a turning point in mythological tradition. Kṛṣṇa represents the common people in every sense of the word. The social tension between "high" and "low" classes has thus found expression in the mythology. The myths also emphasize the conflicts between Kṛṣṇa and the gods of mainstream Hinduism; i.e., Brahmā and Indra (see the myth of Brahmā stealing the cowherds and the myth of Govardhana mountain, respectively).

It is possible that Kṛṣṇa was the god of the cowherds a long time before his acceptance into the elite mythology which treats him as the 8th descent of Viṣṇu who came down to earth to save the common people. The emergence of a new god and its acceptance by the common people generally led to its acceptance in the " great" tradition of Hinduism, which has included even Buddha as the 9th descent of Viṣṇu.

# 7.0 Life of Kṛṣṇa

## 7.1 The birth of Kṛṣṇa

Kṛṣṇa is believed to be the 8th descent of Viṣṇu to earth for the destruction of the evil king Kaṃsa. In the *Harivamśa,* the story of Kṛṣṇa's life begins with the dialogue between the earth and Viṣṇu. Pṛthvī, the earth, was tired and exhausted from carrying the burden of "evil" caused by the sinful acts of the king Kaṃsa. Kaṃsa was arrogant, oppressive and selfish. He did not hesitate to kill anyone who attempted to stop him from committing heinous deeds. Pṛthvī, being unable to bear the burden any further, approached Viṣṇu, the protector and the sustainer of the world, and said, "O Sustainer of the world! You are the protector of all creatures and the three worlds. Earlier, in times of difficulty, you descended in different forms and saved me and the world from being destroyed. The time has come again for you, O wielder of the powerful disc *cakra,* to come down to save the world. Promise me that you will destroy the demon-king Kaṃsa, for I no longer have the strength to bear the burden of him and his evil acts." Viṣṇu could not refuse her request. He promised her that he would destroy the evil Kaṃsa and re-establish peace and order on earth.

This was the purpose of Viṣṇu's descent to earth in the form of Kṛṣṇa. Once Nārada, Viṣṇu's disciple and a wandering ascetic, visited Kaṃsa and informed him, "The eighth son of your sister Devakī will destroy you, O king, so beware of him." "What a joke," said the demon, laughing contemptuously. "No one, not even the god Indra, can defeat me ever, even when I am asleep or intoxicated with wine (and thereby vulnerable). My power is insurmountable."

However, Kaṃsa did not want to take any chances. He advised his ministers to keep an eye on Devakī and her husband Vasudeva, whom he had already imprisoned.

Vasudeva, (who belonged to *yadu vaṃśa* 'lunar dynasty') Devakī's husband, had another wife named Rohiṇī. The seventh time Devakī became pregnant, after Kaṃsa had had Vasudeva's and Devakī's first six children slain, Viṣṇu transferred the fetus to Rohiṇī's womb. (Indeed, this child was none other than Ananta, the giant cobra on which Viṣṇu rests.) Rohiṇī was sent to Gokula, where she gave birth to a son Balarāma at the dwelling of Nanda and Yaśodā, a kind cowherd couple who did not have a child of their own. Vasudeva and Devakī told Kaṃsa that the baby had miscarried.

Finally, it was the time of birth of the eighth child of Devakī. The whole world trembled with joy. The ocean could not contain the waves of excitement, the mountains began to swing, the cool wind began to blow and the clouds of dust and darkness suddenly disappeared. The stars began to twinkle with a soothing glimmer. Viṣṇu appeared on earth as a baby Kṛṣṇa (the dark one) in the middle of the night, when torrential rains were drenching the whole world, as if to put an end to the long hot summer of Kaṃsa's torture.

Viṣṇu appeared before Vasudeva and Devakī and instructed them to transfer Kṛṣṇa to Gokula, where Yośadā had given birth to a baby girl. Suddenly at that moment a strange spell of sleep fell over the guards in the prison and the prison doors opened. Vasudeva set out to carry the baby Kṛṣṇa in a basket to Gokula. As he crossed the river Yamunā, which was in the spate of floods at the time, the waters suddenly receded as the little toe of the baby Kṛṣṇa touched the waves! Having reached Gokula, Vasudeva exchanged Kṛṣṇa for the baby girl of Yaśodā and Nanda. Kaṃsa had ordered the killing of the eighth child of Vasudeva and Devakī who he thought was a son, but he was informed that it was a girl. Kaṃsa decided to kill her nevertheless. The girl was none other than *Māyā* who had taken the form of a baby. As Kaṃsa held her in his hand and forcefully dropped her onto the stony ground, she flew away into the sky announcing, "You can not destroy the one who is going to slay you! He will drag you by your hair and drop you on the ground as you did to me. An evil act never goes unpunished. You have sown the seed of your destruction!"

In Gokula, the cowherd family of Nanda and Yaśodā celebrated the birth of Kṛṣṇa, the baby boy, whose complexion resembled that of the life-giving dark clouds in the rainy season and the thirst-quenching waters of the river Yamunā. An inexplicable joy filled the hearts of the people in Gokula.

## *7.2 The power of the 'little Kṛṣṇa'*

This exchange of babies turned the course of subsequent events, since it appeared that a daughter rather than a son had been born to Devakī. Thus, Kaṃsa fearlessly released Devakī and Vasudeva from prison; but still he was not at peace. He could not forget the words of the little baby daughter of Vasudeva and Devakī. "How will I know where that evil child is born who is bound to slay me?" Kaṃsa thought to himself and finally ordered the killing of all newly-born children. He sent several demons and demonesses to perform this job and ensure the destruction of his would-be killer at an early age so that he could live without fear for the rest of his life. But little did he know about the power of the baby Kṛṣṇa.

Pūtanā, a hideous demoness, once visited Yaśodā. She had been entrusted with the job of killing Kṛṣṇa. Though in reality she was fierce looking and cruel, with her magical powers she changed herself into a beautiful woman of soft voice and of an apparently affectionate disposition. She was determined to kill Kṛṣṇa by feeding him poison through her breast. When everyone was asleep, Pūtanā held the baby Kṛṣṇa in her arms and began to feed him. Kṛṣṇa started sucking her breast harder and harder till finally he sucked the life out of her body. Pūtanā could no longer bear the pain and started screaming. Nanda, Yośadā and the other members of the household came running as they heard her dreadful screams. By then Pūtanā lay on the floor, lifeless, tranformed into her real form of a demoness. Eventually her body while being cremated, emitted a sweet fragrance which filled the air. Her body with its evil deeds was left behind while her soul had merged into Kṛṣṇa.

Another time Kaṃsa sent Bakāsura 'crane monster' to kill Kṛṣṇa. Bakasura stood on the banks of the Yamunā river waiting for the cowherd boys to come around so he could pick them up with his long beak and gobble them up. Kṛṣṇa and his friends took the cattle to the river to drink. They saw the crane and were amazed at its size. Bakasura looked like a piece of mountain which had been cut off by Indra's thunderbolt. Suddenly the crane grabbed Kṛṣṇa with its beak and tried to swallow him. But he had no idea of the power of little Kṛṣṇa, who pushed the two parts of his beak apart and tore it off into two pieces. The monster's body lay dead, but his soul like Pūtanā's found eternal joy since it merged into Kṛṣṇa.

The cowherd boys and girls, Kṛṣṇa's playmates, and the people were amazed to see this feat of power by a tiny boy and exclaimed "The power of the almighty is unfathomable! It abides in all forms, big and small alike."

Once, while the cowherd boys were sporting among themselves on the banks of the river, singing and dancing, fighting and reconciling, there came a dragon demon called Aghāsura. He was Pūtanā's and Bakāsura's younger brother. When he saw Kṛṣṇa, he said to himself, "This is the one who killed my brother and sister. Today I will take revenge on him and kill him along with his friends. When the children die, gradually the entire community of the cowherds will be destroyed." Aghāsura, lay in their path with his jaws open. The cowherd boys, thinking that it was a cave, walked into it. The demon swallowed them as the dreadful fire swallows the blades of grass. As soon as he entered the dragon's mouth, Kṛṣṇa enlarged his body to the extent that it blocked the fierce demon's throat, so that he could not breathe anymore and finally died. Like the other demons, Aghāsura became one with Kṛṣṇa after his death.

There were several other demons, such as Śakatāsura 'the cart demon', Trivikrama 'the storm demon', and others who tried to kill Kṛṣṇa but got killed instead. Such was the power of the little Kṛṣṇa.

After experiencing the continuous attack of demons, the cowherds' community decided to move from Gokula to Vṛndāvana to avoid the tortures of Kaṃsa and other demons. However, they soon realized there was no safe place for them.

## *7.3 Kṛṣṇa—the butter thief*

Kṛṣṇa was a naughty child who loved butter, but it was not always easily accessible. The jars of butter were securely tied up by ropes and were kept hanging from the roof to keep them out of the reach of the children. Kṛṣṇa would gather his friends and using a ladder, would get down the jars of butter and distribute it among the cowherd boys. When everyone in the house was asleep, Kṛṣṇa would get up, steal butter, and run away. There are numerous stories of Kṛṣṇa's tricks as a butter-thief. An interesting story is given below:

Once Kṛṣṇa was stealing butter in his own house. Suddenly he looked up and saw his own reflection in the mirror on the wall. Thinking that there was someone else watching him he said, "O brother, don't tell my mother about this, please! Come, I will share my butter with you." At that moment, his mother walked in. Kṛṣṇa pointing to the reflection, changed the course of his speech and said, "Mother, this thief was trying to steal your butter, and I was trying to stop him. Won't you believe me, Mother, your own son? I really did not have any intention of stealing butter." Yaśodā embraced him with love and forgot to get angry at him.

All the cowherds, men, women, and children, loved Kṛṣṇa dearly. He was their joy. They could not bear his absence. The *gopīs* 'cowherd girls' would complain about his tricks and his stealing. "Your son, O Yaśodā, is a butter thief," they would say, but when she would try to punish him, tears would flow from their eyes and they would themselves implore Yaśodā not to punish Kṛṣṇa. Kṛṣṇa at times would go into hiding just to see how they would react. And sure enough, they could not bear his absence. "Where is our butter-thief? Where is the player of *muralī* 'flute'?" they would ask. The little Kṛṣṇa had charmed whole of Gokula.

## *7.4 Viśvadarśana—'the vision of the universe (in the "little mouth")'*

Once some people came and told Yaśodā, "Mother Yaśodā, your darling *lāl* 'son' Kṛṣṇa has been eating clay." Yaśodā was angry. "Tell me, you naughty one," she said to Kṛṣṇa, "why did you eat clay? You are becoming impossible to control these days. You have been sneaking around and eating clay, haven't you?" "No, mother, I have not," said little Kṛṣṇa innocently, "If you do not belive me, look into my mouth." And Kṛṣṇa opened his tiny mouth. Yaśodā stood spellbound by the vision of the entire universe in his mouth. The sky, the planets, the animate and inanimate worlds were inside his mouth. Yaśodā realized that her little son was the source of the entire universe, and her perceptions, i.e., "I" and "mine" (as in "I am his mother, this is my son," etc.), were illusory—*Māyā*. In the absolute sense everything abides in Kṛṣṇa, the indivisible reality. However, Kṛṣṇa quickly concealed his real nature and Yaśodā was able to see him as her child once again.

## *7.5 Kṛṣṇa—the cowherd*

Kṛṣṇa was a cowherd boy who dressed like the cowherd boys, played with them, took cattle to the forest for grazing and brought them back in the evening. He played the bamboo flute. The enchanting melody of it was dear to everyone, the cattle and the *gopīs* 'cowherd girls' and the *gopas* 'cowherd boys' alike. At sundown Kṛṣṇa would play upon his flute and everyone who heard it would remain spellbound. The *gopīs* would forget their household chores and run to meet Kṛṣṇa. Like souls liberated from the trap of Māyā, the *gopīs* would run toward Kṛṣṇa, as if the sound of his flute was the call of the divine. There was some inexplicable bond between the sound of Kṛṣṇa's flute and the *gopīs*. The sound of the flute would touch the divine essence *(Ātman)* in everyone and remind everyone of the temporariness of the world of *Māyā* which had deluded them into believing that everything and everyone around them was the only reality. The flute was a reminder for everyone of their real identity with "the flute player," the ultimate reality. The *gopīs* loved Kṛṣṇa passionately. They would wait for his call as anxiously as a woman waits for her lover. The *gopas* would love him as a great friend who would love them, protect them and share their joys and pains. Nanda and Yaśodā loved him as a child. There was no one around who did not love Kṛṣṇa in one way or another.

## *7.6 Kāliya-damana 'vanquishing the poisonous serpent (Kāliya)'*

Kṛṣṇa, the mischievous butter-thief, reveals in his behavior towards Kāliya an entirely different dimension to his personality. Indeed, he was a protector of the entire community of cowherds, but that never prevented him from being kind, compassionate, and understanding in appropriate cases or circumstances.

A poisonous serpent named Kāliya had been driven away from his native place (*Rāmāṇaka Dvīpa*) by his arch enemy *Garuḍa* 'eagle' and had been forced to take shelter in the river Yamunā. Kāliya was such a dangerously poisonous snake that by his very breath the water of Yamunā had become poisoned. Once the cowherd boys were playing a game of ball on the bank of the river. When they became thirsty, the cowherd boys and the cattle went to drink the water. They did not know that the water had been poisoned by Kāliya. As a result, they fainted, and were on the verge of death. Kṛṣṇa came around and revived them. As they began to play ball again, Kṛṣṇa climbed up into a tree. When the cowherd boys threw the ball to Kṛṣṇa, it fell into the river, and Kṛṣṇa jumped into the water to fetch the ball. Kāliya was greatly enraged by Kṛṣṇa's audacity in daring to come into his territory. The serpent grabbed him and coiled around him with hundreds of his hoods. But he could not keep Kṛṣṇa trapped for very long, since Kṛṣṇa quickly freed himself from the grips of Kāliya and, jumping onto the serpent's head, began to dance on his hoods. Step by step, Kṛṣṇa began to trounce the hoods of Kāliya. Kāliya began to feel as though he were under the weight of the entire universe. Kāliya tried to shake Kṛṣṇa off his head and to retaliate but with no success.

Soon Kāliya realized that Kṛṣṇa was not an ordinary human being, since no one else had ever succeeded in overcoming the power of his poison. Kāliya's wives could not bear the sight of his approaching death. They went to Kṛṣṇa and beseeched him to release Kāliya. "O, Kṛṣṇa, save our husband, Kāliya. Do not kill him. But if you must, then kill us as well, since the life of a woman is worthless without her husband," said Kāliya's wives. They further reminded Kṛṣṇa, "Kāliya is not really to be faulted, since he was only behaving according to his nature. A poisonous serpent can not but be poisonous. How can you punish him for that?"

Kṛṣṇa forgave Kāliya on the condition that he would go back to his native place, *Rāmāṇaka Dvīpa* and poison Yamunā no more. Kṛṣṇa gave him further assurance that Garuda would no longer torment him in *Rāmāṇaka Dvīpa* when he saw the mark of Kṛṣṇa's feet on his hoods.

## 7.7 Kṛṣṇa's conflict with Brahmā

Kṛṣṇa always identified with the cowherds and therefore it was very important for him to preserve the identity of the community of cowherds. This can be illustrated with the following myths:

Once Brahmā arrived in the forest seated on a beautiful white swan. Kṛṣṇa and his friends, the cowherds, were playing and the cattle were grazing in the forest. Brahma, the god of creation, stole the cattle and the cowherd boys and girls to prove his superiority over Kṛṣṇa by greatly embarassing him. However, as soon as Brahmā flew away on his swan, Kṛṣṇa, realizing the extent of Brahma's mischief, created another set of cattle and cowherd boys and girls identical to the ones which had been stolen. When Brahmā returned after a year to check on the situation, he was amazed to see that Kṛṣṇa had foiled his mischievous attempt to embarass him by recreating the cattle and the cowherd boys and girls.

Brahmā realized that Kṛṣṇa was not an ordinary cowherd; rather, he was the supreme being, all-powerful and all-encompassing. Brahmā prostrated himself before Kṛṣṇa and apologized for his misconduct, asking for his blessings. Brahmā realized that no one could overpower Kṛṣṇa because Kṛṣṇa was the very source of everything in the universe.

## 7.8 The Govardhana mountain: the encounter with Indra

Once Kṛṣṇa asked his father about the purpose of the ritual sacrifice to be offered to the god Indra. "My son" said Nanda, "Indra is our savior. Our farms, our cattle, our whole life depends on Indra, since Indra is the rain god. Therefore, we perform this sacrifice to please him, so he may give us timely and plentiful rains." Kṛṣṇa disagreed and said, "Father, human beings suffer or rejoice due to their own *karma,* do they not? We should respect *karma* and perform proper *karma* according to our position in society and stage of life. The *iṣṭadeva* 'the chosen personal god' ought to be the one who is responsible for the smooth functioning of our life. From this perspective, then, the forest, rivers, and the mountains are our true gods. These are the entities that help create rain-bearing clouds. We must worship them, instead of Indra. Therefore let us offer a sacrifice to the Govardhana mountain."

The whole community was thus persuaded by Kṛṣṇa to worship the mountain instead of Indra. And indeed the sacrifice was ritually performed for the mountain. Indra, enraged by this act, decided to teach Kṛṣṇa a lesson. Indra began to shower torrential rains on Vṛndāvana. Every inch of the village was submerged under water. The storm and the rain created a havoc in the village. The cowherds came to Kṛṣṇa for refuge. 'Do not worry," said Kṛṣṇa, I will protect you." Kṛṣṇa then held up the mountain Govardhana on his little finger and used it as an umbrella to protect the village from the heavy rain. The whole community of cowherds was protected under the mountain. Eventually Indra was forced to accept the superiority of the cowherd Kṛṣṇa.

## *7.9 Kṛṣṇa as a divine lover*

Kṛṣṇa's relationship with the *gopīs* was one of intense love. Each *gopi* loved Kṛṣṇa as her own lover and experienced in union with him all shades of love: desire, jealousy, expectation, agony of separation, anger, joy. When Kṛṣṇa played his flute on a moonlit night, the *gopi* were no longer chained to worldly attachments with family, friends, etc. They ran to Kṛṣṇa as a newborn calf runs naturally towards its mother. Kṛṣṇa loved the gopīs just as passionately as they loved him. One of Kṛṣṇa's favorite *gopīs* was Rādhā, but each gopi had a special significance for Kṛṣṇa. This relationship between Kṛṣṇa and the *gopīs* was unique.

Symbolically, the *gopīs* were the *Ātmans* 'embodied souls' trapped in human bodies and in the world of *Māyā,* and Kṛṣṇa was *Brahman.* The *gopīs*' search for Kṛṣṇa was the natural attraction and inclination of *Ātman* toward *Brahman.* Similarly, Kṛṣṇa's intense love for them was the indication of the natural bond which existed between *Ātman* and *Brahman.* The tension caused in the hearts of the *gopīs* by their relationship with their relatives on the one hand and with Kṛṣṇa on the other depicted the tension between the body and *Ātman, Māyā* and *Brahman.*

Kṛṣṇa often teased the *gopīs* and told them that he did not love them anymore, he was going to leave them, etc. He often tested them. Once the *gopīs* were bathing in the river. Kṛṣṇa stole their clothes and sat on a tree on the banks of the river. "Give our clothes back, Kṛṣṇa, or else how will we come out of the water? Do not be so cruel, give our clothes back," said the *gopīs.* "You must come to me and take your clothes back. You should not be shy, since you have offered everything to me . Why this attachment to clothes?" On hearing this the *gopīs* did as Kṛṣṇa told them; they approached Kṛṣṇa without any clothes, like *Ātmans,* free of all the worldly attachments approach *Brahman.* Kṛṣṇa returned the clothes back to the *gopīs* and asked them to return home with the assurance that they would soon be united with him.

## *7.10 Rāsa Līlā 'the divine dance of Kṛṣṇa and the* gopīs'

Kṛṣṇa would play his flute on beautiful moonlit nights and invite all the *gopas* and *gopīs* to the forest to dance with him. This dance is known as *Rāsa Līlā* 'the dance of the union of *Ātman* and *Brahman*' or 'of the union of the human and the divine'. The forest represented the dividing line between the worlds of *Māyā* and *Brahman*. The sound of Kṛṣṇa's flute charmed the *gopas* and the *gopīs* who left their homes and other worldly ties and ran to the forest. The melody was enchanting and they were spellbound. The forest was shimmering in the mellow moonlight, and Kṛṣṇa was waiting there to dance with them. The melody of the song and the rhythm of the dance indicated that all the *gopas* and the *gopīs* had transcended the awareness of their existence in the phenomenal world, all they were conscious of was their eternal union with Kṛṣṇa. Their song was Kṛṣṇa, their movements were Kṛṣṇa, the forest was Kṛṣṇa, their dance was Kṛṣṇa, the whole world was Kṛṣṇa. Their bodies danced but their souls *(Ātman)* had become one with Kṛṣṇa. Each *gopi* felt that she had her own "personal" Kṛṣṇa dancing with her. just as the *gopīs* had lost their sense of separation from Kṛṣṇa, Kṛṣṇa had merged himself in them too. *Brahman* and *Ātman* were united. The cosmic activity (dance) went on. And the distinction between the dance, dancers and the song disappeared altogether. This dance, which represents the union of the human and the divine, is celebrated even today in India. Men and women participate in the dance and sing the songs of Kṛṣṇa. Although Kṛṣṇa is worshipped in almost all parts of India this tradition of celebrating Rāsa līlā is particularly popular in Gujarat, Rajasthan, and Uttarpradesh (the regions of Kṛṣṇa's mythical birth and life).

## *7.11 Kaṃsa's death*

While Kṛṣṇa and Balarāma (Kṛṣṇa's brother and the incarnation of *Ananta*) were thus living in Vṛndāvana, news of the special occasion of a tournament at Mathura reached them. King Kaṃsa had devised a master plan to kill Kṛṣṇa. He invited kings from different countries to compete in the royal tournament. He knew that Kṛṣṇa and Balarāma would certainly come to attend the tournament and he would be ready with his scheme to kill the brothers. As Kṛṣṇa and Balarāma reached the main gate of the tournament ground, they saw a fierce, intoxicated elephant named Kuvalayapīda running toward them. The maddened elephant lifted Kṛṣṇa by its trunk and tried to whirl him around and kill him by dropping him on the ground. But Kṛṣṇa, who had anticipated the moves of the elephant, turned around, each time avoiding attack. Finally, Kṛṣṇa killed the elephant, and placing the blood-smeared tusks of the elephant on his shoulder, he entered the royal palace where Kaṃsa was sitting with his courtiers. At that moment Kṛṣṇa appeared to the common people to be the best of men. He was the god of love (*kāma deva*) to women, a relative and friend to the *gopas*, an admirable child to the elderly, the ultimate reality to the *yogis*, and death to Kaṃsa.

Afterwards, Kṛṣṇa and Balarāma were confronted by two huge wrestlers named Canura and Muṣṭika. The audience was amazed to witness the fight between the two young boys and the strong wrestlers. But Kṛṣṇa and Balarāma succeeded in killing the two wrestlers.

Kaṃsa was now frightened to see the courage and power of the two brothers and ordered his soldiers to drive them away from the city. At this moment Kṛṣṇa jumped up onto the high throne where the demonic king Kaṃsa was sitting and grabbed him by his hair as tightly as the eagle grabs a snake. Kṛṣṇa thus dragged Kaṃsa along and dropped him on the floor. Soon the evil Kaṃsa died. Interestingly enough, his soul was united with Kṛṣṇa, for every moment of his life had been occupied with thoughts of Kṛṣṇa. Even though his thoughts were full of hatred, jealousy, and anger for Kṛṣṇa, nonetheless Kaṃsa's mind was constantly directed toward him. Hence Kaṃsa became one with Kṛṣṇa in death. This concentration *(dhyāna)* on Kṛṣṇa was not any less than that of a devotee who is always occupied with thoughts of his personal god. The mission of the 8th descent of Viṣṇu was accomplished.

## 7.12 Kṛṣṇa's marriages

When Kṛṣṇa grew up, he married several women. The women he married included Kalindī (the river), Jāmbuvatī (the daughter of a boar), Rukmiṇi, and Satyabhāmā (the princesses), and sixteen thousand women who had been imprisoned by the demon Bhaumāsura.

Kṛṣṇa married some of these women because they dearly loved him while some he married to save them from bondage and trepidations. Kalindī loved Kṛṣṇa passionately, while Satyabhāmā and Jāmbuvatī were offered to Kṛṣṇa by their fathers. The sixteen thousand women needed to be rescued from Bhaumāsura's prison. Kṛṣṇa married them all and granted them release for they symbolized *Ātman,* the embodied souls dwelling in different bodies yearning to be united with Kṛṣṇa, the ultimate reality *Brahman.* Their marriages with Kṛṣṇa symbolized the union of *Ātman* and *Brahman.*

Although Kṛṣṇa loved all his wives, his most favorite woman was Rādhā, a *gopi,* a simple cowherd woman of Gokula. Kṛṣṇa gave himself completely to her for she loved him without any expectations. She did not desire royalty, neither did she expect to be called *Priyatamā* 'the most loved one' of Kṛṣṇa. She did not even expect Kṛṣṇa to marry her. In fact, she was already married. Her love for Kṛṣṇa transcended all worldly attachments, needs, and expectations. It was a natural, intense instinct which connected her with Kṛṣṇa. She loved Kṛṣṇa because she could not do otherwise. She performed her worldly duties with a mind totally detatched from the actions and their results. As a cowherd woman, she was part of *Māyā* and fulfilled her duties—but she did this as a pure soul. She could not remain separated from Kṛṣṇa even for a moment. Similarly, Kṛṣṇa could not bear separation from Rādhā. Their love encompassed all shades of human love, i.e, anxiety, waiting, pangs of separation, jealousy, passion, etc. And yet, it transcended all of these emotions. Rādhā loved Kṛṣṇa in spite of his many marriages and Kṛṣṇa loved her inspite of her being someone else's wife. It was as if at the level beyond *Māyā* they were one; there was no Kṛṣṇa and there was no Rādhā; only *Brahman,* the absolute one.

## 7.13 Kṛṣṇa: Sārathī 'the charioteer' of Arjuna

Kṛṣṇa was the Pāṇḍavas' cousin. Vasudeva (Kṛṣṇa's father) was Kuntī's (mother of the Pāṇḍavas) brother. Kṛṣṇa was always very close to the Pāṇḍavas. He was their friend, advisor, and protector. It was Kṛṣṇa who (by supplying her with garments) protected Draupadī from being utterly humiliated in the court (see chapter 5, section 3.7). He was the one who was worshipped by the Pāṇḍavas as the most honored dignitory at the celebration of their newly established kingdom in Indraprastha. Finally, Kṛṣṇa, after trying (without success) to prevent the war between the Kauravas and the Pāṇḍavas, decided that the only possible solution to the conflict between the two royal families was to support the Pāṇḍavas in the war. Kṛṣṇa volunteered to be Arjuna's charioteer in the war at Kurukṣetra; his role as the spiritual guide of Arjuna is well documented in the *Bhagavadgītā* (see chapter 6). When the war was over and the Pāṇḍavas victorious, the whole atmosphere at Kurukṣetra was filled with grief over the death of loved ones. Duryodhana's mother, Gāndhārī, who had lost all her sons, could not contain the pain of the loss of her children and said to Kṛṣṇa, "Kṛṣṇa, why did you not stop the war? Did you not know that it would lead to this catastrophe? How could you be so blind? Kṛṣṇa, since you, the all-powerful one, ignored the consequences and prescribed war, I pronounce this curse on you: Your entire family will be destroyed as mine was, and you will die a miserable death, alone, separated from your loved ones."

## 7.14 Kṛṣṇa's death

The time had come for the curse to come true. When Kṛṣṇa returned to Dvārakā, (where his family and his entire Yādava clan had moved) he found that all his ralatives and friends were dead, as a result of fighting among themselves. Kṛṣṇa's brother Balarāma, who was the incarnation of *Ananta* (the giant cobra on which Viṣṇu rests) was ready to withdraw from the world of *Māyā* to depart to his original abode. He went away to the forest, where Kṛṣṇa watched him seat himself in a meditative posture. Suddenly a huge serpent emerged from his mouth and went away toward the ocean. Kṛṣṇa's brother had disappeared from the world of *Māyā* ! Later, Kṛṣṇa, while sitting alone, was contemplating the past events of his life. He was lost in thoughts of his loved ones whom he had lost forever. At that time, a hunter came by. In the darkness of the evening, mistaking Kṛṣṇa for a deer, he shot an arrow at him. The arrow hit Kṛṣṇa's foot. The hunter, after realizing his mistake, came to Kṛṣṇa and asked for his forgiveness. Kṛṣṇa consoled him, for he knew that his mission on earth was over and it was time for him to leave the world of *Māyā*. Once again Kṛṣṇa withdrew from his worldly form and returned to his original abode, where he lay on *Ananta,* the endless one.

CHAPTER 8

# The Mythology of Śiva: Destruction as Divine

## 1.0 Introduction

As we move from the Kṛṣṇa myths to the Śiva myths, we move from the mythology of the beautiful and serene to the mythology of the terrible and fierce. Śiva is one of the three gods of the Hindu trinity; he is the god of destruction. The mythology of Śiva focuses on the following questions: (a) Why does destruction exist along with creation and sustenance? (i.e., what is the explanation for the destruction of all existence); (b) What is the relationship between destruction and creation? and; (c) Is destruction evil? (i.e., what is the definition(s) of good and evil).

## 2.0 Death as divine

The mythology of Śiva stresses one major point, i.e., death is divine—as divine as creation and sustenance. Death, decay and destruction are not only inevitable but are necessary. This positive view of destruction finds expression in the very name of the god of destruction, *Śiva*, which literally means 'auspicious'. On the timeless cycle of creation, sustenance and destruction and recreation of the universe, destruction is viewed not only as the necessary outcome of all existence, but also as the necessary condition for the recreation of the universe. Without destruction, there can be no recreation of the universe. This inseparability of the three necessary elements of creation, sustenance and destruction finds expression in Hindu mythology in the form of the tripartite godhead.

Unlike Greek mythology, Hindu mythology does not attribute death, decay and destruction to any sin; nor does it view them as deviant or undesirable. On the contrary, they are viewed as natural and essential, and therefore, Śiva is viewed as auspicious. The myth of the "birth" of death clearly illustrates this point. This myth portrays the misery of the people in heaven when there was no death. It also illustrates heaven's inhabitants' desperation to reach out to touch the end of all existence. The myth expresses the desperate need to slip away from immortality—to give meaning to life and existence by escaping from a state of endless existence. For without death there is no past or future, and if there is no past or future, the present becomes a dull and dreary stretch of monotony. The Śiva myths depict the celebration of the so-called "negative forces" of death, decay and destruction.

## 3.0 The birth of death and cyclical time

There are several myths in the epics and the Purāṇas which provide explanation and justification for why death and destruction was essential and why and how the concept of cyclical time was introduced.

One of the important myths in the *Mahābhārata (12.248–13.*14) is as follows: A long time ago, Brahmā created the world and the people therein. Brahmā's creation went on incessantly, and the number of people kept on increasing. At that time there was no death (i.e., death did not exist as a natural corollary to life); there was only creation, because Brahmā could not create mortals (i.e., he could only create immortals). As the time went by, all three worlds (heaven, earth, and hell) were filled with people, tall and short, good and evil, happy and sad. They were all blessed with immortality but did not have enough space even to move around. The immortality of human beings became a torment for everybody. The earth, unable to carry the burden of the ever-increasing creation, began to sink into the ocean. Brahmā got worried about the unlimited creation. He was angry at himself. His anger produced fire, which began to burn and scald the people. Śiva could not bear the pain of the people who were being burnt by Brahmā's wrath. "O, god of creation," said Śiva, "this is your own progeny. How can you burn it like this? Have mercy on them." Brahmā answered, "I have no desire to torture them. But I am angry at myself, since I do not know how to stop this ever-growing population. What can I do?" Then Śiva suggested to Brahmā that there was a solution to the problem. If he would agree to accept it, neither would he have to stop creating nor would he have to worry about the overcrowding of the three worlds. "O, Brahma, do not panic. It is true that the creatures whom you have burnt to ashes will not return. Instead, please allow those who are alive to return to this world for repeated births and repeated deaths." Brahmā was consoled by this advice.

Then Brahmā restrained the flow of his creative energy (which was incessantly flowing outwards) and absorbed it back within himself. From then onwards, Brahmā followed a pattern of exhaling and inhaling his own creative energy. This cycle of creation *(pravṛtti)* and withdrawal from it *(nivṛtti)* was necessary for the continuation of the periodic creation, destruction, and re-creation of the universe.

This myth not only emphasizes the necessity of death, but also points out that death is not viewed as annihilation; rather, it is viewed as a point on the continuous cycle of life and death. Moreover, death is not interpreted here as a punishment for some wrong-doing on the part of human beings. It is a compassionate act on the part of the regulator of the universe. Death is a predecessor of new life, a forerunner of a new beginning, a pause between two creations to allow Brahmā to re-energize himself to re-create a universe full of vitality. Therefore, it is not surprising that the name of the god who is responsible for destruction, i.e., Śiva 'auspicious' conveys a positive meaning.

## 4.0 Śiva as Nilakaṇṭha (the one with the blue neck)

Since Śiva is the god of destruction, all destructive forces (i.e., *mrtyu* 'death', *kāla* 'time', *jvara* 'disease', etc.) are viewed as forms of Śiva. However, much like creation, death and destruction can not be unrestrained either. They have to be timely, restrained, and well-regulated. Therefore, to prevent untimely destruction, Brahmā, and Viṣṇu often summon Śiva to contain the destructive forces within himself. According to the mythology, there have been several such occasions in the long history of the universe when Śiva's help was desperately sought by Viṣṇu and Brahmā. He always responded to their call and remained true to his name, Śiva, 'the auspicious one'. The Vāyu Purāṇa narrates a myth which throws light on this compassionate" aspect of Śiva's personality.

Once Śiva's wife, Pārvatī, asked him "Tell me, O auspicious one, why is your neck the color of a blue cloud? Why does it radiate blue light? I am curious to know." Śiva replied, "It is a long story, my beloved. It was a long time ago, when the gods and the demons were churning the ocean to obtain *amṛta* 'the drink of immortality' from the ocean. The mountain Mandāra was their churning stick and Kūrma 'tortoise' (who was in fact Viṣṇu as an incarnation, see chapter 3, section 12.2) was their pivot. As the churning continued, out came *Hālāhala Kālakūṭa* 'the deadly poison', of a dark blue color, resembling the dark clouds of the deluge. The poison radiated fire as if to consume the whole universe. The gods and the demons were as scared as a deer frightened by the sight of a tiger. The shadow of death was spreading over the universe. Viṣṇu (in the form of the tortoise) himself became dark due to the poison. Brahmā foresaw the untimely destruction of the universe by the poison and in his desparation, called Śiva, 'Save us all, Śiva, for no one else besides you has the power to contain the poison. If it is not contained, it will devour the whole universe.' After hearing those words, I drank that blue poison and held it within myself in my throat. Therefore, my beloved, my throat is blue."

## 5.0 Cosmic destruction

With a serpent around his neck, poison in his throat, a tiger skin around his loins, and a spear in his hand, Śiva projects an image of terror and destruction. At the end of the fourth yuga (the last part of the cycle) the universe is ready to be destroyed; it has lived its life. All orders—physical, moral, and ethical—are breaking down. Even Viṣṇu is incapable of saving the universe! Śiva begins to dance the dance of death, Tāṇḍava. There are cosmic floods, the waves rise high and the whole universe is in a turmoil. There is a cosmic rhythm to this dance. The universe goes back to its source, the Eternal Waters.

The destruction of the universe is viewed in the Śiva myths as the mirror image of creation. Creation is viewed as the separation of *many from one* (i.e., multiplicity from singularity). The universe with multiple forms is created from a single source—the Eternal Waters which are a metaphor of energy. Creation is the separation of the elements from their source and from each other.

Another dimension of creation is that it separates opposites from each other, such as darkness from light, earth from sky, man from woman, and so on. In contrast to this, destruction is viewed as the merger of the many into one. It is a gradual return to the source. It is also viewed as the fusion of opposites, where distinctions of every kind vanish. Destruction unifies all diversity. Thus, destruction is the divine force which, according to Hindu mythology, is the unifying substratum of all diversities.

Since Śiva is the personification of destruction, it is not surprising that the iconography of Śiva reflects the concept of destruction as the fusion of opposites at various levels. This is the explanation of the apparent paradox in Śiva's personality depicted in the iconography and mythology. Śiva's icon, *lingam* (a pillar of the shape of phallus placed on vulva), shows both male and female reproductive organs. This symbol is ambiguous when interpreted as the fusion of the male and female reproductive organs. This union of the reproductive organs represents creation, and Śiva is interpreted as the god of creation. Yet, if the symbol is stripped of its specificity, and is interpreted as the symbolic fusion of all opposites (of which male and female reproductive organs form a subset), then the same symbol is interpreted as the representation of destruction where all opposites merge. Thus the paradox of the fusion of creation and destruction is well-founded.

## 6.0 Socio-historical background of the Śiva myths

The historical development of the mythology of Śiva is extremely controversial. There are two major opinions regarding the origin and development of this mythology. According to one, Śiva is a non-Āryan god whose origin dates back to the Indus Valley civilization (about 3000 B.C.). Three major arguments are presented in favor of this hypothesis: (a) Śiva is also a god of fertility (besides destruction) and the seals found in the excavation of the Indus Valley shows clear evidence for the existence of a fertility god; (b) Śiva is called *paśupati* 'lord of animals'. The fertility god in the Indus civilization shows a close relationship with animals; i.e., he has horns and is surrounded by tigers, elephants and other animals; and (c) the name Śiva is not found in the Vedas, which are the earliest sourcebooks of Āryan mythology. The above evidence indicates that Śiva was not part of the early Āryan pantheon but was added to it later.

In addition to the above, there is internal evidence within the mythology of Śiva which shows that perhaps there was a tension between the two Indus Valley civilizations, i.e., Āryan and non-Āryan regarding the position of Śiva.

According to another view, Śiva was originally a Vedic god, and, although the name Śiva is not mentioned in the Vedas, the fierce god of the Vedas, *Rudra* 'howler' later on became Śiva. The major and compelling reason for this hypothesis is the fact that the very epithet Śiva 'the auspicious one' is a Sanskrit word and hence it could not have been the name of a pre-Vedic god. Moreover, it refers in the Vedas to the god Rudra, who though terrible and destructive, is beneficent as well. He is called a bull and is the father of a great golden troop of young male gods, the Maruts, whose mother was a cow. Maruts hold the lightening in their hands, are richly adorned with ornaments, and are as broad as the sky through which their chariots thunder, spilling rain. However, it is only the destructive personality of Śiva which can be traced back to *Rudra*, the god of destruction in the Vedas, and there is no evidence to believe that Rudra was ever treated as a fertility god.

Hence, in the final analysis, scholars are compelled to trace the origin of Śiva's personality as the "fertility-god" to the non-Āryan-Indus Valley civilization. The above hypothesis assumes that Śiva's ambivalent personality has a twofold origin and that during the epic period (7–5th century B.C.), the god of destruction of the Vedas *(Rudra)* and the fertility god of the Indus civilization merged into one, giving rise to Śiva, who was viewed as the god of destruction as well as creation.

Although the above hypothesis is very plausible, the question that still remains to be answered is what the motivation was for the merger of these two independent gods. A close examination of the historical developments shows that the Āryans, who arrived in India around 2000–1500 B.C., were gradually assimilated into the local indigenous culture, thereby including non-Āryan beliefs and mythologies in their own system of beliefs. The following two myths clearly illustrate this point.

## 7.0 The conflict between Śiva and Dakṣa

The mythology of Śiva often depicts tension between Śiva and the Āryan mainstream gods (Brahmā and Viṣṇu). Moreover, Śiva's conflict with the Āryan priest Dakṣa is vividly described in several myths in *Vāyu Purāṇa* and *Śiva Purāṇa*. Many scholars have taken this tension /conflict in the myths to be evidence for Śiva's non-Āryan origin. It has been claimed that Śiva belonged to the group of the non-Āryan deities and only later found his way first into the Āryan (Vedic) and then the Hindu pantheon of gods.

In the following myth the tension between Śiva and the Āryan priest Dakṣa is described:

Dakṣa was the son of the *Prajāpati* 'the creator'. He had a beautiful daughter named Satī. Dakṣa had a grudge against Śiva, since Śiva had not paid respect to him on the occasion of a sacrificial ritual. Dakṣa considered Śiva to be an outcast, unworthy of any association, a beggar, barbarian, an unsophisticated vagabond who lived in the cremation grounds, and who was always surrounded by ghosts, spirits and ugly creatures. Dakṣa pronounced a curse on Śiva, according to which Śiva would not be allowed a share (any portion) of the sacrificial ritual with other gods, and would not be invited to any rituals either. Dakṣa's daughter, Satī, however, was in love with Śiva and was determined to marry him. Dakṣa did not invite Śiva to his daughter's Svayaṃvara ceremony. However, Satī prayed to Śiva and requested him to appear at the ceremony for she would marry no one else. Śiva appeared at the scene and married her against the wishes of her father. "Why do you want to marry a barbarian?" asked the father. "He is the evil one who does not even know the proper (Āryan) traditions and customs." But Satī did not pay any heed to her father's suggestions.

Dakṣa never pardoned Śiva for his marriage to Satī. Once Dakṣa performed a sacrifice and did not invite Śiva. Satī advised Śiva to attend the ceremony, but Śiva refused to attend the ceremony without an invitation. However, Satī herself decided to go to her father's house and attend the ceremony. By the time she reached there the sacrificial ritual was already in progress. She was affectionately greeted by her mother and sisters, but her father Dakṣa completely ignored her. Satī was enraged at her father's behavior. She said, "Śiva is the source of all the creatures of the world. How could you not invite him? Do you not know his power? Father, you have lost your sense of propriety. You will have to bear the consequences of your behavior." "Go away," said Dakṣa to his daughter. "Why did you come here? I did not invite your husband because he does not have a respectable lineage; he is *Vedabāhya* 'does not belong to the Vedic tradition'. He is the god of ghosts and goblins. Therefore, I deliberately did not invite him. I was a fool to have allowed you to marry him. Calm down, take your portion of the ritual and go home."

Now Satī's anger knew no bounds. She was trembling with anger and insult. She decided to kill herself at the sacrificial ritual rather than return home. "You have insulted the most powerful god on earth for no reason. You will pay for this *karma.* I am leaving this world now." With these words, Satī immolated herself, jumping into the sacrificial fire in the presence of her father, the gods and the other guests.

When Śiva learned about Satī's death, he was greatly enraged. Angrily he pulled out a strand of his hair. From that strand of hair emerged a strong and powerful warrior, Vīrabhadra, whom Śiva instructed to destroy Dakṣa's sacrifice and cut off the priest's head. Vīrabhadra followed Śiva's orders to the letter. However, Brahmā and Viṣṇu requested Śiva to have pity on Dakṣa, since he was the creator. Śiva replaced Dakṣa's head with a goat's head, and brought him back to life. Satī's words had come true. Dakṣa had paid the price of his *karma.*

## 8.0 The superiority of Śiva

Another myth which depicts the tension between Śiva and the two major gods (Brahmā and Viṣṇu) of the Āryan tradition is described in the *Vāyu Purāṇa.* This myth shows that Śiva had to prove his superiority over Brahmā and Viṣṇu (the Āryan gods).

Once Brahmā, the god of creation and Viṣṇu, the god of sustenance, were fighting over the issue of their respective superiority. Each was convinced of his own superiority. As they were arguing with each other, Śiva appeared. He placed his *lingaṃ* (a pillar of the shape of the phallus which was Śiva's symbol) between Brahmā and Viṣṇu and asked them to find the end points of the pillar. "Brahmā, you find the upper end, for you can fly up on your swan," Śiva said to Brahmā. To Viṣṇu he said, "You can dive down to find the bottom end of the pillar. This will be the test of superiority. The one who finds the end of the pillar will be the acclaimed superior."

Brahmā and Viṣṇu each went in their appointed directions. They each spent one thousand years trying, but neither could find the end of the pillar. Exasperated, they returned to Śiva and said, "We accept your superiority since you are the victor. It is because of you that the endless cycle of creation, sustenance, and destruction goes on forever." Thus they admitted that he was superior to both of them.

The development of the trinity in Purāṇic Hinduism marks a major development, since it treats each of the three gods as being dependent on the other two for their existence and function to the extent that each is interpreted as being identified with the other two. For without Brahmā (creator), Viṣṇu (preserver) and Śiva (destructor) can not exist, nor can they function. Without Śiva there can not be any Brahma. Therefore, the interpretation of the god of destruction being the god of creation was clearly justified within the theological framework. Thus Śiva, who originally within the Āryan tradition symbolized the destructive aspect of the divine now came to be interpreted as the god of creation as well.

During this period (7–5th century B.C.), the tension between the Āryan and non-Āryan people in general and their beliefs in particular was moving toward the assimilation of the two. The god of fertility, whose symbol was the phallus, and whose origin was primarily non-Āryan, came to be interpreted as the god of creation, who gradually merged into Śiva. Śiva's personality in the mainstream Āryan system justified this fusion of the Āryan god of destruction and the non-Āryan god of creation. The dual nature of Śiva as a fusion of destruction and creation now was manifested in this merger.

## 9.0 Śiva's *wives—blending of opposites*

Śiva's wives, Satī, Pārvatī, and Durgā (Kālī) are indeed personifications of his three powers (i.e., creation, sustenance, and destruction). The mythology describes them as *śaktis* 'powers of Śiva'. Śiva is a blending of all three.

### *9.1 Satī—the śakti 'power' of creation*

After Satī, Dakṣa's daughter, killed herself, Śiva could not bear to be separated from her. He tore out his hair in anger. Śiva could not concentrate on anything. Without Satī the world meant nothing to him. The *Sādhu,* ascetic Śiva could no longer involve himself in the functioning of the world. As a result of Śiva's preoccupation with Satī's death all creation in the world ceased. Śiva held on to Satī's corpse as a child holds on to its mother. As Śiva wandered around with Satī's corpse on his back *Viṣṇu* thought of a way to save the world. He walked behind Śiva and began to cut Satī's dead body into pieces. As the pieces fell down on the ground, they were transformed into Śiva's *lingam* (symbol of Śiva's creative energy) and creation began again, so that the world, which had been overcast with the shadow of death, was revived with new life.

### *9.2 Pārvatī—the śakti 'power' of love and sustenance*

Pārvatī, the daughter of the Himālaya mountain, represented Śiva's power of love and sustenance. She was none other than Satī reborn! She represents Śiva's power to sustain a family in this world. When he is with Pārvatī, Śiva is a householder engrossed in talking about their two children and their welfare, etc. The mythology of Śiva shows that it was Pārvatī's *tapas* (severe austerities) which finally convinced the ascetic Śiva to get involved in the worldly affairs of love, marriage, and family.

Some myths particularly emphasize the need for Śiva to get involved in the affairs of the world. Without this involvement, the world would perish. For example, the birth of Śiva's son Kārtikeya (with Pārvatī) was essential for the destruction of the demon Tārakāsura. As the myth explains, Tārakāsura could have been killed only by the son of the god of destruction, Śiva, and no one else. However, according to the myth, Pārvatī did not bear the baby herself. Śiva's "seed" (semen) was placed into a fire which transferred it to the Ganges, who in turn offered it to six *kṛttikas* 'group of stars forming a constellation'. The *kṛttikās* were flying in the form of birds when they noticed it on the river; they took it to their "nests" and preserved it for nine months. Kārtikeya (son of *kṛttikās)* was born in their nest and was later found by Śiva and Pārvatī, who raised him. After he grew up, he killed the demon Tārakāsura.

## 9.3 Gaṇeśa—the elephant-headed son of Śiva

Matsya Purāṇa mentions the birth of Gaṇeśa, the elephant-headed son of Pārvatī. According to myth, Pārvatī created a son from the ointment which she had used to wash her body. She then infused life into the child and appointed him door-keeper to guard the door and not let anybody in until she was through with her bath.

It so happened that Śiva returned home and was prevented by Gaṇeśa from entering the house. Śiva got very angry and cut off Gaṇeśa's head saying, "Who are you to prevent me from entering my own house?" When Pārvatī learned of her son's death, she could not bear the pain. Śiva promised her that he would replace Gaṇeśa's head with the head of the first living being he encountered. This happened to be an elephant, whom Śiva met as he set out in search of a living being. Śiva cut off the elephant's head and installed it on the dead body of Gaṇeśa. Thereafter Gaṇeśa became the elephant-headed god.

According to another myth, Pārvatī, the proud mother, asked Śani (the planet Saturn) to look at her son Gaṇeśa whom she loved dearly. She had forgotten the fiery hot glances of Śani. As a result Śani inadvertantly burned Gaṇeśa's head to ashes. Pārvatī requested Brahmā to revive the child and it was Brahmā who installed the head of an elephant on the body of the child. Therefore, Gaṇeśa became the elephant-headed son of Pārvatī.

Gaṇeśa is called *Vināyaka* 'the one who was created without the spouse *(nāyaka)*'. He is worshipped as the god of wisdom and as the remover of obstacles in any venture undertaken by human beings. Thus Gaṇeśa is worshipped before starting any major undertaking to ensure its success.

In general, Śiva's involvement in the worldly life is shown not to be for his own personal enjoyment of family life, rather, it is for the welfare of the world. Śiva's mythology emphasizes this point by showing that his progeny was not created by physical union with his wives.

## 9.4 Kāli-the śakti 'power' of destruction

Kālī represents Śiva's power of destruction. She is the killer of Mahiṣāsura, a buffalo demon who had conquered the three worlds and had driven the gods away from heaven. She is the destructive power who received all the powerful weapons from the various gods: the trident from Śiva, the *cakra* 'disc' from Viṣṇu, a fiery arrow from Agni (the fire god), the *vajra* 'thunderbolt' from Indra, a lion from the Himalayan mountains, and poisonous snakes from *Ananta.* She destroyed Mahiṣāsura and rescued the whole world. She had ten arms and wore a garland of skulls, with her hair dishevelled and her flaming red tongue trembling with energy, In order to destroy the demon, she had to mount a lion. In general, she is the very picture of the "terrible" and destructive aspect of Śiva's personality which destroys evil to recreate a new universe, safe and full of vitality.

## 10.0 Symbols/forms of Śiva

The ambivalence in the nature of Śiva is seen in his symbols. The lingam, which represents a fusion of male and female reproductive organs, is one of the prominent symbols of Śiva. This symbol clearly represents Śiva as the god of creation. Other symbols of Śiva include Time *(Kala),* Death *(Mṛtyu),* and Fever *(jvara).* All destructive forces in the world are viewed as manifestations of Śiva.

The above symbols have a philosophically oriented explanation in the mythology of the Purāṇas. The lingam represents both the conceptual and substantive manifestation of Śiva. At the conceptual level, the Lingam symbolizes the state of total dissolution *(pralaya).* The term *linga* is derived from *layana/laya* 'dissolution', because everything is absorbed into it (*Linga Purāṇa* 1. 19.16). It is the fusion of all opposites. All potentialities abide in *linga.* It is the beginning and end of all existence and thereby depicts creation and destruction. As an iconic object, carved in wood or stone, *lingaṃ* represents the operational aspect of Śiva's personality. It represents the power of creation which operates through the fusion/union of male and female energies.

Śiva is called 'the maker of time' (śvetāśvetara Upanisad 6.2.16). Time is viewed as the substratum of creation, sustenance and destruction of all existence. Kāla 'time' is the all consuming, dark, world-destroying form of Śiva, who reduces everything to ashes (Kena Upanisad 2.44.2–3). In *Śiva Purāṇa* (7.1.7.4), Śiva is viewed as death *(mrtyu),* the ender, time, (past, present and future). He is the universal fatality. The wheel of creation and destruction whirls in his mouth. And yet Śiva is viewed as Mahākāla the absolute (literally, great) time, which transcends time-the all-consuming force.

## 11.0 Śiva as an ambivalent god

As mentioned earlier, Śiva is an ambivalent god both in his appearance and his behavior. The following two myths show that Śiva is seen both as an intense lover and a withdrawn ascetic.

Once Śiva, who had renounced and severed all connections with the phenomenal world of *Māyā,* was in a state of meditation. He was totally oblivious to all activity around him. Year after year passed in this way. Śiva remained silent, unmoved, unattached, like *Ātman,* completely liberated from the world of *Māyā.*

However, all was not well with the world. Tārakāsura, a demon, was torturing the world and it was deemed right by Brahmā and Viṣṇu to ask Śiva to produce a son who would destroy the demon. But who would have the courage to disturb Śiva's meditation and draw him back to the world?

Kāma 'the god of love' was entrusted this task. Kāma was ready to do his job, but he waited for the right moment. Soon the spring arrived, filling the atmosphere with the beautiful scent of newly-blossomed flowers. Kāma shot his arrows of love at Śiva, thinking that the beautiful, romantic season, the fragrance of the flowers, would charm him and lure him away from his meditation. But lo and behold! Śiva was fuming with anger. When Kāma did succeed in distracting and diverting his mind from his meditation, Śiva opened his third eye and used its blazing energy to burn the god of love to ashes. Such was Śiva's contempt for worldly attachments. Kāma's wife Rati smeared her husband's ashes on her body and decided to kill herself. But Śiva assured her that Kāma would be reborn; however, he would be *ananga* 'bodiless' hereafter. The angry Śiva had regained his balance of mind and realized that for the world to continue to exist, Kāma 'the god of love' had to be revived.

There are several myths about Śiva's asceticism and his withdrawal from the world of *Māyā*. And yet there are several others which depict him as a passionate lover.

The *Skanda Purāṇa* narrates a story about Śiva's passion. Once Pārvatī and Śiva had a fight while they were playing a game of dice. Pārvatī left Śiva and went away to the forest. Śiva could not bear to be separated from her. Pārvatī took the form of a beautiful mountain girl and wandered around in the forest. When Śiva saw her, he could not control his desire for her and tried to grab her and force her to marry him. She however, suggested that he should ask her father's permission to marry her. When Śiva found out that her father was the Himālaya mountains, he realized that Pārvatī had tricked him and that the mountain girl was in fact Pārvatī. Śiva's passionate love for his other wives such as Umā, Satī, Durgā, and Gangā, and other women such as Sāvitri and Anasūyā emphasize his involvement in this world of *Māyā*.

CHAPTER 9

# Buddhist Mythology and Thought

## 1.0 Introduction

Buddhism as a religious system emerged in India in the 6th century B.C. This was a turbulent period in the political, social, and religious history of India. There was political unrest caused by continuous invasions by the Greeks, Śakas, Hūṇas, and Kuṣāṇas, who not only ruled over northwestern India, but also brought with them their religious and social systems. The political instability was also enhanced by constant conflicts among the small kingdoms whose kings were trying to gain more political power. This situation had caused insecurity among the people.

The political unrest was coupled with social unrest. The caste-system (sanctioned by the Brāhmaṇical religious system) had become extremely restrictive in terms of its membership. Membership in a caste was determined strictly by birth and interclass mobility was prohibited. (See discussion in Chapter 5.) This gave enormous power to the two higher castes, the *Brāhmaṇas* and *Kṣatriyas.* The *Śūdras* were denied any hope of bettering their lives in their present birth. This discrimination against the lower classes of society was justified by the "spiritual impurity" of the *Śūdras* (their birth in the lower caste was viewed as the proof of their "wrong /undesirable" deeds in the last birth). Thus the Brāhmaṇical religious system had closed its door on the lower castes.

The Brāhmaṇical system, based primarily on religious rituals, was further proved to be unsatisfactory because (a) it excluded the *Śūdras* from participating in the religious rituals of the upper castes, (b) its efficacy was challenged (since it did not seem to provide political or social security), (c) it allowed animal slaughter in the rituals (which could not be justified within the belief-system of the all–pervasiveness of *Brahman;* i.e., every existence was a part of *Brahman)* and thereby went against the notion of 'equality of all existences.' The Brāhmaṇical religious system, based on the concepts of the permanence of *Ātman* and the spiritual equality of all existences, did not seem to provide answers to immediate "this worldly" concerns about the impermanence of life (threatened by constant wars) and social discrimination. Society in general was ready for an alternative which would provide solutions to the immediate problems of the time. Moreover, by the 6th century B.C., the masses were excluded from learning the language (Sanskrit) of the religious scriptures and thereby had lost contact with the original religious system presented in the texts. Their contact with the system was mainly through religious rituals, which did not provide a well-defined path to be followed by individuals to attain the spiritual goal of life (i.e., *mokṣa* 'liberation'). It was against this background that Siddhārtha Gautama Buddha founded a new system of religion which rejected the caste system, religious rituals, violence of any kind, and, more importantly, provided a well-defined path to attain the spiritual goal of life.

## 2.0 The life of Buddha

Though Siddhārtha Gautama Buddha was a historical figure, the story of his life depicted in 3rd–4th century texts (such as *Mahāvastu* 'the book of great events,' and *Lalitavistara* 'the history of the sport' (of the Buddha), etc.) is shrouded in legends and myths. In the following sections (2.0–2.13) some of the major episodes in the Buddha's life are presented (along with their legendary/mythical elements) to facilitate understanding of the personality and the teachings of the Buddha.

## *2.1 The descent of the white elephant: the birth of the Buddha*

In a beautiful capital city named Kapilavastu, located in the foothills of the Himālaya Mountains, there lived a king of the *Śākya* clan named Śuddhodana. His queen wife was Māyā—often called Māyādevī due to the fact that she possessed superior qualities like those of the goddesses *(devī* 'goddess'). She radiated purity, beauty, and strength of body and mind. The royal couple was happy and content, enjoying the life of householders, caring for their family and the citizens of the kingdom.

One day Māyādevī had a strange dream in which she saw a beautiful white elephant descending from heaven and entering her womb. She related this dream to her husband, who asked the *paṇḍits* (the learned priests) to analyze it. They concluded that the dream signalled the forthcoming birth of a child to the couple. "O king!" said the *paṇḍit,* "Your wife has conceived a male child. The white elephant, carrying on its tusks a beautiful lotus flower, is indeed a divine being descended from heaven. The baby is blessed with divine powers. If he leads the life of a householder, he will be the sovereign king and rule over the world. However, if he is drawn to the spiritual life and is detached from the life of a householder, O king, he will be a monk. He will renounce all worldly pleasures and become Buddha—the enlightened one. He will then release the people from their fetters of ignorance and sin and lead them to the ultimate freedom. In either case, he will guide the world." The king and the queen rejoiced to hear of their baby's potential greatness and were determined to spare no effort to ensure a future full of worldly power and pleasure for their child, whom they ardently wished to become the *samrāṭ* 'universal emperor,' as opposed to a wandering ascetic.

Little did the couple know of the "master plan" of the heavenly powers which determined their and their baby's future. The predicted birth of the "divine being" in Śuddhodana's royal palace was no accident. It had been planned in the sixth *Tuṣita* heaven (the heaven of utmost delight). The *Bodhisattva* 'future Buddha,' who had chosen to be born several times previously on earth for the sake of helping all those in despair, had declared, "The time has come for me to be born on toward *Nirvāṇa* 'the final release from the miseries of death and decay of human life'. It was this Bodhisattva who had assumed the form of the white elephant to enter the womb of Māyādevi.

When the baby was in her womb, the mother's body became transparent and she could see the divine baby growing inside her. Finally, the moment of the baby's birth arrived. Māyādevī had been on her way to her parents to rest and deliver the baby in peace, but the baby was instead destined to be born in the Lumbini forest under the shade of a *palāśa* tree. Soon after the birth, the baby stood up and took four steps, pointing toward four directions. It is said that, at each step, a lotus flower sprung up and held the baby tenderly on its petals. The whole world experienced peace and joy. The skies showered life-giving rains for mankind, the flowers bloomed, the birds sang songs of joy, melodies vibrated from musical instruments, and the whole world was filled with divine light! The sick were cured, the hungry fed, and the naked were clothed. Misery was replaced by joy, as if the whole world was bathed in the divine light which had descended from heaven to earth. The baby was ceremoniously named Siddhārtha Gautama.

## 2.2 The four faces of misery: Siddhārtha's encounter with reality

Siddhārtha's mother died seven days after his birth. Śuddhodana grieved painfully over the death of his wife. Nevertheless, he was determined to prevent the child from becoming an ascetic, for, thought Śuddhodana, "A *kṣatriya* prince can find fulfillment only in the life of a powerful king—not in the life of a begging ascetic."

"What will cause Siddhārtha to renounce the worldly life?" asked the concerned king of the learned *paṇḍit*.

"The four signs," replied the learned priest. "They are old age, sickness, death, and an ascetic. When the prince witnesses these four signs he will renounce the world."

"Then he shall never behold the "four signs" that would cause him to renounce the world," said the king, "for I shall protect him from them."

The king, with strong resolve, did everything to guard his son from witnessing the "four signs." Siddhārtha, the young prince, was endowed with exceptional intelligence, and in a very short time he had learned the skills of weaponry, archery, horse riding, wrestling, and other martial arts. He also easily acquired knowledge of the literary arts, mathematics and logic. However, Siddhārtha, the prince of superior knowledge, was still totally ignorant of the nature of life as manifested by the four signs which he had never encountered. The young prince at the age of sixteen consented to marry his cousin Yosodharā, the daughter of Suprabuddha, after proving himself to be a superior warrior.

Siddhārtha had accomplished everything which a young prince could aspire to knowledge, power, and a beautiful loving wife. But Siddhārtha was not at peace. Deep down he was restless and dissatisfied. The world and all its pleasures remained external to him and failed to bring him inner peace and contentment.

One day the young prince expressed a desire to visit the royal gardens. His favorite charioteer, Channa, made preparations for the trip. The streets were properly cleaned and decorated to prevent the young Siddhārtha from seeing any signs of misery or pain, for the prince was to be protected from everything which manifested the inauspicious dimensions of human life. But as the prince was driving along, he was suddenly confronted with an unusual sight! This was an old man, weary and worn out, broken and bent, wrinkled, with his nearly bald head shining through a few strands of white hair, trotting away with a stick, feeble and thin, trying with great effort to carry the burden of life.

"Oh, charioteer, what is this? How can there be a man, so weak and feeble, barely moving, even with a stick?"

"It is old age, Prince, which has weakened his faculties. Therefore, he is weak and feeble. He can not help himself. He needs a stick to help him carry his body through the suffering of old age."

"Is this a peculiar lot of his and his family, or is it the rule of the world? Tell me, charioteer, I want to know," said Siddhārtha.

"Prince, know that it is not peculiar to him or his family. This is the truth: youth is inevitably defeated by old age. No one escapes it. It attacks everyone. You, your parents, and your relatives will experience old age. This is the nature of humanity."

"How can youth be so blind and foolish? How can youth not see the future and its transformation into old age? Of what use are the pleasures of the body when the body itself is going to be taken over by old age? I do not wish to visit the pleasure gardens. Take me back to the palace," said the prince to Channa.

King Śuddhodana was greatly distressed to learn the news of his son's encounter with old age and punished the old man.

After some time, the prince was persuaded to visit the royal pleasure gardens again. Despite all the King's efforts, the prince, who was again being driven by Channa, happened to see a sick man, weakened by fever, fatigued, emaciated, and decrepit, abandoned by his friends.

After being asked by the prince to explain why the sick man looked so miserable, Channa replied, "This is sickness, Prince, which takes away strength. Sickness is not peculiar to this man alone. Everyone has to experience it some time in their life. The man is sad because he has lost his health."

"If health is so transitory," said the prince, "why do people indulge in transitory delights of the body? Turn back, O charioteer, and take me back to the palace."

Siddhārtha's mind was perturbed and his whole being was shaken by these sights, and yet another sight was still in store for him. When Siddhārtha was being driven to the summer palace by Channa, he saw a corpse being carried to the cremation ground by the relatives of the dead, who were lamenting the death of their dear one.

"What is this? O, charioteer, tell me," said the prince, "why is the body being carried away? Why is it so rigid?"

"This is death," said Channa, "The man is dead. He is gone to the land of *Yama* 'the king of the dead'. The dead will never walk or talk again. Death is the irreversible event in life. This is the end of everyone and everything that is alive. Death is the destined end of everything that is born—including you and me."

Siddhārtha's heart sank in despair. "How can anybody enjoy the pleasures of a body which is so fragile? Take me back, I must seek freedom from this misery," said the prince to Channa.

When Siddhārtha, driving with Channa once again, saw a monk, he was touched by the sight, for the monk radiated peace and calmness. He had a begging bowl in his hand and he showed no signs of a perplexed mind.

"Who is this man?" asked the prince.

"Prince," said Channa, "this is a monk, an ascetic who has understood the transitory nature of the human body and life and therefore has abandoned all attachment to the body. He does not seek any pleasures of the body. He is peaceful because he does not suffer the loss of transitory possessions. He has understood the true nature of existence. He does not grieve since he is not attached to pleasures.'

"This is the path," said Siddhārtha, "which leads to peace. This is the way I want to go. Freedom from these miseries will be my pursuit. This alone will deliver me from the sufferings of transitoriness and lead me to immortality."

This was a "new birth" for Siddhārtha, who had witnessed the "four signs" which revealed to him the impermanent nature of existence. Siddhārtha's quest had begun—the quest to find the cause and nature of *dukkha* 'misery,' and more importantly, the solution to this misery. And no power on earth could hold Siddhārtha back from pursuing this goal. His journey had begun.

## 2.3 The bonds are broken: the great renunciation of Siddhārtha

Siddhārtha had been in a pensive mood ever since he had witnessed the "true nature" of human life. "I must find the solution to the problem of misery: but how? Where should I begin?" thought the prince to himself. Suddenly he had a flash of insight, and he thought, "How can there be freedom for someone who is caught in the net of worldly attachments? Each desire, each attachment, is a bond which binds one to fragile and transitory existence. Existence vanishes like a spark which is extinguished in an instant. What remains behind is *dukkha* 'misery' caused by the loss of what is dear, including life itself. In the bonds of love for one's family, friends, relatives, and everything else in the world, lies the seed of *dukkha* 'misery'. As long as I am bonded to them, there is no hope for freedom. The bonds must be broken. As the lotus must rise beyond the muddy water to receive sunshine, its life-force, I must cut off those connections—however painful the process may be." And Siddhārtha, determined to pursue his quest, decided to relinquish all connections with his family and the royal palace. These connections, those intimate bonds, had many faces. Some were tender and passionate—his love for his new born child (in fact, he renounced everything right after his son's birth), wife, and parents; others were tempting—his royal comforts, precious gems, and luxurious clothes and foods. Though some were more difficult to renounce than others, Siddhārtha was determined to give them all up. Different they might be in forms and shapes, but bonds they were nevertheless.

Siddhārtha went to say good-bye to his father. "I must go father, the time of departure has come. Please allow me to depart peacefully."

"What do you wish to gain, my son, by leaving the home of your loved ones? What is it that your heart is seeking? just tell me and it will be yours!"

"My father, I need to attain freedom, release from illness, old age and death; I want to go beyond the life of waste and decay. I want to escape the torments of rebirth. I want to be immortal. No one can grant me immunity from the passage of time, which is so cruel and ruthless! Let me go, I want to explore the path to freedom!"

"Alas! My child! I am incapable of granting you your wish. Perhaps you are destined to be a spiritual guide to the whole world, which is seeking answers to the problems of transitoriness and *dukkha* 'misery'. "

The king Śuddhodana had no argument to convince his son and prevent him from departing, so he appointed hundreds of soldiers to guard the four gates to stop Siddhārtha from leaving.

Siddhārtha's mind had already taken flight from the palace. Now his body had to leave. But that night singers and dancers tried their best to amuse Siddhārtha and keep his mind involved in the pleasures of the world. They were beautiful women indeed, but Siddhārtha's mind was pining for peace more permanent and therefore more beautiful than any thing which would wither away with the passage of time. In the middle of the night Siddhārtha woke up and saw around him women with dishevelled hair and garments, their jewelry scattered, creating a vision of disorder and clumsiness. They suddenly revealed to Siddhārtha their true nature—disorderly, ugly and transitory; for the beauty, charm, and order which they seemed to display when they were awake was revealed as a façade to Siddhārtha. It could not be sustained even during the few hours of night! "It is all *dukkha!* Let me go away from here at once!" said Siddhārtha and called his charioteer Channa to prepare Kanṭaka, his horse, for departure. "Let me take a look at my son. That will be the last bond to be broken, and then, my dear Channa, I will depart." Siddhārtha entered the palace where his beautiful wife was asleep with a protective arm around her sleeping son Rāhula. "I will not lift her arm to pick up my son," thought Siddhārtha, "for she might be awakened, and it would then be harder for me to leave. I will leave while they are asleep and will see them again when I return after finding answers to my questions—after I am enlightened!" With those thoughts Siddhārtha moved away from the palace. "My friend Kanṭaka, you are my first guide out of *dukkha* toward the path of freedom!" said Siddhārtha to his favorite horse and commanded Channa to take him out of the guarded palace. It is said that a strange silence fell on the palace. The guarding angels opened the gates for the horse to leap out, and soon Siddhārtha was out of the city near the river Anomā. Siddhārtha descended from his horse and was ready to bid farewell to Channa and Kantaka when Channa pleaded with him to return home for the sake of his family, friends, and the country.

"My friend, my return to Kapilavastu is meaningless, for, even if I come back now, there is no power on earth which will prevent our separation. Life may create the illusion of union, but death is the ultimate end of life. Death causes separation and that is reality. So, my friend, go back and convey my message to my people: 'Siddhārtha has gone; he may find the answer to the problems of *dukkha* "misery" and soon return, or he may fail in his quest and die, never to return again!'"

Channa gave Siddhārtha his own sword, which he used to cut off the long and beautiful locks of his hair and his shiny, glamorous crown. Siddhārtha thought to himself, "The bonds of attachments are broken now, and Siddhārtha is free to pursue his goal of freedom from the passage of time!"

## 2.4 Siddhārtha's struggle

Siddhārtha's goal was certain, but the path which would lead him to that goal was not. In search of a guide, he decided to go to Rājagṛha (the major city in the kingdom of Magadha), where there were well known hermitages of the sages. Siddhārtha had only a begging bowl, which was his source of livelihood. When Bimbisāra, the King of Magadha, learned that Siddhārtha had abandoned worldly pleasures in favor of becoming a monk, Bimbisāra requested that he return to the world of the common people as a king. He offered Siddhārtha his entire kingdom as a gift, for the world needed a righteous king, an able ruler. But Siddhārtha refused. He entered a hermitage in Rājagṛha, where the monks were practicing penances; they were fasting and denying their bodies any kind of sensual gratification. When Siddhārtha asked them the purpose of their penance, they told him that they were suffering here in order to attain heaven. Pain and suffering was the key to heaven. "Pain and suffering of the body," thought Siddhārtha, "is not the way to freedom from the bondage of *dukkha,* for the pain is for the sake of pleasures—pleasures which are not permanent and therefore are the cause of *dukkha.* That which is not permanent should not be sought. Restrictions on the demands of the body will not prevent the wanderings of the mind and its attachments to mundane pleasures and the objects of pleasure.

The 'purification' of the body (i.e., making the body abandon its demands) is not the path to freedom. Pilgrimages, bathing in a holy river, etc. do not purify the mind, and without purifying the mind there is no escape from attachments which lead to *dukkha.*

Siddhārtha was dissatisfied with the methods of the learned monks who were seeking the answer to the question of *dukkha.* He went from one hermitage to another, trying to find the correct answer. He visited the famous sage Ālāra Kālāma, who taught him the Hindu doctrine of *Ātman* and *Brahman* and tried to impress on his mind that the doctrine of identity with *Brahman* was the supreme one. This doctrine did not attract Siddhārtha, since *Ātman* (in this doctrine) seemed to be subjected meaninglessly to the conditions and pains of rebirth which always resulted in *dukkha.* His quest continued. He visited Uruvelā where he met Uddaka, the disciple/son of Rāma, who taught him the method of *Yoga* which involved severe mental and physical exercises. Those teachings were motivated by the goal of rejecting the bodily existence, or so it appeared to Siddhārtha. He tried the method of *Yoga* along with five other sages. He fasted and put his body through severe pain for six years. The time came when his body was so emaciated that there was no flesh left and only the skin and the bones remained! "Siddhārtha Gautama is dead!" people told Śuddhodana, who with utmost faith in his son said, "No, that cannot be true; my son cannot die without attaining enlightenment!"

## *2.5 Sujātā's food offering*

While Siddhārtha Gautama was in Uruvelā fasting and starving himself to the point of death, he was offered milk and rice by Sujātā, a girl of the Śūdra caste. She always offered food to people, as she was such a pious soul. She had long cherished the desire of offering food to a *Bodhisattva* (the future Buddha). In a golden bowl, she offered him milk mixed with rice. Siddhārtha accepted it, dividing it up into forty-nine portions to last him for forty-nine days. He emptied the golden bowl and set it afloat on the river. "If it goes upward with the stream, I will attain enlightenment today," said Siddhārtha. And it did!

## *2.6 The temptation: Māra's attack*

By now, Siddhārtha had realized that nobody (i.e., a guide, a teacher, etc.) could lead him to freedom. He had to find it himself. Also, freedom could not be achieved by mere emaciation of the body. It was a state to be reached through the mind. It was "inner" freedom, to be achieved by one's effort, and not by any externally imposed methods. Indulgence in worldly pleasure was just as bad as mortification of the body. Neither lead to freedom. The answer was elsewhere; it was in one's own experience—it had to be one's own path. And it could be found through one's own hard striving.

Siddhārtha's mind thus turned inward for the answer. He went away from the people and the crowds to a solitary Bo-tree (which was later on called *Bodhi*-tree 'the tree of enlightenment'). There he sat with his eyes closed contemplating the meaning of life, its bondage and freedom. Siddhārtha became his own guide. While he sat with his mind engrossed in analyzing events in his own life and in those of others, the interconnections between the past, present; and future and what lies beyond, Māra came around. Māra is the lord of the fifth heaven, he is the 'tempter'. He follows the *Bodhisattva* and tries to tempt him with wordly pleasures; and thereby tries to prevent him from attaining enlightenment. He has several weapons, beautiful and terrible, tender and hard! He is both the tempter and the tester. He is a tempter because he tries to lure the *Bodhisattva* to "this world" of pleasures by presenting to him attractive objects such as precious treasures and beautiful women. He is a tester because he presents a challenge to the *Bodhisattva* to test the power of his mind. If the *Bodhisattva* wins, he is released from the bondage of worldly pleasures and is ready for enlightenment; but if Māra wins, the *Bodhisattva is* proved to be too weak to go beyond "this world of *dukkha*." Thus Māra is a barrier on the path to freedom from *dukkha* which a *Bodhisattva* must cross to enter the land of freedom. Or perhap Māra is the gateway to the land of freedom, since it is Māra who ensures detachment of the *Bodhisattva* from worldly pleasures!

As Siddhārtha, seated under the tree, contemplated on the meaning of life, Māra arrived several times in different forms and tried to persuade him to return to the world of pleasures. First he came as a messenger from Kapilavastu. "I have come from your city with sad news of your family. Your cousin Devadatta has forcibly seized your wife and kingdom and imprisoned your father, Śuddhodana." said Māra (the messenger), "Will you not consider returning home to rescue your loved ones from the tyranny of Devadatta?" This was a plea to Siddhārtha's emotions toward his loved ones. Siddhārtha was silent for a while and then replied, "Devadatta, like the rest of the people, has acted out of passion for the worldly pleasures of power and wealth. I intend to cut the bond of attachments, may they be to pleasures or people. Devadatta's deeds have only made me see the truth more vividly. I will not return."

Māra felt helpless but he did not give up, for he knew the weakness of human beings only too well. Māra tried another device, more attractive than the first one, to dissuade *Bodhisattva* from pursuing his goal. He sent his three beautiful daughters to lure Siddhārtha to the world of attachments and pleasures. They are *Tanhā* (Sanskrit tṛṣṇa) 'desire,' *Rati* 'passion,' and *Rāgā* 'love /attachment.' They tried to seduce Siddhārtha using their nearly divine charm. Their passionate singing and dancing only reminded Siddhārtha of the frailties of human life. He thought "These charms are like flashes of lightning. They will pass away in no time! I want to go beyond them!"

Māra, now disappointed more than ever, tried to threaten Siddhārtha by challenging his generosity. "You are sitting on my seat. This seat is for the one who has been very generous! Is there proof of your generosity?" asked Māra. And, it is said, the deep voice of Earth was heard, "I am the witness. Siddhārtha was Vessantara in his earlier birth, when he gave away everything he owned, including his kingdom!" Māra's weapons had failed. Siddhārtha was truly detached—no emotion could sway him away from his resolve. Siddhārtha was ready to pass beyond the realm of bondage. "You may attain your goal," said the three daughters of Māra to Siddhārtha.

## 2.7 "The builder of the house"

Siddhārtha was now left alone to realize truth on his own. He meditated on the nature and cause of *dukkha* and its solution. The night was filled with thick, blinding darkness. The first "watch" of the night presented to Siddhārtha the vision of his previous births. The memory of endless previous births was revived. He remembered one, two, three, hundreds, thousands of births, many million ages of manifestation and dissolution of the world. He existed in each of them (i.e., in the manifestation and dissolution of the world) in different forms and names. They were apparently disconnected lives, and yet there was a connection—a causal connection, for one birth directly led to another. Siddhārtha was not merely groping in the dark anymore; the path to knowledge was becoming more visible.

The second "watch" of the night brought to him the vision of the lives of all creatures, passing away, reappearing in new forms and names. The vision of passing and reappearing was not limited to his own life but was the fact of every creature's life. And there was something more significant about those dream-like visions of passing away and reappearing, there was an intimate connection between the successive lives. The actions in one life caused the next life. There was a chain of lives, each one caused by the previous one and causing the next. His life and others' were all bound and governed by this law of causation.

With concentrated effort Siddhārtha went through the third "watch" of the night when he understood the cause and nature of suffering and the solution to the problem of *dukkha*. This realization (which later came to be known as the Four Noble Truths and which included The Eightfold Path) of the true nature of his own as well as other existences made him

*Buddha* 'the enlightened one.' The knowledge was not external to him anymore; it was direct experience of the truth, of the meaning of life. It was so intimate and intense! "When there is no birth, there is no aging and death; with the cessation of birth, there is cessation of death."

-When there is no being, there is no becoming.

-When there is no attachment, there is no being,

-When there is no craving, there is no attachment,

-When there is no feeling, there is no craving,

-When there is no contact, there is no feeling,

-When there are no senses, there is no contact,

-When there is no name and form, there are no senses,

-When there is no consciousness, there is no name and form.

"With the cessation of name and form, consciousness ceases to be."

Thus, Siddhārtha was transformed into *Buddha,* having understood that as long as there is being there is going to be *dukkha.* This was the prerequisite for the cessation of being and thereby the cessation of suffering (more discussion in section 3.2). He realized that the cause of and the solution for *dukkha* was within himself. He himself was the "builder of the house" in each birth. Constantly supplying the material for building it anew in each birth, he had himself kept the chain going. His quest was over now. The house stood on a foundation of craving; with the craving gone, the house would stand no more.

Buddha said,

"Always struggling to find the builder of the house,
I journeyed through the circle of innnumerable births,
How painful is rebirth!
O, Builder of the house, I have found you.
No house shall be built by you again.
Your center pole is destroyed
Your beams have been broken down.
My mind has attained the formless *nirvanā,*
the realm beyond every craving is reached at last!"

*(Dhammapada: 153–4)*

Siddhārtha grieved no more. He had realized that one had to put a stop to one's craving in order to be free from *dukkha.* The Buddha, who was completely detached from worldly attachments, was suddenly overcome with intense compassion for all human beings, for he had realized that it was their ignorance about the nature of things which caused *dukkha* and that he could help them to be free from *dukkha. He* could help them attain the ultimate freedom—*nirvanā.*

## 2.8 Turning of the "wheel"

The Buddha, the enlightened one, arose from his seat under the Bo-tree. It was then called the *Bodhi*-tree 'the wisdom tree'. He returned to the Deer Park in Banaras to meet his five friends, the wandering ascetics. The whole world would receive the knowledge from him later, but the five ascetics were the first to obtain it. "My friends," said the Buddha to them, "if one wants to be free from *dukkha,* one must avoid the two extremes—an extreme attachment to worldly pleasures and the extreme mortification of the body—for neither leads to freedom. Follow the Middle—the Eight-fold path of Right Views, Right Aspirations, Right Speech, Right Conduct, Right Course of Livelihood, Right Effort, Right Contemplation, and Right Meditation. The one who follows this path escapes from the craving and eventually reaches a state of freedom." (For discussion on the Eight-fold Path, see section 3.2) This first sermon by the Buddha is called the "Turning of the Wheel of Law" (*Dhamma*). It contained all the basic ideas of the later teachings of Buddha. (Siddhārtha had attained enlightenment and become the Buddha at the age of 35. The Buddha gave up his mortal frame at the age of 80. Thus, he went about teaching for 45 long years.) Buddha's message was clear. One must become one's own guide and terminate craving, and thereby the chain of causation, which is the key to the ultimate freedom. The Eight-fold Path emphasized, in general, the way to cultivate the attitude of non-craving (see section 3).

The Buddha was followed by several disciples who joined him in establishing a monastery for those who aspired to gain knowledge of the Four Noble Truths.

Siddhārtha returned to Rājagṛha to meet Bimbisāra, who earlier had offered him his kingdom. Bimbisāra now became Buddha's disciple. Śuddhodana's joy knew no bounds when he learned about the spiritual attainments of his son. He sent his courtiers to the Buddha to request that he visit home. Buddha agreed to visit his old home which once had been his capital city and which had held all his worldly bonds.

## 2.9 The Buddha-Prince Siddhārtha no more!

The Buddha returned to what once had been his home. Kapilavastu was promptly decorated to welcome the Buddha. The pleasure gardens were prepared once more with the hope of reminding the Buddha of the life he had led there. His father could not contain his happiness. But when he saw his son followed by hundreds of disciples and surrounded by a divine glow like that of the sun around him, radiating light in the world, he knew that he had lost his son. The person he was seeing was not human; he was divine. "I worship you, O Buddha," said he, "for I know you are the great enlightened one. Although I am your father, treat me as your disciple." Tears rolled from his eyes as he looked at his son. The princes also paid homage to the Buddha.

The Buddha visited his wife and son. His wife, Yaśodharā, did not know what to expect from the Buddha, who once had been her husband and with whom she had had their son Rāhula. Though she knew he had abandoned every attachment to the world, she also knew that her tie of love was real. She loved him all the same. In fact she had been following him in everything—shaving her head, when she heard that her husband had shaved his head, keeping herself away from all pleasures of life and leading the life of an ascetic, just as her husband had been doing, "Will he accept me or his son as his own?" she thought to herself. As soon as he arrived, she flung herself at his feet and began to cry. The Buddha restrained her and consoled her. Yaśodharā sent for her son Rāhula. "Ask your father, dear son," she said, "what you will receive as your inheritance."

"Father, I am your son," said Rāhula. "Grant me my inheritance."

"You shall be granted entry into the order of monks," said the Buddha. And it was done! Rāhula became the Buddha's disciple, for what could be a better inheritance for a son than that of the knowledge which his father had received.

## 2.10 The Buddha prevents a war

The Buddha wandered from place to place spreading his knowledge through sermons. Many kings and noblemen had become his followers by then. The Buddha was spreading a message of peace through the Four Noble Truths. Kings such as Sāriputra and Mogallāyana became his disciples and learned the importance of giving up political power as opposed to gaining it, since, as the Buddha taught them, such craving for power would only cause more *dukkha.*

There are several legends about the impact of the Buddha's teaching on the conduct of the people. One of the prominent ones is about the conflict between the kingdoms of Kapilavastu and Koli (i.e, the Śākyas and the Kolis, respectively). This dispute was over the water of the river Rohiṇī, which was the only source of water for both kingdoms. Each kingdom claimed exclusive rights to it, and neither side was willing to compromise. Both parties had decided to solve the issue through war. The Buddha arrived at the site of the battle and asked both parties to lay down their weapons. Then he asked them the cause of the dispute. After listening to their complaint he said to them, "What is more important, human beings or water?" "Human beings" was the answer of both sides.

"Then why are you bent on destroying what is more valuable for that which is less valuable?" It is said that the two kingdoms agreed to share the water from then onwards.

## 2.11 Devadatta's plots

Devadatta was the Buddha's cousin. He was always envious of him, of his royalty, power and beauty when he was Siddhārtha the prince, and he was later envious of his grandeur as a learned Buddha. Devadatta managed to gain a great deal of political power by indulging in conspiracies and deceits, but his ultimate goal was to kill the Buddha and get rid of him once and for all. Devadatta's platter of destiny was filled with countless evil deeds, such as murdering the king by conspiring with the king's son Ajasat, and using his powers to torture those who lived in the monastery, etc.

He tried to kill the Buddha by sending an intoxicated elephant toward him, throwing sharp rocks at him, and by other such malicious plots. But all his efforts failed, and soon Devadatta realized that the Buddha was invulnerable to his tricks. He finally decided to ask for his forgiveness and approached him with that intention.

"Who am I to grant him forgiveness?" said the Buddha. "He cannot evade the results of his evil actions. They will bear fruit and Devadatta will be punished. No one can save him."

The Buddha denied him permission to see him, but Devadatta ignored this and proceeded to see him.

The legend says that as he came close to the Buddha a column of raging fire arose from the underworld. This flame broke through the ground and wrapped up Devadatta, who was soon reduced to ashes. Thus was the power of his evil actions.

## 2.12 The Buddha's compassion toward women

The Buddha, the enlightened one, was compassionate toward the whole world but did not allow women to enter the monastery as nuns, for he thought they were distractions, a barrier for the seekers of enlightenment. But Gotami, the old widow from the royal palace of Kapilavastu, along with the wives of the five hundred princes who had been ordained as monks, approached the Buddha and asked permission to enter the order. The Buddha denied it several times, but then his favorite disciple, Ānanda, argued, "Are women incapable of spiritual knowledge? If they follow the rules of the hermitage and renounce worldly bonds, can they also not become bhikṣuṇī 'female ascetics'?"

The Buddha had no argument against this. With some reluctance, he finally opened the doors of his monastery for women as well. Women, including his wife Yaśodharā, were admitted to the religious order of the Buddha.

## 2.13 Parinirvāṇa 'the final release'

Forty-four long years had passed during which the Buddha had preached the *Dhamma* 'the law' to thousands of people—men and women, kings and beggars. For the Buddha the time for his final departure had come.

The Buddha was living in a city called Pāwa. He was served by a goldsmith called Chunda. Once Chunda expressed his desire to feed the Buddha. When the Buddha gladly accepted his invitation, Chunda made him a special pork dish. Soon after he ate the meal, the Buddha became very sick. He had violent pains and he started throwing up blood. He felt that he was not going to survive for too long. So, he called his favorite disciple Ānanda and said to him, "My friend Ānanda, someone may blame Chunda for feeding me a spoiled pork dish, which they will say, caused this sickness. Do tell the people that Chunda's dish was a blessing indeed; if I die of this sickness, he should be praised because he only hastened the process which leads to death. Two types of food should be treated as equally meritorious—the one through which the Buddha attains enlightenment and the other through which the Buddha dies—or becomes free from the physical bondage of the body. Chunda's meal is going to help me reach my goal easily. Tell him not to feel guilty for what has happened." The Buddha had asked Chunda to bury the remainder of the dish in a hole so that no one could find it. The Buddha lay on a couch underneath a śāl tree in a town named Kushīinagar (where Ānanda had brought him at his request). He, as well as his disciple Ānanda, could sense his approaching death. Ānanda could not bear the pain of the anticipated departure of the Buddha, for how could he lead his life without his teacher, his guide? Ānanda wept, leaning against the door of his teacher's room. The Buddha called him and said to him, "My dear Ānanda, do not weep.

Do not lament. The separation, division from and loss of the dear one is inevitable. Do not grieve. This is the ultimate law of the world. That which is born must die. How can you expect any exception to this law? If you understand this, you will not grieve. You have served me with kindness and care. You have been my dear friend. You are pure—physically and mentally—in actions and thoughts. You have acquired merit and you will be duly rewarded." Then the Buddha addressed the monks, saying, "*Bhiksus!* (monks) be your own guiding light. Work out your *nirvanā* yourself with strength and perseverence."

Legend says that the Buddha entered successive stages of meditation until he reached the point where distinctions between perception and non-perception are dissolved. He had attained the final *nirvanā*. The passing away of the Buddha is known as *Parinirvāna.*

## 3.0 Teachings of the Buddha

The Buddha's teachings were communicated to the people for the first time in his sermon in Deer Park (in Banaras) after his enlightenment. His sermon was later interpreted several times by his disciples and followers. Therefore, it is difficult to know the exact words of his sermons. Nevertheless, it is certain from all of the Buddhist writings that the central theme of the Buddha's teaching was the Four Noble Truths and the Eight-fold Path.

It is important to note here that, unlike the contemporary systems of Hinduism, the Buddha's teachings do not include lengthy discussions on philosophical or metaphysical problems. He was always at pains to emphasize that questions such as the following were not of utmost concern to him: (a) Is the universe eternal? (b) Is it finite?, (c) What happens to the Buddha after his death? Does he continue to exist or not?, and (d) Are body and soul identical?

This did not mean that the Buddha deemed those questions to be insignificant, but rather, people usually asked these questions either casually or used them as a pretext for postponing *nirvāṇa.* The Buddha himself focused more on the immediate condition of the world and people, which he called *dukkha* 'misery,' and devoted his time to helping people obtain release from *dukkha.* Thus he was more concerned with the practical issues of attaining *nirvāṇa* than discussing abstruse metaphysical problems. If a person is hit by a poison arrow, according to the Buddha, speculations regarding questions such as who shot it, how the person was hit , and how the arrow was made are unimportant for someone who wants to save the person from death. The doctor's first concern is how the arrow should be taken out of the body so that the person's life may be saved. Similarly, the Buddha saw himself as a doctor whose primary responsibility was to rescue the world from the perpetual misery caused by the countless cycles of rebirth. His doctrine of the Four Noble Truths (which according to the tradition were revealed to him when he was meditating under the *bodhi*-tree) then is the analysis of the condition /problem of the world, its diagnosis, and the remedy for the problem. Thus the Buddha's teachings are primarily in the form of ethical and moral principles consolidated in a system which is meant to guide the individuals to *nirvāṇa* 'enlightenment' and thereby rescue them from the misery of life. It is the doctrine of the Middle-path, which avoids the unrestrained or extreme indulgence in worldly pleasures and a complete withdrawal from it (i.e., severe asceticism); it is a doctrine of balancing the two.

## 3.1 The Four Noble Truths

The Four Noble Truths are: (a) Everything is *dukkha* 'misery' or 'suffering,' (b) The cause of suffering is *tṛṣṇa* 'craving,' (c) The cause (i.e., craving) can be annihilated, and *(d)* The means to this annihilation is the Eight-fold path.

### 3.1.1 The first truth : everything is dukkha 'misery'

According to the Buddha, the simple truth of life is that everything is *dukkha.* Birth, decay, sickness, and death are *dukkha.* To be related to all of these is *dukkha.* To be separated from what one likes is *dukkha.* Not to get what one wants is also *dukkha.* Any conceptualization of the above is in fact *dukkha.* The above analysis is not meant as a pessimistic evaluation of all existences, It is meant to be the acceptance of the true nature of all existences and objects; i.e., they all are of the nature of *dukkha.* Again, the Buddha's analysis of *dukkha is* to be viewed in connection with the nature of things; i.e., they are impermanent. It is the impermanence of everything, it is the finitude of all existence which is being emphasized here and not merely the *dukkha.* It is not merely the dissatisfaction and frustration in life which are being stressed; rather, it is the inherent nature of things which is being focused on.

Moreover, it is crucial to note here that the Buddha presents this truth not merely to express objective reality outside oneself but also subjective reality as well. All existence is impermanent, and therefore everyone must accept that their existence is too, One's being, feeling, and desires all are impermanent. The goal of presenting this truth is to identify the cause of *dukkha* and thereby find a way to get rid of it.

### 3.1.2 The second truth: the origin of dukkha

It is *tṛṣṇa* 'craving' which causes *dukkha. Dukkha is* the subjective experience caused by the craving for an object (which by definition is impermanent). The gain and loss of the desired objects, which leads to happiness and/or pain are caused by a deep attachment (craving) to the object. If one never craved for anything, there could be no *dukkha.*

In this Truth, the Buddha focuses on the subject-object relationship between the experiencer (subject) and the experienced (world of objects). The emphasis is on the fact that it is the attitude of the experiencer (subject) of intense attachment to the objects which is the root of *dukkha.*

### 3.1.3 The third truth: removal of tṛṣṇa 'craving'

The solution to the problem of *dukkha* is the annihilation of craving. The Buddha identifies all types/kinds of craving as the root of *dukkha;* i.e., the craving for sensuous experience, the craving for immortality, the craving for extinction of existence, etc. One must understand the true nature of things (i.e., everything is impermanent). Only then can one annihilate craving. By understanding the true nature of things, one's perspective on them changes. In this Truth the Buddha emphasizes the fact that *dukkha* cannot be removed by trying to change or replace objects (which are impermanent). *Dukkha* can be removed only by changing one's attitude toward the objects; i.e., by removing the craving for them.

### 3.1.4 The fourth truth: the Eight-fold path

The method of removing the craving is described in the Eight-fold Path. The Eight-fold Path presents a system of regulating one's mental and physical behavior whereby one can remove the craving and eventually *dukkha.*

## *3.2 The Eight-fold Path*

The Eight-fold Path presents a system of eight dimensions. These are not necessarily viewed as sequential steps, but rather as proper modes of behavior. The eight parts are as follows: (1) right views, (2) right aspiration, (3) right speech, (4) right action, (5) right means of livelihood, (6) right effort, (7) right awareness, and (8) right concentration. The first two clearly outline a system to regulate the attitudinal, the next four the behavioral, and the last two the meditative dimensions of human life. The *Madhyama Sūtra* elaborates the Eight-fold Path as follows: right views imply knowledge of the Four Noble Truths. Right attitude means renunciation *(naiṣkramya),* non-violence *(avyāpāda),* and harmlessness *(avihiṃsā).* The implication in the above two is clear; i.e., if one has accepted the Four Noble Truths, then one should develop the above attitude to remove craving.

Right speech, right action, and the right means of livelihood primarily focus on regulating the mode of behavior. Right speech involves abstaining from falsehood, malicious speech, harmful speech, trivia or nonsense. Right action involves abstaining from taking life, from taking what is not given. The right means of livelihood again involves maintaining oneself without harming others. This system implies that the above-mentioned code is "right" in the sense that it removes craving. The one who craves objects alone indulges in lying, harming others, and leading a self-centered life. The observance of the above practices is not an easy task. One has to constantly strive to follow it. Therefore "right effort" is included as a major path. Effort is essential to prevent evil from emerging, to remove evil, to cultivate good and to increase the good which exists. (Evil is viewed as any obstacle in the path to enlightenment, while good is viewed as that which is conducive to progress on the path toward enlightenment.)

Right awareness and concentration refer to regulating mental behavior. Five types of mental faculties are involved: (a) faith *(śradhā);* i.e., one must have faith in the enlightenment of the Buddha, (b) energy *(vīrya);* i.e., one must develop energy or strength to abandon wrong principles, (c) memory *(smṛti);* one must have the memory of what has happened before, (d) concentration *(samādhi);* one must withdraw from every kind of distraction and concentrate on the Four-fold Truths, and (e) knowledge (*prajñā*); the knowledge of the Four-fold Truths.

The Eight-fold Path provides a practical system which, according to the Buddha, leads an individual to the state where all craving ceases to exist. Consequently, the individual becomes free from *dukkha* and attains *nirvāṇa* 'enlightenment'.

The Eight paths are integral complements of one another. It is assumed in the system that absolute adherence to any one path both presupposes and invariably leads to adherence to the other paths. For example, if one develops the "right attitude," then it is expected that he will translate it into his behavior; i.e., the person will not lie, steal, or harm others.

The Eight-fold Path thus presents a cohesive system in which attitude, behavior and thinking together aim at the achievement of the goal. It emphasizes the importance of regulating one's way of life (with all of its facets) in accordance with the goal. One must refrain from both extreme indulgence and extreme asceticism and follow the Middle Path—the Eight-fold Path which calls for regulating one's attitude, actions, and thinking in accordance with the nature of reality (*yathā bhūtam*) and the goal.

The following story of Kisā Gotamī shows the method which the Buddha often used to preach the Eight-fold Path. The story also shows how knowledge/awareness of the nature of things (impermanence) leads to the removal of craving and *dukkha.*

### *3.2.1 "As a mighty flood sweeps away a village asleep…": the story of Kisā Gotamī*

She was a weak and frail woman. Her name was Gotamī, but they called her Kisā Gotamī—'the frail Gotamī.' Kisā Gotamī was born in an extremely poor household. When she got married nobody cared for her, for she had come from a poor home.

It was the birth of her son which finally brought happiness to Kisā Gotamī, for the birth of a son meant prosperity for the family and honor and respect for the mother. The sight of her growing son always filled Kisā Gotamī's heart with tender affection and motherly pride. But her happiness was unexpectedly terminated by the death of her son, who had barely started walking and playing. Once again Kisā Gotamī's world was filled with darkness. "With the son came respect and joy, and with him it will go away," she thought to herself. "The village folk will take my son away from me and I will have no one and nothing to live for."

Kisā Gotamī refused to part with her son. She carried his dead body on her hip and moved from house to house, asking everyone in desperation, "Please give me medicine for my son!"

"How can you find any medicine for the dead?" said the village folk to her with smiles full of sarcasm. Kisā Gotamī was totally oblivious to their answer, for she thought only of reviving her son. One learned man guided her to *Tathāgata* (the Buddha), for he knew that no one else would have the knowledge of medicine which could bring the dead child back to life.

"Go to the one who is the master of ten forces, he will give you medicine," said the wise man. "He lives in the monastery."

Kisā Gotamī wasted no time in approaching *Tathāgata* at the monastery. Her request was direct. "Please give me medicine for my son, O learned one," she said to him.

"Be assured, O woman," said *Tathāgata.* "I will give you the medicine, but there is something I would like you to do before that. Please bring me a handful of tiny mustard seeds from any house where no one has ever died."

Kisā Gotamī rejoiced at this request and began her search of the mustard seeds. At the first house she said, "Please give me a handful of mustard seeds if no one has ever died in your home. The honorable *Tathāgata* has asked me to bring him the mustard seeds and he will then give me medicine for my son."

"Alas! Gotamī, innumerable people have died in this house," said the owner.

"I cannot accept the seeds then," said Kisā Gotamī and moved on to another house. Thus she went from house to house only to find that it was impossible to find a house where no one had ever died. She then thought that *Tathāgata* must have knowledge of the way of the world!

She carried her dead son out of the city and placed his body on the cremation ground and said, "My dear little son, I thought you were the only one taken away by death. But everywhere this is the law without any exception. Every house is invaded by death, Death is the law of all mankind. It is not restricted to a house or a village. It is the universal law that everything is transitory and perishable. One must understand this and accept it."

Kisā Gotamī returned to her teacher, *Tathāgata*. "Gotami, have you brought the mustard seeds?" asked *Tathāgata*.

"Enough!" said Kisā Gotamī. "There is no need to discuss the mustard seeds. Please give me shelter in your order."

*Tathāgata* gave her advice in accordance with the *Dhammapada:* "The one who is intensely attached to children and cattle is swept away by death like the stormy flood which sweeps away a whole village while everyone is asleep." Kisā Gotamī had understood the inevitability of death. She requested *Tathāgata* to allow her to enter the order of Buddhist monks. *Tathāgata* permitted her to be a member of the convent of nuns. Kisā Gotamī practiced meditation and pondered over the true meaning of life and death. According to legend, Kisā Gotamī, the frail one, thus accomplished enlightenment and became a saint.

## 4.0 Philosophy of Buddhism: the main concepts

The Buddhist system of belief is founded on four major principles: Impermanence *(anicca)*, Non-self *(anatta,* unreality of *Ātman,* 'self'), Misery *(dukkha)*, and Enlightenment *(nirvāṇa)*. These four principles are interrelated and together they define the goal of life, the method to attain it, the ethical and moral code of behavior, etc.

Impermanence *(anicca) is* the true nature of all existences. Everything is subject to decay, aging, and death. There is nothing which exists permanently. Everything is in flux. There is no permanent being. There is only constant becoming. There is no permanent, undying *Ātman* or self. There is only a chain of existences in which one existence leads to another. This impermanence, this constant becoming is the perpetual cause of *dukkha* 'misery.' Here Buddhism is similar to Hinduism in that they both aim at transcending impermanence. *Nirvāṇa* 'enlightenment' is the state beyond impermanence where there is no becoming and the chain of causation and rebirths is terminated. It is a state of permanent peace (i.e., freedom from *dukkha*).

### 4.1 Dependent origination: the chain of causation

The rationale behind the above analysis of the world is presented in the Buddhist system by the theory of dependent origination. This theory explains the origin and emergence of *dukkha* by the logic of causation in the following way. There is a chain of twelve links (i.e., states), each being the effect of the preceding and the cause of the following link (i.e., state).

The first, primary cause of being (coming into existence) is ignorance about the impermanence of the world and the self. This ignorance in the individual personality is a carryover from the last birth (death without attaining *nirvāṇa* inevitably results in birth in ignorance) which determines the dispositional traits *(saṃskāras)*. Due to these dispositional traits, one becomes aware of oneself and the world. In other words, the faulty perception of the world and "I" arises due to the predisposition of each individual. One then defines one's individuality (of name and form) separately from everything else. This individuality is expressed in terms of the mind and the five senses of the individual. These interact with other selves (individual existences) and things. Due to this contact with other external objects (i.e., other names and forms), there arises sensation. Sensation then becomes the cause for desire or craving *(tṛṣṇa)*. The craving gives rise to attachment or clinging to names and forms (i.e., one's own of becoming a constantly changing being. And it is this becoming which causes a new state of being to come into existence whch is different from the earlier existence and has its own old age, decay, and death. Human suffering begins anew. This is the chain of new being, becoming and being—the everlasting cycle of suffering. Since each state depends for its origin on the preceding state and causes the following states, this chain of cause-effect-cause is called the chain of dependent origination. If suffering is to be terminated, then one has to annihilate the root of all suffering; i.e., ignorance about the real nature of the world and self.

If there were no birth, no old age, decay or death could occur. The birth would not have occurred if the factors giving rise to becoming did not exist. This clinging to existence and craving are viewed as the evil (in Buddhist thought) which causes the chain of rebirths. The craving would not take place if there was no contact between senses and external objects. The contact would not take place if the senses and the mind were regulated differently. Again the behavior of senses and mind would depend on the consciousness or awareness of the individual with regard to the nature of the world and self which was carried over from the last birth. The twelve links in the chain of dependent origination depict the interconnection of the past, present, and future births. While the first two states (ignorance and disposition) are the consequence of past births, the next seven (from consciousness to clinging to cravings) relate to the present birth, and the last three (becoming, rebirth, and aging and death) project consequences of the actions of this birth to future birth. (See the diagram on page 116.)

## 4.2 Karma and saṃsāra

*Karma* and *saṃsāra* are two of the major concepts in the Buddhist system of beliefs. The doctrine of Dependent Origination as well as that of the Eight-fold Path assume the Buddhist faith in *karma* and *saṃsāra*. Similarly, the mythology of Buddha's earlier births *(Jātaka)* crucially refers to belief in the above two.

Though Buddhism has retained the basic meaning of the original Hindu concepts of *karma* and *saṃsāra*, it has done so without adhering to the concomitant belief in the existence of *Ātman* 'soul' as well. *Karma* (literally, action) in Buddhism, much as in Hinduism, is the theory of causation, according to which actions must bring results and the doer is responsible for the results of his actions. *Karma* includes mental (thoughts) as well as physical actions. *Karma* has the power to cause a new birth , the form/character of which is determined by

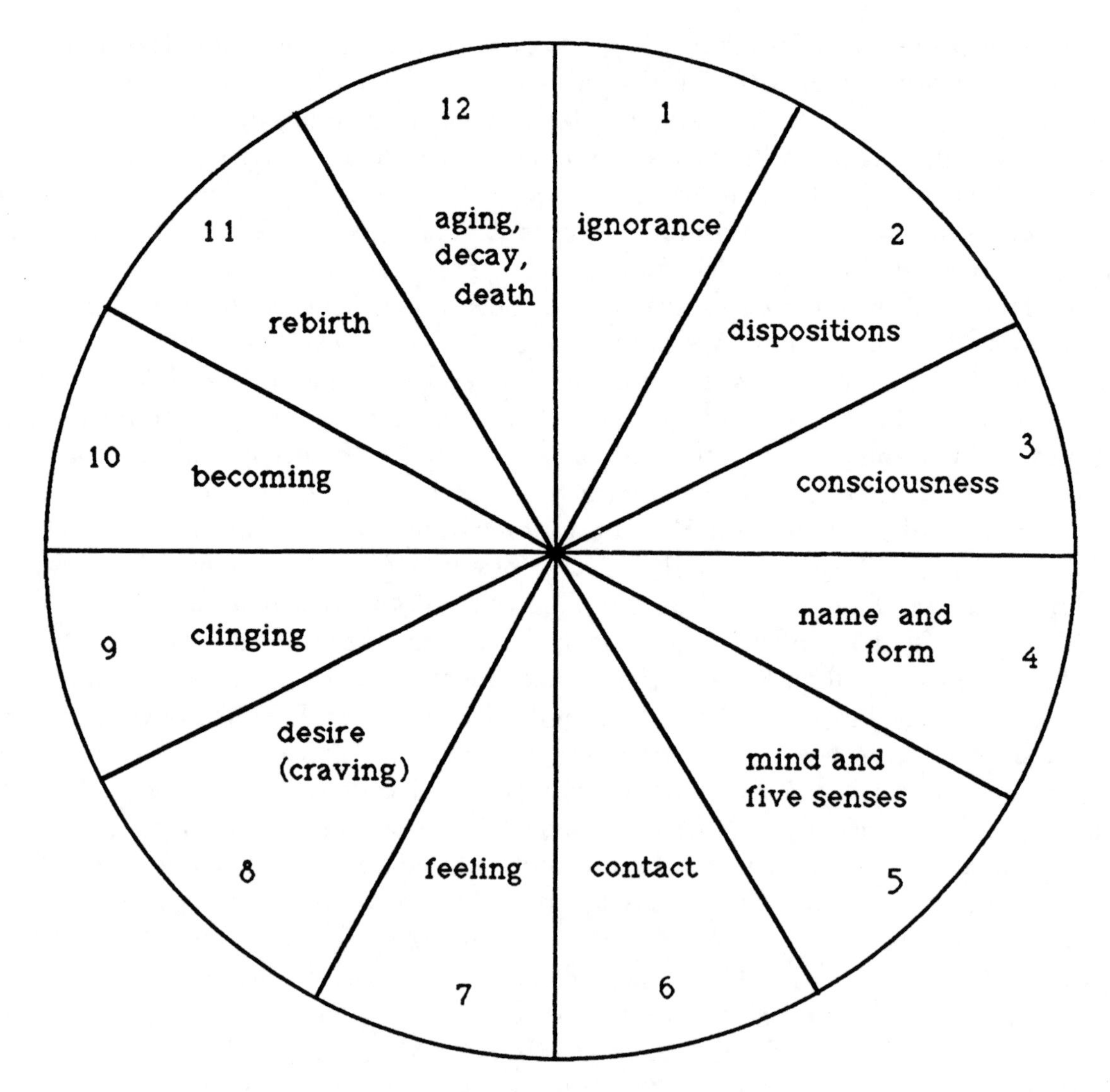


The Buddhist View of Saṃsāra

the *karma* of the earlier birth. This causation thus operates across births, creating an unbroken causal chain in which each birth is simultaneously the consequence of the earlier birth and the cause of the next birth. This cycle of births is called *saṃsāra.* Due to its faith in the power of *karma,* the Buddhist system, much like the Hindu, emphasizes "right" thought/motivation and action to ensure a better rebirth. In the ultimate analysis, however, birth (or coming into being) itself is held to be responsible for *dukkha* (the misery of life), and therefore adherence to the Eight–fold path is emphasized to regulate behavior so as to terminate the root cause that sustains the cycle of rebirths.

The Buddhist doctrine of *karma* and *saṃsāra* does not imply the existence of any permanent being (i.e., *Ātman* 'soul'*) or* a "subtle being" which migrates from one body to another across births. Thus, for example, A's *karma* in a birth causes the birth of B and the only definite connection between A and B is a causal connection. Nothing permanent in the body transmigrates from A to B. The causal connection between the two births is as follows: just as the flame of candle A lights candle B, *karma* in one birth causes the next birth. Nothing has been transferred from A to B. There is no retention of identity between A and B. However, the absence of identity (of the doer) across births does not take away the responsibility of the doer for the actions he has performed. The doer must bear the "fruits," the responsibility, for the consequences of his action because he has willed it and thereby creates the potential cause for the perpetuation of *saṃsāra*; that is, he, by performing actions in ignorance brings one more being into existence and suffering. Thus the Buddhist's concern is not motivated by the consideration of being reborn in a higher caste (in fact, there is no caste-system in the Buddhist system) or of going to heaven.* In the Buddhist view, as long as one is performing actions in ignorance and sets the chain of rebirths in motion, one is not performing "right actions." An action which directly or indirectly leads to the attainment of *nirvāṇa is* the "right action." We can trace this view of "right action" to the life of Buddha himself. As a young prince, the one goal Siddhārtha was ready to live or die for was the knowledge of how to attain freedom from *dukkha* in this very birth. This overriding concern of the Buddha for attaining *nirvāṇa* explains his general reticence toward spelling out the karma theory to its last detail. For the Buddha, it was the individual action of attaining *nirvāna* that mattered, and not endless discussions on the details of the *karma* theory.

*Nirvāṇa is* viewed as the goal of life from yet another point of view. All individuals who die without attaining *nirvāṇa* become the root cause for perpetuating *saṃsāra* and bringing endless beings into existence and *dukkha.* Hence an individual has truly fulfilled his responsibility to the larger humanity by annihilating this root cause of all suffering.

## 4.3 Nirvāṇa

According to Buddhism, *nirvāṇa is* the ultimate goal to be attained by a human being. *Nirvāṇa is* a Sanskrit term (Pāli, *Nibbāna)* which literally means 'extinction, dying out' and generally refers to the process of the dying out of a flame. In Buddhism, *nirvāṇa* refers to the state experienced by the Buddha, in which all craving has died out (like a flame extinguished). It is also the moving away *(vāṇa)* from all attachments to worldly pleasures. The metaphor of flame is often related in the Buddhist doctrine as follows: the fire of *rāga* 'attachment,' *moha* 'delusion,' and *doṣa* 'faulty perception' sets the whole world on fire. *Samsara* (perpetuation of births) or constant becoming is the transfer of the flame from one candle to another. *Nirvāṇa is* the dying out of this fire and thereby of the flame. Thus *nirvāṇa is* the state which marks the point of termination of *saṃsāra.* It is the end of the karmic effect. Since no rebirth is possible after the attainment of *nirvāṇa,* it is also viewed as the state of liberation or freedom (similar to *mokṣa* in Hinduism) from *saṃsāra* and thereby from *dukkha* of old age, decay and death.

*Though the Buddha had explicitly and vehemently rejected heaven as the goal of life, ironically enough, in some of the later schools of Mahāyāna Buddhism heaven became an important concept.

*Nirvāṇa is* also viewed as the state of knowledge of the true nature of reality (including oneself), i.e., the knowledge of 'emptiness' *(śūnyatā)* of all existences, of their relative / dependent origination and their impermanence. It is the state where the apparent separation between "I" and "not I" (subject and the object of experience) disappears, since such distinction is based on the assumption of the existence of independent unrelated existences. In the Buddhist literature, it is often mentioned that the experiencer of *nirvāṇa* does not say, "*I* attained *it (nirvanā),*" since there exists no duality (not even between the experiencer and the experienced). *Nirvāṇa is* the experience of ultimate freedom, knowledge, and peace. This state was attained by the Buddha while he was alive. His craving had been completely terminated. He was "enlightened." Although this state does not prevent the *jīvan-mukta* (free though alive) from dying, it puts an end to the cycle of rebirth for that individual. There is no rebirth for the *jīvan-mukta.* The physical death of the Buddha is called *parinirvāna* 'final dying out' because the death of his physical body removed the last barrier between him and *śūnyatā* 'emptiness.' It is believed in Buddhism that *nirvāṇa* remains the goal of the seeker who may attain it in one or after many births. In this sense, it continues to provide a motivation for a constant betterment of one's life across births.

## 5.0 Schools of Buddhism

After the death of the Buddha, according to the tradition, several councils (including the one held in about 247 B.C. by King Aśoka) were held by his disciples to evaluate the authenticity and interpretation of the existing teachings of the Buddha. There must have been a great debate regarding the interpretation of the doctrines and practices among different groups of disciples of the Buddha. Around the 4th century B.C. there were two major established schools, Theravāda and Mahāsanghika (later known as Mahāyāna), and by 200 B.C. there were already over fifteen to eighteen different schools. With the spread of Buddhism into countries outside India, many more schools of Buddhism came into existence, each adapting to the local tradition(s) and culture(s), and each interpreting the doctrine and/or practice of Buddhism differently. The discussion in the following sections focuses primarily on Theravāda and Mahāyāna schools, because these two were some of the oldest schools of Buddhism and have been extremely influential in the Buddhist history as well as in the development of the other later schools of Buddhism in different countries.

### 5.1 Theravāda and Mahāyāna Schools of Buddhism

Theravāda 'Doctrine of the Elders,' and Mahāyāna 'The Great Vehicle,' are two of the major schools of Buddhism. The Theravāda school flourished mainly in South Asian countries such as Sri Lanka, Burma, Cambodia, and Thailand, while the Mahāyāna school has been very influential in China, Japan, and Korea.

Although the exact date of and motivation for the division of the two schools is controversial, the scholars agree that by the first century A.D. these two were established as separate schools of Buddhism. Theravāda 'Doctrine of Elders,' the oldest Buddhist tradition, was formerly called Hinayana 'Lesser Vehicle' by followers of the later Mahāyāna 'Great Vehicle' school. In more recent literature, the Theravāda 'Doctrine of Elders' school has abandoned the name Hinayana 'Lesser Vehicle' (which they deemed condescending) and adopted the name Theravāda 'Doctrine of Elders.'

Both schools commonly share the basic tenets of Buddhism originally introduced by Gautama Buddha, i.e., belief in the theory of *karma, saṃsāra,* and *nirvāṇa.* Furthermore, both regard the Buddha as the founder of their system. However, they differ from each other with regard to their interpretation of the concepts in the sacred texts, and some of the religious practices. While both schools accept *tripīṭaka* 'three baskets' (a text dealing with the life and teachings of the Buddha) as their sacred text, different groups within the Mahāyāna school went on further illustrating, reinterpreting and codifying the Buddha's life and teachings through such texts as *Saddharma Puṇḍarika Sūtra* 'Lotus Sūtra,' *Prajnā-Pāramitā Sūtra* 'Sūtra of Perfect Wisdom,' *Lankāvatara Sūtra* 'Sūtra of the Descent (of the Buddha) to the island of Lankā.'

As Buddhism spread far and wide within and outside of India, several changes in its doctrine and religious practices were introduced in different countries, giving rise to various schools within both the Theravāda and the Mahāyāna schools.

## 5.2 Theravāda School

The Theravāda doctrine is primarily based on the early texts which, according to the followers of the Theravāda doctrine, were directly and orally transmitted to the people by the Buddha himself. The Theravāda doctrine is generally characterized by the following features: (a) its insistence on the monastic life and asceticism as prerequisites for attaining *nirvāṇa,* (b) its acceptance of only one Buddha (i.e., Gautama Buddha) as a teacher, who, though a mortal, was endowed with superior qualities which enabled him to attain *nirvāṇa,* and who, having attained his final *nirvāṇa,* did not return to the world, and (c) its ideal of *Arhat* 'worthy one' who, after following the path of the Buddha, attains *nirvāṇa.* The term *Arhat* literally means 'a deserving person,' 'a worthy person.' He is viewed as the one who has attained freedom from desires and attachments *(āsavas)* and thereby from *saṃsāra.* He has gone *(pāragata)* beyond old age, decay, and death. He is released from *dukkha.* He has attained *nirvāṇa.* He is also viewed as possessing the highest social rank, worthy to receive gifts and worship from the people. The *Arhat* passes through different stages in which the karmic effect gradually recedes until finally he attains *nirvāṇa.*

## 5.3 Mahāyāna School

The Mahāyāna school of Buddhism emerged in Northern India around the first century B.C. and then was transported to Nepal, China, Korea and Japan, According to the Mahāyāna tradition, its teachings are superior to those of the Theravāda school, since their goal is the enlightenment of all human beings irrespective of their spiritual and social status.

The Mahāyāna objection to the Theravāda doctrine was that (a) the Theravāda doctrine excluded the lay (who generally led the life of householders) from the group of possible

*Arhats,* since monastic life was necessary to become a *Arhat,* and (b) the *Arhat* in the Theravāda school was not necessarily guided by concern for the enlightenment of all beings. In general, the Mahāyāna labelled the Theravāda doctrine as Hinayāna 'Lesser Vehicle' (toward *nirvāṇa)* due to its lack of concern for all of humanity. In contrast to this, the Mahāyāna doctrine is called Mahāyāna 'the Great Vehicle' (toward *nirvāṇa)* because of its primary concern for the enlightenment of all humanity. The major features of the Mahāyāna doctrine are the following: (a) the term "Buddha" is not interpreted narrowly to refer to a historical personality, but rather it is interpreted to mean "the Buddhahood" which is simultaneously the eternal, all-pervasive reality and the true nature of all existences, (b) according to the Mahāyāna doctrine, each individual (lay as well as monk) has the potential to attain *nirvāṇa,* and (c) the Mahāyāna ideal is of the *Bodhisattva* 'Buddha-elect'/ 'enlightened.' The *Bodhisattva,* similar to the *Arhat, is* one who has attained enlightenment and can proceed toward final release *(parinirvāṇa).* However, unlike the *Arhat* (who attains final release), the *Bodhisattva* delays it for several births for the sake of humanity. The *Bodhisattva,* due to his compassion for the people who are ignorant and therefore are subjected *to dukkha,* takes an oath to rescue humanity from *dukkha.* His concern for the world overrides his concern for the attainment of final release for himself. According to the followers of the Mahāyāna school, the *Bodhisattva* ideal is superior to that of the *Arhat,* since the former places universal concern over that of his own, while the latter is concerned only with his own enlightenment. The *Jātakas* stories of the Buddha's earlier births vividly describe the compassionate nature of the *Bodhisattva.* (See sections 6.1–2.)

According to the Mahāyāna doctrine, Buddhahood, or Buddha-reality can be expressed in three ways. This is the *trikāya* 'three-bodies' concept in the doctrine. The first *kāyā* 'body' is called *dharmakāya* 'truth body.' This is the all-pervasive, formless, eternal, one reality. This is the true Buddha-nature. The second form is called *sambhogakāya* 'bliss body.' This "body" is the *dharmakāya* expressed in the form of the heavenly Buddhas (i.e., Buddha has life in different heavens) and *Bodhisattvas.* By worshipping the heavenly Buddhas, people could attain enlightenment after listening to the Four Noble Truths.

The third body is called *nirmāṇakāya* 'created body.' This is the Buddha-nature expressed in the world of names and forms (the reality experienced by the common people). Here the Buddha-nature is expressed in the form of a mortal being (e.g. Gautama Buddha) who demonstrates and teaches the path to enlightenment for the common people.

Although the basic concepts of the Mahāyāna school were founded in India, its different branches originated in China and Japan. The two major branches are *Ch'an* (in China) or *Zen* (in Japan), and Pureland (in China). The *Ch'an/Zen* school focuses on the intrinsic Buddha-nature of all human beings and thereby the necessity to turn inward instead of outward in order to realize one's true Buddha-nature. (For further discussion see Chapter 12).

### 5.3.1 The Pureland

The Pureland *(Ching T'*u *Tsung)* branch of the Mahāyāna school was founded in China by a monk named T'an-luan (476–542 A.D.). Shan-tao (613–681 A.D.) was one of the most prominent masters of Pureland Buddhism in China.

The major belief of this school of Buddhism is that there exists a heaven called Pureland where the Buddha (in the *saṃbhogakāya* 'bliss form') abides as the god *Amito-fo* 'the god (Buddha) of infinite light.' It is further believed that *Amito-fo* has vowed to save all beings (in misery) who perform virtuous deeds and offer their worship to him with sincere prayers of *Nan-Wu/Mo A-Mi-T'o- Fo* 'Praise to Amitabha Buddha'. By the grace and blessing of *Amito-fo,* individuals are reborn in the paradise of Pureland and thereby are released from *dukkha.* In the mythology and religion of Pureland, *Amito-fo is* always assisted by a female Bodhisattva named Kwan-yin ('who listens to the cries of the people') 'the goddess of mercy,' who due to her compassion for humanity has delayed her *nirvāṇa* 'enlightenment.' There are several stories in the Pureland literature about the compassion of Kwan-yin for the people. The doctrine of Pureland retained the basic concepts of karma, rebirth, and release from *saṃsāra* from the earlier Buddhism, but, additionally, it emphasized the grace of the Buddha as an important factor in attaining enlightenment. Pureland Buddhism thus is similar to the *Bhakti-mārga* 'path of devotion' emphasized in the *Bhagavadgītā,* where *moksa* 'liberation' is viewed as being attainable by worship of a personal god. In the Pureland school, the Buddha *(Amito- fo) is* worshipped as a personal god of compassion and mercy.

## 6.0 *Jātaka*: stories of the Buddha's earlier births

*Jātakas* are the collections of the stories of the Buddha's earlier birth. The *Jātakas* in the present form were not compiled until the fifth century A.D. According to the Buddhist tradition, these stories were earlier (at least four hundred years ago) transmitted orally and were written down later. The language of the *Jātakas* is Pāli. The Buddha is shown in these stories as a *Bodhisattva* of infinite compassion for all the creatures in the world, as well as the "guide" who leads the world to "enlightenment." It is because of his compassion for every existence in the world that a Bodhisattva chooses to be born several times to help everyone attain freedom from *dukkha* (i.e. release from *saṃsāra* 'cycle of rebirths'). This has led scholars to believe that the *Jātakas* belong to the tradition of the Mahāyāna school. The following *Jātakas* illustrate the role of the compassionate Buddha as well as his teaching.

### 6.1 *Nigrodha-Miga Jātaka*: take my life for hers—the Banyan Deer

This is the story of the compassionate Bodhisattva who was prepared to die to save one in trouble. For a Bodhisattva, they say, the life of others is more precious than his own.

It was a time before many births, when Brahmadatta ruled over Banaras. Bodhisattva was born as a golden deer, with large sparkling gem-like eyes, huge silver horns, a bright red mouth like the lotus flower, and a nice bushy tail like that of the Tibetan ox. He lived in a forest with a herd of five hundred other deer who respected and honored him and called him the "King of the Banyan Deer." Another beautiful golden deer, known as the Monkey Deer, lived close by attended by another herd of five hundred deer.

The king of Banaras was as fond of hunting as he was of eating meat. He would disrupt the work of the people in his city and command them to go hunting with him or for him. The people thought that, if there were a nearby grove full of deer where the king could find deer to his taste, they would not be constantly disturbed from their day-to-day work to go hunting. So they planted trees and grass in a grove and drove the forest herds of the Banyan Deer and the Monkey Deer into it. The deer were happy to be there where food and water were guaranteed and they were perfectly safe to wander around as they pleased.

The people told the king, "Now, O king, you will not have a difficult time chasing the deer around. We have brought them from the forest into a grove. Also, we will not be disturbed." The king entered the grove and saw the two golden deer—the Banyan deer and the Monkey deer. They were so beautiful that he decided never to kill them. However, the situation was different with the rest of the deer. The king would go to the forest himself or send his cook to shoot a deer for his meal. This created havoc for the deer, whose ears would stand straight up and whose eyes would freeze from fear. The sound or sight of an arrow would frighten them and they would run, gasping for life.

The Banyan Deer invited the Monkey Deer to discuss the matter and to find a solution which would not enrage the king and yet would be beneficial to their herds. In their meeting, the Banyan Deer said, "My friend, Monkey Deer, a lot of deer are being unnecessarily wounded and killed everyday. If we want to stop this, we must request the king to stop the killing. Let one deer each from my herd and your herd voluntarily take turns going to the king, putting his/her head on the block at the place of execution, lying down, and offering himself/herself to the king. In this way, the death of one deer will save all the others from constant fear, torture and wanton attacks. The Monkey Deer agreed to this suggestion, and so did the king. One deer would voluntarily die every day, and the royal cook would take it away to the palace. The king was happy to receive a deer for his meal every day, and the deer were happy to be able to enjoy their life without worrying constantly about the sword of death hanging over them.

One day it was the turn of a young roe from the Monkey Deer's herd to go to the place of execution. The roe was pregnant. She was tormented by the thought that her death would be the cause of her baby's death. She ran to the Monkey Deer in despair and said, "Save my baby, O lord, please let someone else take my place today. I promise that I will be willing to die as soon as the baby is born. Please don't let my baby be killed."

"I can do nothing," said the Monkey Deer. "I cannot ask anybody else to replace you. It is your fate and you need to face it."

In desperation the expectant mother ran to the Banyan Deer and pleaded for her baby's life. "Have no fear," said the Banyan Deer. "I will see what I can do." With these words, the Banyan Deer himself went to the place of execution. He lay there with his head on the block, waiting to be killed. When the king saw him, he asked, "My deer friend, I had granted you your life. Why are you lying here?"

"O, king," said the Banyan Deer, "Today was the unfortunate day for a young and pregnant roe to die for you. I could not ask anyone else to replace her. Therefore, I decided to offer my life instead. Kindly save her; let me die."

The king was amazed to witness this generosity on the part of the Banyan Deer, and he said, "My lord, the golden deer! Never have I seen anyone so kind and compassionate as to give his own life for someone else's. I am pleased with you, I will save you as well as the young roe. Get up and be free!"

"O, king, we are now safe, but what about the other deer? Who can change their unfortunate destiny?"

"Then they will be saved too," said the king.

"What about the other four-footed creatures who dwell in the forest? Will they too be safe, O, king?"

"They also will be free from the fear of death," said the king.

"The birds?" the Banyan Deer asked.

"The birds too," said the king.

"And what about the fish which live in the water? Will they be safe?" asked the Banyan Deer.

"Yes, they will be granted freedom as well," said the king.

The great Bodhisattva, the Banyan Deer, got up and blessed the king. "O, king, by being merciful and compassionate to the mothers, fathers, daughters, sons and to all the creatures and countrymen, you will enter the world of heaven after your body is dissolved at the time of death."

The king, thus advised by Bodhisattva, refrained from killing animals, birds, or fish. He never harmed anybody thereafter. In time, a beautiful son was born to the young roe, and his mother advised him to be in close company with the Banyan Deer, whom she remembered fondly and with great reverence. She said, "One is better off to die with someone like the Banyan Deer, than to spend one's life with the Monkey Deer."

Now the king's kindness had no bounds. No deer could be killed or wounded in his kingdom. The deer became safe but also quite arrogant. They would invade the crops of the people and feed on them or destroy them.

The farmers complained to the king, who said, "I will give up my life but not my promise. No one can kill any deer!"

The Banyan Deer was extremely unhappy to see this situation. He said to the deer, "From now on, no deer shall enter any farm, neither will anyone touch the crops. Let there be no fences put up to guard the crops; let there be only some leaves tied up near the field as a sign."

They say that after this time the crops stood straight in the field, untouched by the deer. There were only signs made of leaves tied around the fields, and it is said that no deer ever trespassed beyond those signs!

## *6.2 Mataka-Bhatta Jātaka: the power of an evil act*

It was the time when the dead were honored by the living, who offered them food of their liking. The living used to have a magnificent celebration called "the Feast of the Dead." The feast was supposed to satisfy dead relatives and in turn bring their blessings to the living. Generally, goats were ritually killed and offered to the dead, and then consumed in their honor.

Once some monks, having watched this ceremony, asked their teacher, the Buddha, "O learned lord, is it proper to kill innocent creatures to satisfy the dead? How can an evil act like killing an animal lead to obtaining merit?"

The teacher said, "You have expressed a noble thought, O mendicant. Let us not offer 'The Feast of the Dead.' There can be no advantage in taking life for the dead. Long ago, the wise men in the sky advised people against it, but this is a new *Yuga* (age) and the practice has started again."

The teacher then told the following story to his disciple monks, illustrating the effect of an evil act (of killing animals in religious rituals).

Long, long ago, when Brahmadatta was the king of Banaras, a learned Brāhmaṇa, well-versed in the Vedic scriptures decided to offer. "The Feast of the Dead." He asked his pupils to fetch a goat. When the goat had been brought, the learned Brāhmaṇa asked his pupils to get him ready for the ritual offering of the animal in the feast. "Bathe the goat in the river, place a garland around his neck, feed him well, and then bring him back," said the Brāhmaṇa.

The obedient students prepared the goat according to the orders of their teacher. The whole process of getting ready for the ritual put the goat in an extremely contemplative mood. He thought of his past lives, his actions, their impact and the future of the Brāhmaṇa who was determined to kill him.

Suddenly the goat laughed loudly—it was like the sound of a thunderstorm! "I am going to be free today from the misery of a goat's life! O, what joy it will be," said he to himself. But the next moment his laughter was replaced with tears flowing from his eyes. It was the pain he experienced within when he thought about the Brahman's destiny. "This poor Brāhmaṇa is going to experience a sad destiny (of becoming a goat) by killing me today. What I did is what he is doing, and for which he will suffer as I have. The power of the evil act won't go without effect," thought the goat to himself and was overwhelmed with compassion for the Brāhmaṇa.

The goat thus laughed and cried. A young Brāhmaṇa watched him and asked, "My dear goat! Your laughter was as sincere as your tears. What, may I ask, is the reason for this behavior? What is it that makes you laugh and what is it that makes you cry?"

"Ask this question in the presence of your teacher," said the goat.

The Brāhmaṇa's pupils took the goat to him and told him the whole story. "Why did you laugh and cry?" the teacher asked the goat.

"Five hundred births ago, I was a Brāhmaṇa as learned and well-versed in the Vedic scriptures as you. And I killed a goat in "the Feast of the Dead." As a result of this act, I have been born as a goat in the last four hundred and ninety-nine births. In each of those births I had my head cut off. But the end of my misery has come. Today my head will be cut off for the five hundredth time, and finally I will be free from this wretched life! Therefore, O, learned Brāhmaṇa, I laughed heartily. It was the laughter of anticipated freedom. But I could not help thinking about your act of killing me, the power of that evil act and the terrible fate that awaits you. Five hundred births as a goat and five hundred painful deaths is too much to bear! So I cried."

"Do not grieve or fear, my friend goat," said the Brāhmaṇa. " I will not kill you," he said.

The goat smiled and said, "You do not understand, O Brāhmaṇa. None can save me from death today. Today is the day of my death as well as freedom."

"I will protect you," said the Brāhmaṇa, "Do not worry."

The goat could not help being amused and said, "You do not know the power of an evil act. No one can protect me today."

The Brāhmaṇa ordered his pupils to release the goat, "We will not kill the goat," he said, and he let the goat wander around.

The goat began to eat leaves off a shrub growing near a huge rock. And suddenly lightning struck the rock, breaking it into pieces. One of the sharp pieces of the stone struck the goat's head and split it. The goat died as destined!

At that time the Bodhisattva was born in the form of a tree. After watching this event he seated himself in the sky and grieved for the multitudes of people with compassion. He thought to himself, "After witnessing the power of an evil act, would these people refrain from killing and destroying of life?"

In his low, smooth, soothing and compassionate voice, he said to the people, "If people only knew that a sinful act will cause a birth in misery, they would not kill the living, for the one who takes life will have to pay dearly with his own life. Such is the power of an evil act."

The people who heard this advice pondered over their own destiny and decided to refrain from taking life. They brought gifts for each other and did good deeds. It was a celebration of good karma. And heaven was filled with kind people.

# CHAPTER 10

# *Confucius: The Wisdom of Heaven*

## *1.0 Introduction*

Chinese mythology, much like Indian, is a mosaic of several traditional and religious beliefs. The three major strands which constitute the Chinese tradition are Confucianism, Taoism, and Buddhism (imported from India). These three systems of thought did undergo a period of sociological adjustments, but the end result was a tradition in which the constituting elements blended into one another so beautifully that to view it now as a homogeneous whole will not be an exaggerated idealistic generalization. While Confucian philosophy provided the guiding principles for ethical and moral behavior, the Buddhist system satisfied the innate human urge to go beyond the concerns of "this world" and ponder over such questions as the essential nature of life, death, time, afterlife, causation, etc. In Taoism the mutually exclusive concerns of Confucianism and Buddhism (that is being an ethically and morally perfect human beings vs. attaining enlightenment) were beautifully reconciled by presenting a world view in which a "gentleman" was not truly perfect without having experienced "Ultimate Reality." And the enlightened one was not truly enlightened unless he was a gentleman as well. These three are so much a part of the Chinese Psyche that any analysis of Chinese cultural traditions, including the mythological, is not complete without a description of the undercurrents of the three religious/cultural systems. However, this is not the place to discuss the relative influence of these traditions on the Chinese people. The aim here is to identify and understand these views, their origin in the sociocultural context of their time, and their contributions to the Chinese mythology. Our discussion on Chinese mythology is divided among three chapters. Chapter 10 focuses on a brief analysis of the Confucian thought. Chapter 11 focuses on the Taoist ideology. The Buddhist system in China has been already discussed in chapter 9 section 5.3–5-3. 1.

### *1.1 Confucius (551–479 B.C.)*

Confucius was born in 551 B.C., the son of a low level military official in the province called Lu (modern Shantung). His parents died when he was very young. Although he was extremely intelligent and ambitious, Confucius had to be satisfied with a job as a cattle and granary guard. He managed to educate himself through the study of the Chinese classics. Confucius believed that education was the key to the welfare of the people. At that time, education was largely restricted to the families of courtiers and noblemen. Later, under Confucius' guidance, the system of education was revolutionized and became accessible to the common people.

Confucius provides yet another dimension to the world of thought which was at the peak of its dynamism in the 5th century B.C. The name Confucius is the Latinized form of the Chinese characters, K'ung Foo-tze, meaning "the master K'ung."

## **2.0 Historical background**

The mythical period of the Golden Age (4000 B.C.) is marked by the establishment of the civilization of China. This was the time when the writing system, marriage codes, agriculture, and medicine were developed in China.

The period between 2000 B.C. to 600 B.C. marks the development of China under monarchy. The period of the Shang dynasty (1765 to 1122 B.C.) in north central China (specifically in the province of Honan) is highly acclaimed as the period of advanced civilization and culture. The Shang dynasty was overthrown by the tribes of the Chou dynasty at the end of the second millennium B.C. The Chou are often described as "barbarian invaders" who lacked the "cultural grandeur" of the Shang dynasty. The Chou dynasty established its empire on the basis of the feudal system. The entire kingdom was divided into smaller states ruled by dukes who were directly under the power of the emperor of the Chou dynasty. Although the system functioned quite well for a few hundred years, by the time of Confucius the political situation had drastically changed. The empire, consisting of more than 20 states spread over a region between the north of the Yellow River and the Yangstze, had become too large to be governed peacefully by the emperor. Also, the fragmentation of the kingdom into states of inequal sizes created an imbalance of power. The states constantly indulged in wars to gain more political power. Even within a state, the prince or duke often lacked controlling power, since lesser noblemen often wielded enormous power over the emperor.

This continuous struggle for power affected the whole structure of society. The aristocrats and the commoners had no common ground. It was the farmers and the common people who suffered the most during this time. In order to maintain the royalty and the noblemen in luxury, the common people had to pay exorbitant taxes without receiving any reward of education, security or personal advancement.

It was during this time that Confucius saw the immediate need for a sociocultural framework which would simultaneously preserve the old traditions and provide ample freedom to create a new system to satisfy the needs of the people. He analyzed the contemporary situation as a breakdown of interpersonal relationships and traditions which, according to him were essential for a stable society. As a remedy, he provided an ideology based on the principles, namely, *li, jen,* and *tao,* (see sections 6, 7, and 8) which was mainly responsible for the foundation of the United Empire of China.

## 3.0 Basic writings of the Confucian tradition

The Confucian tradition is believed to be consolidated in the five classics (*Wu Ching)* and the four books *(Ssu Shu)*. According to tradition, Confucius did not write the entire texts; rather, he wrote parts of them and carefully edited some of the rest. Confucius called himself a conveyor of the classical texts to the people. He had a great reverence for the ancient traditions, philosophical and religious, which according to him were treasures of wisdom to be highly valued by everybody.

The five classics of Confucius are:

(a) *Ch'un Ch 'iu* (Spring and Autumn Annals). (b) I *Ching* 'the book of changes' is the book of divination. It incorporates the principles of *Yin* and *Yang* as the cosmic forces which are deeply embedded in later Chinese thought. (c) *The Shu Ching* (Classic of History). (d) *The Shih Ching* (Classic of Poetry) is an anthology of poetry. (e) *Li chi* (Classic of Ritual) is the book of the principles of ritual.

The four books are:

(a) *Lun Yu* (The Analects), (b) *Mengtzu* (Book of Mencius), (c) *Ta Hsueh* (Great Learning), and (d) *Chung Yung* (Doctrine of the Mean).

It is believed that the first five were authored/edited by Confucius himself, while the four books were put together by his disciples Mencius (or Meng Tzu) (371–289 B.C.) and Hsuntzu (298–230 B.C.). The main thoughts of Confucius are outlined and elaborated in The Analects and the five classics. The Analects are the 'sayings of Confucius'—not necessarily his original thoughts but the concepts which he learned and interpreted in the sociocultural context of his time. They summarize his views on the structure of human society in its relationship to the traditions on the one hand and to individuals on the other.

## 4.0 Confucian philosophy

Confucius' philosophy has been variously called "optimistic humanism," "the sacred as secular" or "the philosophy of the ideal person." These definitions sum up the central theme in Confucian thought, i.e., the "magical power" which controls and shapes human life is human power. Confucius did not reject the "supernatural," nor the role of "spirits," "traditions," etc.; rather, he emphasized "human control" over the events or operations in this world. He did not see human beings as helpless creatures at the hands of powers which transcended human existence. Confucius' "this worldly" approach becomes evident when he insists on human effort being instrumental in shaping the individual's life as well as society. It is not by any supernatural power that human beings can achieve power, rather it is by constant improvement and effort. The "ideal" can be accomplished by "cutting,"filing," "carving," and "polishing."

> It is like cutting bones, polishing elephant's tusks, carving jade;
> it is like grinding stones. (Analects I. 15)

Confucius' focus on "this world" is immediately obvious in the following analect:

Chi-lu asked how the spirits of the dead and the gods should be worshipped. The master said, "You are not able even to treat humans appropriately. How can you treat the spirits appropriately?"

"May I ask about death?"

"You do not understand even life. How can you understand death?" (Analects XI. 11)

In the above analect, Confucius emphasizes the need to analyze and understand what is immediately accessible; i.e., life and human beings. Unless "this world" is completely understood it is not possible to understand issues related to phenomena beyond human reach (i.e., spirits, death, etc.).

## 5.0 The concept of heaven

The worship of ancestors, spirits, and anthropomorphic deities was popular in China from the earliest period of Chinese history. Heaven (or *Tian)* was believed to be the abode of the divine spirits and deities. It was further believed that *Ti* 'divine being' had the power to rule over the human world. The emperor was believed to be the representative of heaven on earth. He had the sanction and the power of heaven. The emperor established and ensured the rule of heaven on earth. He was believed to be irreplaceable, since he represented the *Mandate* (decree) of *Heaven* on earth.

This interpretation of the emperor's position changed when the Shang dynasty was replaced by the Chou dynasty. The replaceability of kings was justified by changing the interpretation of the concept of '*Mandate of Heaven*'. Firstly, the Chou rulers claimed that their takeover was still in consonance with the *Mandate* (decree) *of Heaven* since heaven, being the abode of the good and auspicious, sanctions what is good on earth. Royalty could claim authority and the right to rule only if it was good. Heaven was thus equated with the impersonal "good" rather than with an abode of anthropomorphic deity/deities. If the king was evil and opposed good, the *Mandate of Heaven* would promote "good" on earth by allowing the emperor to be replaced by another emperor.

This new interpretation reflected a change in the view of heaven, its power, and its relationship to human beings. The power of heaven was viewed as the power of virtue (goodness) and not of some inexplicable divine being. Moreover, this interpretation equated human virtue with divine virtue (i.e. only a virtuous king would be sanctioned by heaven).

Confucius accepted the earlier belief in divine beings. However, he rejected the unquestioned authority of heaven and emphasized its "moral" and "virtuous" character. He further stressed that by developing virtue (which is the attribute of heaven as well), human beings can create heaven on earth. Confucius thus ascribed the power to change and perfect society to human beings and not to any other external agency.

## 6.0 Society as a link between traditions and individuals

Confucius saw society as a product of, and therefore related to, traditions. Moreover, he argued that society was also the realm where individuals could fully develop and realize their potential. The underlying assumption in this ideology is that (a) society is influenced by both traditions and individual effort and (b) society maintains both traditions and individual innovations. This view was based on Confucius' belief in the all-pervasive principle of *Tao*. *Tao*, according to ancient Chinese beliefs, was the principle of harmony in the universe which Confucius treated as the highest virtue. Every individual, he felt, had the inherent capacity to cultivate this virtue *(jen)*. This virtue could be accomplished by adhering to the rules of propriety which he called *li*. Although *li* encompassed the rules of appropriateness (according to the principle of harmony) at all levels—cosmic, social, and interpersonal "Confucius emphasized the role of society in accomplishing *li*. He believed that "the perfect society" would be the one which would establish harmony between traditions (social, political, and religious) and individual innovations. Traditions for him represented the connection of society with the larger universe (i.e., heaven) as well as the rules of *li* (religious rituals) which would ensure harmony between society and the larger universe. Similarly, society as a whole provided a framework within which the individuals could cultivate *li* (rules of social behavior) which would ensure harmony among individuals. Confucius stressed the importance of *jen,* which he interpreted as the individual's potential to function in harmony with other individuals in society. Furthermore, Confucius argued that the accomplishment of virtue in the context of society and the cosmos is possible only if individuals cultivate it at the interpersonal level, within the family and among friends. This, he believed was the beginning of the attainment of *jen*. Thus he believed that *shu* 'fellow feeling' (the rules of propriety at the individual level) and the rules of "five relationships" within the family help individuals to develop virtue at the individual and social levels. In the following discussion, we will take a brief look at these principles of propriety at different levels.

Thus the basic philosophy of Confucius revolves around the following three concepts:

(a) the concept of *li*
(b) the concept of *jen*
(c) the concept of *tao.*

## 7.0 Li

The term *li* in its root meaning is "holy ritual," "sacred ceremony." *Li* refers not only to the sacrificial rituals which then existed in China, but also to the entire body of conventions and traditions of society.

By using the metaphor of *li* 'holy ritual', Confucius explains the structure of society by which individuals, much like sacrificial vessels, occupy certain positions according to their overall functional value(s). The function of a vessel in a holy ritual is defined in terms of its role in the overall ritual as well as in terms of its relationship to other vessels. Similarly, when individuals in society occupy appropriate positions according to their potential and their contribution to the society and maintain an appropriate code of behavior while interacting with each other, the society flourishes, like a well–accomplished holy ritual.

By using the metaphor of *li,* Confucius also linked and explained the social patterns of behavior with the traditional framework (including holy rites, etc.). Just as a ritual object exists and functions in harmony with other ritual objects and thereby fits into the overall structure of the ritual, similarly the individuals in a society must exist and operate in harmony with other individuals. It is this *li* 'the rules of appropriateness (harmony)' which ensures the success of the ritual (at the religious level) and the stability of the society. Moreover, the metaphor clearly focused on shared beliefs, their role in society, and the importance of "working together," which is part and parcel of *li* in any society. As Confucius points out "when employing the services of the common people behave as though you were conducting an important sacrifice" (Analects XII.2).

Thus *li* focuses on the creative and powerful dimension of human beings who, according to Confucius, have the power to create a "perfect society." Confucius did not deny the connection or harmony between heaven and earth, the divine and the human; on the contrary, he emphasized the role of human effort in actually realizing that connection at all levels (social, political, and individual). Virtue, the principle of harmony, is the quality which human beings share with heaven. The more they cultivate it, the closer they get to creating a replica of heaven on earth.

## 8.0 Jon 'benevolence, virtue'

*Jen* is the intrinsic capacity of the individual to live in harmony with the outer world. This potential makes it possible for individuals to live in harmony with other individuals in society. Thus at the social level, Confucius did not interpret *li* 'the rules of propriety' as the enforcement of social laws (needed for the stable society), but rather as the natural context of a system where individuals have an opportunity to develop/realize their inner capacity *(jen)* to live in harmony with others. Confucius further points out that *jen* can be cultivated/realized by developing reverence for all stations (e.g., king, nobleman, duke, farmer, etc.) in society, and more importantly, by assuming responsibility for one's position in society. For example, a king should respect his subjects and must not forget his responsibilities towards them as a king. Similarly, his subjects should respect the king and understand their responsibility toward him and toward society.

The ideal *jen*-person (the person who has fully accomplished *jen*), according to Confucius, would treat himself as a vessel in a religious ritual, and willingly follow social law, viewing the laws not as externally imposed demands on him, but rather, as the medium through which he can realize his own *jen*. According to Confucius, society becomes stable when this connection between the individual's *jen* and social laws is established and it falls apart when this connection is lost.

The Master's comment on Tzu-chien was "What a gentleman this man is! If there were no gentlemen in Lu where could he have acquired his qualities?"

> Tzu Kung asked, "What do you think of me?"
> The Master said, "You are a container."
> "What kind of container?"
> "It is a *húlién* (sacrificial vessel)." (Analects V.3)

Confucius assumed that there is a difference in the potential of the individuals in a society and thereby argued for a division of society into two groups: leaders (kings) and common people. However, he consistently emphasized that the ruler and the ruled should be in perfect harmony with each other like the different vessels in the sacrificial rites.

Confucius, while discussing the method of cultivating the virtue of *jen*, points out that one cannot develop *jen* as long as one leads a self-centered life. To develop *jen* or to learn to live in harmony with others, one has to first overcome one's selfish needs, desires, and ambitions, which interfere with the attitude of living in peaceful harmony with others. This view is elaborated in the following analect:

> Yen Yuan asked about *jen*.
> The master said, "To regulate one's conduct in accordance with *li* constitutes *jen*. If for a single day a person could regulate his conduct according to *li*, then that *jen* person will be in unison with the feelings of the people in the whole empire. One attains *jen* by practicing it on oneself, and not by relying on others." (Analects XII. 1)

Thus Confucius lays the ground work for the necessity to cultivate (as opposed to simply inherit) *jen*. The observance of rites (i.e. following *li*) is essential, but the guarantee of good human relationship is acquired by developing *shu* "fellow–feeling."

Confucius argues that human suffering is caused because human beings fail to understand others' needs, feelings, and potential, and this results in their imposing unjust demands on others. One would not hurt others (e.g., the king would not torture the citizens) if he placed himself in others' shoes. It is the ability to understand others by identifying with them that is called *shu*. One should treat oneself as the measure for judging the appropriateness of one's behavior toward others. *Shu* is thus viewed as the foundation of *jen,* since it is self-evaluation, self-understanding and self-criticism which leads people to a better understanding of others. The following analect illustrates the concept of *shu:*

Tzu-kung asked, "Is there a word which can guide us throughout our life?" The master said, "It is perhaps the word "*shu*." Do not do unto others what you 'Yourself do not want others to do unto you."

(Analects XV:24).

## 9.0 Tao 'the way, path'

The concept of *Tao* "the path, way" in Confucian thought is intrinsically related to the concepts of *li* and *jen* discussed above. Tao is interpreted as the harmony of society and the individual, conventions and individuality. While *li* can be viewed as the external framework for behavior, which is conventionally established, *jen* emphasizes the individual's moral and ethical development according to his/her position, role, and potential. When the external codes of conduct and the internal competence or capacity are in consonance with each other, the result is the "right tao"—the "right path."

## 10.0 Excerpts from Confucius' analects*

In this section, the major themes and concepts of Confucian philosophy are further illustrated with the help of appropriate analects.

### 10.1 The gentleman and the ordinary person

(i) Chi K'ang asked Confucius how to govern people, "If I kill a person who does not follow Tao for the sake of those who follow Tao, what would you think of it?"

Confucius said, "If you want to govern the people, why do you want to kill anybody? If (as an administrator) you want there to be virtue in the world, then people will become virtuous. The virtue of the gentleman is like wind. The virtue of common people is like grass. If the wind blows over the grass, it will bend. (XII: 19)

(ii) The master said, "The gentleman understands what is right (and wrong). The common people understand what is beneficial for them (and what is not beneficial for them)." (IV. 16)

### 10.2 Confucius on the supernatural and heaven/destiny

(iii) Po-niu was ill. The master paid him a visit. He held his hand through the window and said, "We are going to lose him. It must be destiny. What other reason could there be for a man like him to be attacked by such a disease?"

*Translations based on Chien, Mu. 1964. *Lun Yu Hsin Chieh* (New Interpreation of the Analects). Hong Kong: Hsin Ya Yen Chiu Suo.

(iv) Ssu-ma-niu looked worried. He said "Everybody has brothers. I am the only one who does not have any." Tzu-hsia said, "I have heard the saying that destiny determines life and death. Heaven determines wealth and honor. If the gentleman is respectful of everything and everybody, (for example) if he has *li* (observes all rites) everyone within the four seas is his brother. A gentleman does not worry about not having brothers." (XII: 5)

(v) Chi-lu asked how the spirits of the dead and the gods should be worshipped. The master said, "You do not know how to treat people (appropriately). How can you treat the spirits appropriately?"

"I beg to ask you about death."

The master said, "You do not understand life. How can you understand death?" (XI: 11)

(vi) Fan Chih asked about *'zhi'* (wisdom /knowledge). The master said, "To govern the people appropriately according to the ethical and moral responsibility *(yi)*, worship gods and spirits while keeping distance from them can be called wisdom. (VI.20)

(vii) The master does not talk about extraordinary, violence, disorder, and gods. (VII:21)

## *10.3 Li 'holy ritual'*

(viii) When sacrificial rituals are performed, one must worship the gods as though they were present at the ritual. The master said, "If I do not have reverence for the gods, it is like I am not performing a ritual (i.e., the ritual becomes meaningless)." (III: 12)

(ix) The master said, "Lead them by law, control them by punishments, and they will follow the law but they will not be ashamed of their wrongdoings. If you lead them by virtue, control them by *li*, they will be ashamed of their wrongdoings and they will eventually reach the goal intended by the leader. (II: 3)

*(x)* Tzu-kung wanted to eliminate the sacrificial sheep at the first day of the new moon (month). The master said, "You love the sheep but I love the *li* (ritual). (III: 17)

(xi) Meng Yi Tzu asked about filial piety. The master said, "No disobedience." Fan Chih was driving. The master told him, "Meng-sun asked me about filial piety and I have told him 'No disobedience.' Fen Chih asked, "What does that mean?" The master said, "When your parents are alive, treat them with *li,* when they die, bury them with *li* (afterwards) worship their spirits with *li.* (115)

## *10.4 Jen 'benevolence'*

(xii) Chung Kung asked about *jen*. The master said "When away from home behave as though you are meeting an important guest. The administrator should treat common people as though he is performing an important sacrificial ritual (in which they are participating). Do not do unto others what you yourself do not want others to do unto you. By doing so, you will be free from complaints and criticism in the country or in the family."

Chung Kung said, "Though I am not very smart, I shall try my best to do what you have said." (XII. 2)

(xiii) The master said, "Everyone wants wealth and a high position in the society. But unless I acquire them through the righteous way, even if I get them, I do not want them. Nobody likes poverty and lower status in the society. If I get poverty and lower status in the society, even when I do not follow the path which leads to them, I will not try to escape from them (at the cost of virtue). If the gentleman gives up *jen* then how can he be called a gentleman? The gentleman never leaves *jen* even for a short time required for eating a meal. A gentleman will not leave *jen* even when he is in a hurry or in a difficult situation." (IV.5)

(xiv) The master said, "I have never met a man who likes *jen* or a man who dislikes unbenevolence. If one likes *jen* he would realize that *jen* is the most important virtue. The one who dislikes unbenevolence is benevolent because he would not let unbenevolence touch him (he will not do anything that is unbenevolent)."

"Is there anyone who is willing to spend one day on benevolence? I have not met a man who did not succeed in doing this. Perhaps there are people who are not capable of doing it, but I have not met them." (IV.6)

## *10.5 Shu 'fellow feeling' (forgiveness)*

(xv) Tzu-kung asked, "Is there a word which can guide us throughout our life?" The master said, "It is perhaps the word '*shu.*' Do not do unto others what you yourself do not want others to do unto you." (XV:2 4).

## *10.6 Chung 'doing one's best' (loyalty, faithfulness)*

(xvi) Tseng Tzu said, "Everyday I evaluate myself by asking these three questions, 'While serving others have I failed to do my best? In my relationship with my friends, have I been honest and kept my promise? Have I taught others what I have not practiced on myself?' "

(xvii) Duke Ting asked, "How should the emperor treat his employees and how should the employees serve the emperor?"

Confucius answered, "The emperor should treat them with *li* and the employees should serve him with loyalty and full capacity (Chung)." (III. 19)

# CHAPTER 11

# *The Way of Tao*

## 1.0 Introduction

Taoism, alongside Confucianism, marks another important mood of Chinese thought, philosophy, and folklore. Taoism as a system of philosophy was developed in the 6th century B.C. in China as a reaction to the then existing sociopolitical and religious ideologies. The feudal system, which had been so extravagantly propagated and justified by Confucius, gave way to the oppressive autocratic government. The autocratic rulers were constantly at war with each other. The "wise gentlemen" of Confucius had preserved the "form" but had lost the spirit of the *li,* which allowed the traditions to continue but at the same time insisted upon the proper interpersonal relationships.

Confucius' philosophy did not seem to have brought peace and happiness to the common people. Society was ready for a new ideology which would introduce a new way of life. Taoism emerged both as an alternative as well as a complimentary philosophy to the existing Confucian world view. It was an alternative to the Confucian system in the sense that it rejected the Confucian method of creating a perfect society through exclusive reliance on deliberate human effort, without paying any attention to the natural and universal *Tao* of existences and their operation. However, it was still complimentary to Confucian ideology in that it did retain the central idea of "*Tao,*" albeit freeing it from its narrow Confucian interpretation of *Tao* as a method for creating virtue and morality.

## 2.0 Lao Tzu

Long before the development of Confucianism or Taoism, the concept of *Tao* was interpreted as the way to establish communication between heaven and earth. It was believed that shamans, kings and magicians had this "mystical" ability to establish the link between earth and heaven. By the time of the East Chou dynasty (770–256 B.C.) the term *Tao* had come to mean "the proper way" to do things, "the doctrine" of doing things the proper way (i.e., the extension of the meaning 'way'). The Tao, the proper way, thus was equated with the principles which govern the universe—the universal laws.

Although the blanket term Taoism refers to the branch of philosophy developed by various "masters" (teachers), Lao Tzu, a philosopher in the 6th century B.C. is generally accepted as the earliest founder of philosophical Taoism. The Chinese character for Tao has two parts. One part means "head" and the other means "to run." Together they mean the "way," the "path," "the principle" (i.e., that on which someone or something runs). *Tao* is the principle which governs everything in the universe. It is an abstract principle which is responsible for the beginning, existence, operation, and destruction of everything in the universe.

Lao Tzu's thoughts have been compiled in a text named after its author. The *Lao Tzu* is divided up into 81 chapters grouped in two books. Book one consists of 37 chapters and Book two includes 44 chapters. By the second century A.D. the text came to be alternatively known as, Tao-te-ching 'the way of virtue'. The discussion which follows is based primarily on this text.*

## 3.0 Tao and Te

*Tao* is a set of principles which govern the entire universe but are beyond the power of human beings. *Tao* is also viewed as the substantive source of the universe. It is often referred to as the "mother," "source," "ancestor," and " substance" of the universe. The universe is born of *Tao* (and according to Tao). Tao as a creator is similar to the "Eternal Waters" in Hindu mythology, according to which, the undifferentiated "Eternal Waters" is the source of the universe. *Tao* is *ṛta* 'cosmic order' and the "Eternal Water" in one—the source of the universe and the laws of the operation of the universe. It is the cause as well as the principle of existence of multiple forms, which emerge from it and go back to it after death. It is also the cause and the principle according to which the universe functions (i.e., the change of seasons, days and nights, the cycle of seed-plant-seed, water-vapor-water , etc.). It is in essence the underlying principle of the static (existential) as well as dynamic (operational) aspects of the universe. Thus, though *Tao* is abstract, its manifestations can be observed in the cycle of the seasons, day and night and other natural phenomena.

Lao Tzu distinguished *Tao,* the universal order, from man-made order of every kind; i.e., social, political, or religious. According to him, *Tao* is universal, natural, all-pervasive, and immortal. In contrast to this, man-made order is localized, artificial, limited, and temporary. *Tao* excludes man-made order, which is opposed to and interferes with *Tao*. Within the system of Lao Tzu, to conform to *Tao* is to adopt the attitude of *Wu Wei* (no action or inactiv-

*It should be noted that philosophical and religious Taoism are often discussed as independent systems due to their different emphases. While philosophical Taoism founded by Lao Tzu and his disciple Chuang Tzu stressed the universal principles of existence and operation of the world/universe, religious Taoism focused primarily on the religious rituals and practices needed to ensure longevity and immortality. In this chapter, the main focus is on philosophical Taoism. However for a brief summary of religious Taoism see section 13.

ity). *Wu Wei* is viewed as the essential feature of *Tao* which naturally creates and sustains everything without any intentional activity.

Lao Tzu's denial of man-made order is based on the assumption that all man-made orders imply a structure (of the universe) which is based on the differences among existences (e.g. human beings, animals, plants, etc.). Inequality, suppression, and hierarchical positions in a society emerge as a result of the basic ignorance regarding the underlying unity of all existences which are rooted into and regarding the underlying unity of all existences which are rooted into and governed by *Tao*. The understanding of *Tao* is the understanding of the underlying unity of all existences. Such understanding, according to the Taoist view, naturally leads one to the acceptance of all existences as equal. To understand *Tao* is to understand that there is no essential difference between the withering of a flower and the death of a human being or the first sprout of a seed and the birth of a baby. For all of these existences and functions are parts of an all-pervasive system of *Tao*. No existence is superior or inferior for they are all the "children" of the "mother" (*Tao*). The "holy man" understands the "children" (differences) but does not forget the "mother" (*Tao*).

Related to the concept of *Tao* is the concept of *Te*. *Te* is generally understood as 'virtue'. However, it does not refer to any acquired quality; rather, it means a natural quality, tendency, or potency in each individual existence, which makes that existence (human beings, plants, animals) what it is. The etymological meaning of *Te* is 'to get'. In this sense, it means the natural quality which individual elements in the universe receive/get from *Tao*. Since everything emerges from *Tao*, which is itself of the nature of *Wu Wei*, each existence accordingly receives or inherits this nature of *Wu Wei* (non-activity or naturalness). *Te* is thus *Tao* in particular existences, and it is in this sense the realization of the universal *Tao* in particular existences. It is due to this quality that all existences naturally conform to *Tao*. *Tao* and *Te* are thus two facets of the same phenomenon—one universal and the other particular. It is in this context that *Te* can be interpreted as 'virtue' in the moralistic sense, since *Te* is the quality within each individual which causes it to naturally conform to Tao—the highest principle responsible for the well-regulated patterns of existence and operation of the universe.

The recognition of Te is the recognition of the connection of individual existences with *Tao*, as well as the interconnectedness of all existences and phenomena. It is emphasized that every existence can develop its *Te* only in the context of the *Te* of other existences, and thereby each naturally belongs to *Tao*, which does not exclude anything.

*Te* is also interpreted as skill or a special talent which is the natural ability to harmoniously interact with other existences or with all existences in general. Thus a carpenter's *Te* 'skill' lies in working harmoniously with the grains (or the *Te*) of the wood; a teacher's *Te* 'skill' lies in working with the disposition (or the *Te*) of the students and so on.

## 4.0 The idea of harmony in Taoism

The ideal universe, according to Taoism, is the universe which functions in and according to *Tao*. The world of nature is the expression of *Tao* in which everything by definition follows natural laws without any deliberate effort being involved. Everything naturally accomplishes its potential (plants, trees, etc.). There is thus a natural harmony in nature, everything exists and functions only in conjunction with other aspects of nature. There is a natural order. Naturalness (as opposed to cultivated intendedness) and harmony (as opposed to separateness) are the key words for Taoism. Anything artificial and isolated from (artificial and therefore isolated) the laws of nature is viewed as a deviation from *Tao.*

## 5.0 Artificial is deviation

According to Taoism, when the harmony of nature is disturbed by human laws which separate human beings from other aspects of nature, there is deviation from the *Tao.* Any human effort to achieve anything or create anything in an unnatural way is viewed as deviation from *Tao.* The basic belief in Taoism is that human beings, if left alone and allowed to act naturally, will naturally choose a social, moral, and ethical order which is in conformity with *Tao.* For this reason, social order, aesthetic and moral laws arbitrarily created by human beings are viewed as deviations. Human order creates duality of values, i.e., good-bad, beauty-ugliness. It creates duality of positions: high prestigious rulers and lowly commoners. As opposed to this, according to Taoism everything fits into the universal structure of *Tao.* There is no duality of values in the world of nature. This view is observed in the following excerpt from *Tao te ching:*

*The relative opposites*

When the whole world calls the beautiful beautiful
There arises ugliness

When the whole world calls the good good
There arises evil.

Thus existent and non-existent create each other;
The difficult and easy
are always together.

The long and the short
are always relative to each other.

The high and the low
complement each other.

The sound and the
note are inseparable.

The past and the future,
the back and the front,
follow each other.

Therefore, the wise man acts without action
and practices without preaching.

*[Book One: II]*

## ***6.0 In praise of weakness***

In the above excerpt Lao Tzu dismisses the duality of values. He further follows this line of thought by dwelling on the positive aspects of apparently worthless objects and qualities. For example, in the following, Lao Tzu brings out the latent strength of the weak.

*(a) Strength of the weak*

Supple and weak is the person who is alive,
In death he becomes hard and stiff.
Grass and trees are soft and crisp when alive;
In death, they become dry and shrivelled.

The stubborn and strong are bound to die;
The supple and the weak are bound to live.
The aggressive use of weapons will not win.
The tree which is strong will be chopped off to make tools.

The strong and the big takes the lower position.
The supple and the weak takes the higher position.

*[Book Two: LXXVI]*

Another example that Lao Tzu uses to illustrate his point is the real usefulness of the seemingly worthless 'nothing"; that is, an empty space, which is considered to be nothing, is the absolute prerequisite for the usefulness of a wheel or a vessel, etc.

*(b) Usefulness of 'nothing'*

Thirty spokes
are joined
at one hub.
Because of the void
between the spokes

the wheel becomes useful
for the cart.

Knead the clay
in order to make a vessel
Because of the void
(inside the vessel)
the vessel becomes useful.

Cut out doors and windows
in order to make a house.
Because of the void
(inside the house)
The house becomes useful.

Therefore, it is because of nothing (void)
that something becomes useful.

*[Book One: XI]*

This philosophy of not categorizing anything as high or low, useful or useless (in general, avoiding all value-judgments), coupled with the fundamental assumption that every existence must live by and realize its own *Tao*, underlies the Taoist views of all ethics, morality and sociopolitical structures. In fact *Tao* does not remain merely an abstract philosophical concept; rather, it becomes the guiding principle of all human interactions. *Tao* in fact is supposed to be used as a political ideology as well. That is, a ruler must take into consideration the individual *Tao* of his subjects. Since the ruler and the ruled both belong to one *Tao*, the only way the ruler can justly rule is by 'yielding" to the wishes of his subjects. The following excerpt illustrates this concept:

*(c)* *To rule is to yield*

The highest accomplishment
seems incomplete.
Yet, when used
it will not be used up!

Great fullness
seems empty.
Yet, when used
it will not be drained!
Perfect straightness
seems curved.

Great talent
seems flawed.
Great eloquence seems silent.
Constant movement overcomes cold.
Immobility overcomes heat.
Passive and poised,
one can lead the empire.

*[Book Two: LXV]*

## *7.0 The nature of Tao*

*Tao* is all-pervasive. Therefore, it is not possible to define or fully describe it because definitions such as "this is *Tao*" necessarily imply that "something is not *Tao*," a view which goes against the very nature of *Tao*. It is for this reason that *Tao* is usually described by pointing out the inherent inadequacies of all types of definitions, using such descriptions as "*Tao* is nameless," "*Tao* is shapeless," and "*Tao* is immortal," etc.

The following excerpts illustrate the nature of *Tao* by emphasizing the limitations of the "names" and "shapes" in describing it, since names and shapes are capable of describing only entities bound by space and time. Since *Tao* is all–pervasive and timeless it transcends names and shapes.

*(a) Tao is nameless*

The *Tao* that can be spoken of
is not the absolute Tao.
The name that can be given
is not the absolute name.

*[Book One: I]*

The nameless was the origin of
heaven and earth
The named was the mother of everything.

*[Book One: I I I*

Therefore, empty yourself of desires
in order to understand
the subtle truth.
But you should have desire
to observe its manifestation.
The two are the same
but they have two different names.

They are deep and mysterious,
They are doors to the secrets.

*[Book One: III & IV]*

(*b*) *Tao is shapeless*

This is called the shape which is shapeless.
This is the image without an image.
This is called subtle and hazy.
If you confront it, you can not see its head.
If you follow it, you can not see its back.
Follow this law
Which has existed for a long time
And apply it to the present.
If we understand this origin of the law,
Then we can understand the essence of *Tao.*

*[Book One: XIV]*

Tao is viewed as not only beyond time and space but also beyond the limitations of life and death. Hence *Tao* is immortal. Consequently, the one who understands the true nature of *Tao* also becomes immortal and is free from the threats of the rhinoceros and the tiger, both of which symbolize death.

(*c*) *Tao and immortality*

Tao is immortal
From birth to death—
three out of ten live peacefully,
three out of ten live in misery,
three out of ten indulge in the pleasures of life
and dig their own grave.
Why is it so?
Because they place too much value on life.
For someone who knows how to protect his life
does not encounter a rhinoceros or tiger
while traveling on land.
He will not be touched by a weapon.
The rhinoceros will not be able to pitch its horn into him.
The tiger will not be able to use its claws,
nor will the soldiers be able to use their weapons.
(Because he himself will not indulge in any action).
Why is this so?
Because he will never get into a situation which will cause
danger or death.

*[Book Two: L]*

## *8.0 Metaphors of Tao*

Another method of describing *Tao* is the use of a series of metaphors, with each metaphor illustrating one of the dimensions of *Tao*, and thereby providing a glimpse into the all-pervasive nature of *Tao*.

*(a) Tao as the mother of the universe*

Since the universe of multifold existences emerges from *Tao*, it is not surprising that *Tao* is often described as the mother of the universe. The metaphor of the mother is particularly pertinent, since it is suggestive of the caring and nourishing qualities of *Tao*:

> Everything had a beginning.
> This beginning can be called the mother
> of the universe.
> Once you know the mother,
> you should know the child.
> After having known the child,
> You should return to the mother.
> Thus you will not confront any
> danger till the end of your life.
>
> *(Book Two: LII)*

*(b) Tao is like water*

*Tao* is often described as water due to its power of sustaining life. According to the Taoist system, both *Tao* and water share the quality of non-aggressiveness. Water flows toward the lower planes (without insisting on being on a higher level) while maintaining its vitality and life-nourishing quality. Similarly, *Tao* is not restricted to "higher" levels or orders of things, beings or phenomena. Also like water, *Tao* has no fixed shape of its own.

> *Tao* is like water.
> Highest virtue is like water.
> Because water nourishes every existence
> Without competing with them,
> And settles where everybody dislikes to be,
> it closely resembles Tao.
>
> *[Lao Tzu: Book One: VII: 20]*

*(c) Tao is empty*

*Tao* is called empty; by virtue of its being empty it can not be drained, and yet it has the capacity to hold anything inside. *Tao* is shapeless and yet contains all shapes—like an empty space that may contain or hold any shape. It is its formlessness, its nature of empty space, which gives rise to all structures or shapes in the universe.

It is by virtue of being empty (i.e., not being limited /restricted to a particular form) that *Tao* can encompass the whole universe. Thus, understanding *Tao* requires getting rid of the perception of all duality and distinctions such as sharp vs. blunt, order vs. disorder, light vs. darkness, etc.

*Tao* is empty
And yet its use will not drain it.
It is bottomless,
It is the origin of everything.
Blunt the sharpness.
Untie the knots.
Dim the light.
Dark and hazy it remains deep like water.
I do not know whose son it is—
An image of the ancestor of the Gods.

*[Book One: IV]*

## 9.0 What is not Tao

The essential character of *Tao* is further emphasized in *Tao-te-ching* by explicitly discussing what is not *Tao*. *Tao-te-ching* strongly stresses the harmony of all existences as the essential feature of *Tao* by arguing against disharmony. Disharmony at the social level is viewed as deviation from *Tao*. In particular, the unequal distribution of power and resources between the nobility and the common people, according to the Taoist view, goes against the very principle of *Tao* which implies harmony among all existences. Natural harmony should be manifested in equality among the people in a society. This ideology is illustrated in the following excerpt:

*(a)* *This is not Tao*
If I had only a bit of knowledge,
I would follow *Tao*.
I would be afraid to take the short cut.
The real *Tao* is straight and safe
but people like shortcuts.

The government is corrupt,
The fields are overgrown with weeds
(because no one wants to work on the farms)

The granaries are empty.
And yet there are people
who wear glamorous clothes

with swords by their sides,
They eat and drink
And they have too much wealth.
This is robbery.
This is not *Tao.*

Another quality of *Tao is* (see section 11) its non-judgmental attitude toward opposite forces. No value (i.e. good or evil) is placed on either force (e.g., high and low, day and night, etc.), since it is claimed that every existence has a place in the natural world. Thus a man-made parameter for judging existences as "good" or " evil," "clever" or "foolish," etc. is artificial and goes against the basic foundation of the principle of *Tao.* Thus according to *Tao*, a social system based on the artificially defined values of benevolence, smartness, righteousness, etc. indicates deviation and the fall of *Tao.* This thought is elaborated in the following excerpt:

***(b) The Fall of Tao***

When there are people
who abandon *Tao*
There are people
who have benevolence and righteousness.

When some people are capable and smart
There are others
who are hypocrites.

When six relationships are in disharmony,
There are still filial children
and caring parents.

When the government is corrupt
There are faithful ministers.

*[Book One: XVIII]*

## 10.0 Remedy for society

When *Tao* is not understood, there is disharmony in society which breeds corruption, and this leads to the oppression of the common people. The remedy for this problem is the "return to *Tao.*" According to the Taoist view, all "evil" arises from the (mis)perception of the universe as a structure of unrelated elements. Such perception places different absolute values (e.g., high-low, good-evil, etc.) on existences, thereby creating unequality among them. This misperception of unequality at the existential level further extends unequality at the level of importance. That is, some levels (e.g. human) are viewed as more important than others, and eventually some individual human beings are viewed as more important than other human beings. Thus an imbalance of power at the social level indeed emerges from the misperception of the world.

The remedy for the problem is the proper understanding of *Tao*, which treats all existences as equal. On the one hand, this understanding would lead human beings to create a society which recognizes the importance of harmony with other existences (e.g., animals, plants, etc.) and the importance of harmony and equality among the individual members of society. On the other hand, a society based on the principle of *Tao* would be *naturally* conducive to the development of the *te* of the individuals.

The Taoist message is to go back to *Tao* by "shutting the doors" to the artificial (man-made) world and returning to the natural world. The following verse illustrates this point:

### *(a) Remedy for the society*

Those who know *Tao*
do not say anything (They are silent).
Those who say something
Do not know the *Tao*.
Block the openings
Shut the doors.

*[Book Two: LVI]*

According to the Taoist view then, the key to happiness is to live in harmony with everything else in the world. Accomplishment results not from imposing one's will or action on others, but rather from "doing nothing" (not emphasizing one individuality over others). By understanding and accepting the *te* of others one lives a harmonious life and accomplishes everything. What appears to be small, easy, insignificant, and flavorless should not be treated with disdain for in such are the seeds of big, difficult, prominent, and delicious. The recognition of the "trivial" as "important" is the recognition of *Tao*. The ultimate virtue thus is "to be good to him who has harmed you" for this is the proof of understanding of the oneness of all phenomena. The person who harms others shows evidence of ignorance (of the oneness of all phenomena). On the other hand the person who exchanges a good deed for a harmful act shows evidence of the knowledge (of the oneness of all phenomena). The latter has understood the *Tao*, the former has not. This concept of "inaction" (non-imposition) is elaborated in the following verse:

### *(b) Action of no-action*

If you want to accomplish everything
Then start from doing nothing.
If you want to do everything
Then start from doing nothing.
If you want to enjoy flavor,

Then start with no flavor.
The big starts with the small,
many start with a few.
Do good to him who has harmed you.
If you want to accomplish
something difficult,
You need to start with something simple.
The difficult things in the world have their origin in something easy.
Big things have their origin in the small.
Therefore, the wise man never tries to be great;
that is why he becomes great.
One who makes hasty promises rarely keeps them.
For someone who usually thinks
that things are easy,
generally encounters difficulties.
Therefore, the wise man treats things as being difficult.
Therefore, at the end, he does not confront difficulties.

*[Book Two: LX I I I]*

## 11.0 Yin and Yang: the principles of existence and operation of the universe

The principle of *Yin* and *Yang* occupies the central position in the system of Taoism. It is the principle which, according to the Taoist view, governs the existence and the function of the universe. The terms *Yin* and *Yang* literally refer to the shady and sunny sides of the hills, respectively. However, during the development of Taoist thought, these two terms acquired several other meanings which describe the mutually opposite features of the universe i.e., active (*Yang*) and passive (*Yin*), warm (*Yang*) and cold (*Yin*), male (*Yang*) and female (*Yin*), etc. Thus eventually *Yin* and *Yang* came to be known as the principle which captures the nature of the universe in which existences can be categorized as pairs of opposites. Each existence, according to this view, came to be viewed as either *Yin* or *Yang*.

However, it is very important to note that *Yin* and *Yang* are not viewed as conflicting forces in Taoist thought, rather, they are viewed as complementary aspects of Tao, the universal order, since the existence of one presupposes the existence of the other. Thus the Taoist system describes the two as two sides of the same coin—*Tao.* This assumption is supported by the frequent references to the interdependent nature of the two, where it is claimed (Book one: II) that being and non-being, difficult and easy, long and short, front and behind are relative opposites.

A close affinity between *Yin* and *Yang* is further justified within the Taoist view on the basis of the belief that all existences (and thereby opposites) emerge from the same source (see the creation myths). They represent two dimensions of the universe. At any given point

Diagram 1. YIN and YANG

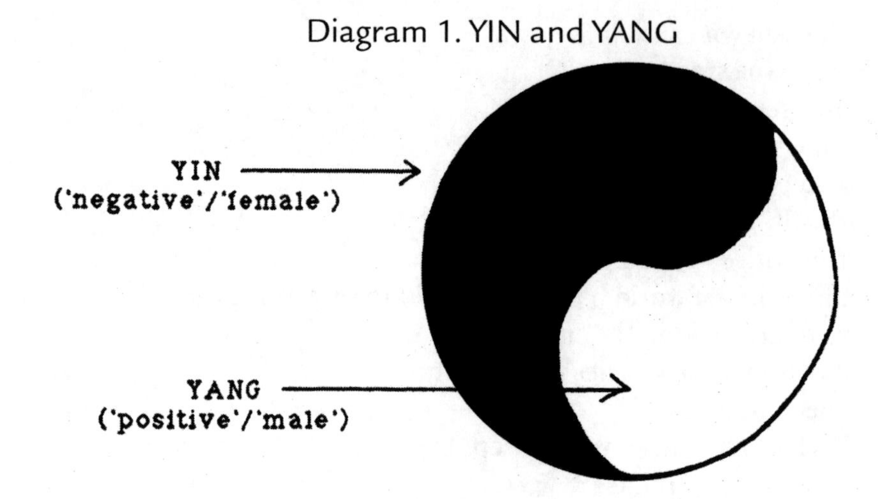


in time, the balance of *Yin* and *Yang* is necessary for the existence and continuation of the universe. The following diagram illustrates the balance of the opposites in the universe.

The principle of *Yin* and *Yang* is further viewed as the principle behind the operation of the universe. The cyclicity assumed in the operation of the universe is due to the fact that the balance of opposites must be maintained in order to sustain the universe. In other words, if creation and destruction are both necessary, then the former must be followed by the latter and vice versa. Once the creation of the universe took place, according to the Taoist view, the cyclical chain of operations started (e.g. creation-destruction-creation /day-night-day, etc.). This chain will continue as long as the universe continues to exist. Thus the *Yin* and *Yang* principle assumes that the occurrence/ existence of an event/element is always rooted into its opposite (its antithetical counterpart). This concept of mutual dependency is indicated in the diagram where a bit of *Yin* is present in *Yang* and vice versa.

This belief in the mutual dependency and inseparability of *Yin* and *Yang* has largely influenced the view of "good" and "evil" in Taoist thought. Since all existences can be categorized as *Yin* or *Yang*, and since *Yin* and *Yang* are interdependent, inseparable, and equally essential for the universe, their division into "good" and "evil" categories is meaningless. Thus no particular existence is viewed as "good" or "evil."

Diagram 2. Dynamic Aspect of YIN and YANG

*Tao* rejects not only all distinctions between "good" and "evil" but also "useful" and "useless," etc. It is for this reason that "the strength of the weak," "importance of inaction," and the value of 'low and dark,' etc. become some of the major themes of Taoist thought (see section 7.0).

Thus Taoist thought values opposites as equal and prescribes the same treatment to both. If one is to understand the universal *Tao*, one must understand the importance of both components of the pairs of opposites. "Knowing the male but keeping the female one becomes a universal stream." (Book One: XXVIII)

The concepts of "good" and "evil," according to the Taoist view, arise only as a result of a particular point of view. They are relative and not absolute concepts. It is only when a particular existence is viewed as beautiful, according to *Tao,* that the concept of ugly emerges. To understand *Tao* is to understand the equal importance of all existences which function harmoniously in the global network of *Tao*.

The only "evil," according to *Tao*, is not accepting the equality of all existences and thereby imposing one's own views/power on others. This is a deviation from *Tao*. Ostentation, pride, oppression of those who are weaker, and boasting all are viewed as deviations and therefore undesirable. The Sage never discriminates between the high and the low—whether in the context of trees or human beings. He judges all opposites as equal. He does not rejoice in happiness nor does he grieve in sorrow. He treats happiness and sorrow alike—as two sides of the same *Tao*. The following excerpts illustrate (a) the role of *Yin* and *Yang* in the creation of the world, and (b) the importance of treating opposites alike.

### *(a) The role of Yin and Yang in creation*

From the Tao emerges one: from one emerge two,
From two emerge three,
and from three—innumerable creatures.
Those multitudes of creatures carry
on their backs the yin and embrace
in their arms the yang and are a
blending of the generative forces of the two.

*[Book Two: X L I I ]*

### *(b) Know the male but keep the female*

Know the male
but keep the female;
Then eternal virtue
will always be with you.
And you will return
to the state of childhood.
Know the white
but retain the function of the black
And you will be the empire's ideal
And eternal virtue

will be with you
And you will return to freedom.
Know pride (high)
But retain the function of humility (low)
And be a valley to the empire.
And if you are a valley to the empire
Then eternal virtue
will be with you.
And you will return to
the unchiseled block.

*[Book One: XXVIII]*

## 12.0 Creation myths

The following creation myths of Taoist origin illustrate some of the basic aspects of the Taoist world view. The existence of chaos before the creation of the universe refers to the undifferentiated state of mass which has the potential to create a well-structured world full of multitudes of forms. Creation in these myths is viewed as the emergence of structure out of chaos. It is also the creation of many forms from one source. The death of *Hun-tun* (in the first myth) and the death of *P'an Ku* (in the second myth) suggest the disappearance of chaos at the time of the creation and, more importantly, the close affinity of creation and destruction, life and death.

Another dimension of the creation myths is their repeated emphasis on the necessity of opposites for creation as well as for the sustenance of the world. The principle of *Yin* and *Yang* which underlies the Taoist view of the world thus suggests that (a) opposite forces (e.g. light and darkness, man and woman, heaven and earth, etc.) rely on each other for their existence, (b) they emerge from a common origin, and (c) they are equally necessary for the maintenance of the world.

In this view of the creation of the world lies the explanation for the acceptance or desirability of opposites in Taoist ideology, according to which the very existence of an element (being) depends on its opposite (non-being). A mountain is viewed as tall and huge because a blade of grass is short and small.

### 12.1. Creation from Hun-tun 'the chaos'

Before the beginning of the universe, there was an undifferentiated chaos; there were no plants, no buds, no animals, no human beings—the world of infinite structures did not exist at that time. *Shu*, the god of the southern ocean, and *Hu*, the god of the northern ocean, always met each other in this land of *Hun-tun*. *Hun-tun* was very kind to them, and always treated them well. *Shu* and *Hu* wanted to return *Hun-tun's* kindness. They said, "Everybody has seven orifices for the purpose of seeing, hearing, eating, and breathing. This kind Hun-tun does not have any. Let us try to dig those orifices in *Hu-tun*."

Thus *Shu* and *Hu* together dug seven orifices in Hun-tun, one each day for seven days. And at the end of the seventh day, *Hun-tun* died.

### 12.2 P'an Ku—the creator of the world

It was the time before heaven and the earth were separated. There was only a formless all-pervasive mass; it might be thought of as an egg waiting to be hatched. It was the time before the birth of the world of forms. There was no separation of *Yin* and *Yang* then—only one undifferentiated chaos pervading the universe.

After 18,000 long years, one day P'an Ku was born after breaking the egg. He was a dwarfish looking man with an axe. Soon after he was born, he separated the egg into two parts—*Yin* and *Yang*. *Yang* was the lighter of the two. Hence it went up. This was heaven. *Yin* was the heavier of the two. Hence it stayed down. This was earth. Thus P'an Ku created heaven and earth. But because he was worried that they might get back together, he kept pushing them apart with his hand; he pushed heaven up and with his feet and he pushed the earth down. This was the beginning of the world. Afterwards, P'an Ku created the sun, the moon, and the bright and shiny stars. In this task he was helped by a dragon, a unicorn, a tortoise, and a phoenix. Each of these supernatural creatures had a function of its own—the dragon was made of *Yang* and the unicorn was both *Yin* and *Yang*. And the tortoise possessed the secret of life and death. The phoenix helped create harmony in the universe, since its feathers were a blend of five different colors. These four creatures represent the necessary ingredients of human life.

Thus creating a harmonious universe, P'an Ku grew ten feet every day for 18,000 long years. And then came the time for P'an Ku's death. Ceaselessly continuing his mission of creation till the final moment, at last P'an Ku died. His head was transformed into the mountains; his breath became the wind and the clouds; his voice became the thunder; and his limbs the four directions of the atmosphere. His skin and hair were transformed into herbs and trees. His teeth turned into various kinds of metals, his bones into rocks and the marrow into precious gems. His blood flowed in the form of the rivers; his heart became the soil. His long beard changed into bright constellations, and his sweat turned into the rain and insects crawling on his body became human beings. P'an Ku thus became the fashioner of this universe both in his life and death.

## 13.0 Religious Taoism

In the preceding sections we have discussed what is generally viewed as philosophical Taoism. Religious Taoism, which represents the practical dimension of Taoism, is different from philosophical Taoism.* While the philosophical Taoism of Lao Tzu and his disciple Chuang Tzu is primarily concerned with describing and explaining (to the extent it can be 'explained')

*The history is not clear regarding the exact relationship and relative chronology of philosophical and religious Taoism. However, scholars believe that religious Taoism did not develop before the 3rd to 4th century B.C.

the nature of *Tao* and its relationship with all forms of existence, religious Taoism is more concerned with the methods/rituals of achieving immortality. However, these two are not completely separate from each other. Philosophical Taoism emphasizes the immortal nature of *Tao* as well as the transient nature of all existences. It is also argued in philosophical Taoism that the *Tao* exists in every existence, in fact it is the immortal essence of all transient phenomena. Thus the realization of identity with *Tao* is the realization of one's true identity and thereby immortality. Although there are several references to the real *Tao*-nature and the immortality of all existences in *Tao-te–ching,* there is no clear, concrete method suggested which would 'liberate' the true 'immortal' spirit of *Tao* from the perishable form of the body. Religious Taoism assumes the philosophical Taoist ideal of "becoming one with the *Tao* by liberating the spirit," but focuses more on the methods to be used to achieve immortality.

## *13.1 The search for immortality*

The goal of religious Taoism was to preserve the immortal essence *chi* 'primordial breath' within the human body by following Taoist techniques, which included internal techniques such as meditation on the "immortal" essence, as well as drinking the elixir of immortality. The two techniques came to be known as *wai-tan* 'outer/external alchemy' and *nei-tan* 'inner alchemy' respectively.

The term *wai-tan* 'alchemy or elixir of immortality' also represents the religious practices related to the preparation as well as consumption of the drink of immortality. The drink was ritually prepared by mixing carefully selected ingredients, including special kinds of stones and metals. It was believed that these contained magical "divine" powers. It was further believed that a knowledgeable priest must carefully choose a holy place for the ritual, select the right ingredients, and ritually carry out the operation of mixing and blending the ingredients in a caldron. Prayers were also to be offered and magical formulas chanted by the priest to ensure the success of the process. It was believed that the ritual blending of the ingredients symbolically suggested the return to their elemental or original state of the diverse existences in the phenomenal world. The ingredients would lose their individual character in the process and were symbolically transmuted into the fundamental undifferentiated state of immortality which existed before the creation of the world of multiple transitory forms. The drink, according to the belief of the Taoists, had the power of blessing the drinker with longevity or immortality.

The method of *Nei-tan* primarily concentrated on preserving the eternal spiritual essence within the body by following physical as well as mental exercises.

According to Taoist belief, the *chi,* primordial breath, the all-pervasive void, or cosmic energy, created the world through the separation of *Yin* and *Yang* (which were earlier blended together in *chi*). *Chi* exists in all existences. It was further believed that the human body had three primary components—*chi* (primordial breath), *ching* (pure essence), and *shen* (soul). These, according to the Taoists, are located mainly in the mind, heart, and the part below the navel. The life force *chi* is used up when the body and mind indulge in worldly actions (eating, breathing, sex, etc.). Once the *chi* is used up, *shen* (which is often called *Yang*) leaves the body. This is viewed as death. Thus, in order to achieve immortality, it is necessary to conserve the *chi*. It was considered important to assume the attitude of nonindulgence (mental or physical) while operating in the world. This, it was believed, would lead to the preservation of *chi* and thereby immortality, or at least longevity. The positive method of breath-control was also prescribed for the preservation of energy. It fact, it was claimed that mental exercise which involved meditation and concentration on one (*Tao*—as opposed to being distracted by many objects in the external world) was a necessary ancillary to conserve *chi*. Many scholars believe that the causal relationship (in the Taoist view) between meditation and the strengthening of mental power was influenced by the *Ch'an* Buddhist (see Chapter 12) emphasis on meditation. Similarly, non-ejaculation of the semen, it was believed, would contribute to the conservation of energy and the extension of life. Like the practice of Yoga in Hinduism, religious Taoism emphasized several exercises (mental and physical), to avoid the influence of the body (which was viewed as *yin*) so that the vital energy could be preserved and *shen*, the soul, would not abandon the body.

Another noteworthy development in religious Taoism is the deification of Lao Tzu and *Tao*. Symbols (e.g. idols, diagrams, etc.) were introduced to help the followers' concentration on one *(Tao)* and thereby avoid getting lost in the world of many forms (i.e., innumerable reflections of *Tao*).

Underlying the diverse practices of *wei-tan* and *nei-tan*, the basic goal (to become one with *Tao)* remained unchanged. The fundamental analysis of the world—that is, its creation and operation—was not altered in religious Taoism. Religious Taoism thus provided a bridge between the philosophy (i.e., the conceptual framework) and the practice of the principles of Taoism.

# CHAPTER 12

# *Zen: Looking Inward*

## *1.0 Introduction*

Zen teaching is believed to have originated with the Buddha himself. Lecturing in Vulture Park, the Buddha wanted to communicate the experience of the ultimate reality to the people who had gathered to listen to his sermon. The Buddha kept silent while the audience waited to hear his sermon. Finally, he held up a lotus flower in his hand. Most of the people did not understand what the Buddha meant, but one person, (according to the legend, Bodhidharma) did understand and simply smiled. The Buddha wanted to convey that there can be no substitute (i.e., nothing like a definition or description) for the living flower. Similarly, there can be no words for the experience of reality. Direct experience cannot be fully grasped or communicated in words.

The above story is held to be the basis of the Zen ideology according to which the experience of the ultimate reality (enlightenment) cannot be communicated through any medium (e.g. words, symbols, etc.) or by any method. Philosophical, religious, and linguistic frameworks only distort the experience, since each brings in its inherent conceptual and methodological bias to the analysis of the experience. Therefore, there is no substitute for the direct, unmediated experience of the ultimate reality (enlightenment).

Bodhidharma, the Indian Buddhist monk mentioned above, is reported to have brought *Ch'an* (the Chinese equivalent of *Zen*; both *Ch'an* and *Zen* are derived from the Sanskrit word *dhyāna* 'meditation') from India to China in about 500 A.D. Bodhidharma, according to a Chinese legend, insisted that he had no name. He said that it is the name and form which hamper the knowledge of reality. We try to determine the nature of reality through the prism of our mind, which lacks clarity due to its preoccupation with millions of thoughts about infinite objects and also by a method (scriptures) which is constrained by its very conceptual framework. Thus we never understand the "real" nature of the reality of which we are part. Direct knowledge of reality (Buddha-nature) can be gained only by getting rid of the "impurities" of mind and going beyond method.

## *1.1 Basic philosophy and the development of Zen Buddhism*

The major feature of Zen is its assumption that any method or training is a process of conditioning. It creates a barrier between reality and the mind. The mind is conditioned into conceptualizing reality within a particular framework. In the process, the mind loses its ability to experience reality directly. The mind experiences only what can be formulated within a given framework. Zen thus treats all forms of conceptualization, including words and ideologies, as traps which do not leave the mind free for direct contact with reality. It is important to note that Zen is not against any methodology, per se; rather, it insists that any methodology reveals only a form which should not be taken to be the true reflection of reality. Once one realizes the limitation of any process of conceptualization, one is free of it. Reality is the content, the substance which one must grasp directly; its conceptualization is the process of giving reality a garb, a form. One must be able to see the reality after stripping it of the form.

According to the Zen ideology, a description of a lotus flower is only a description—not the lotus flower itself; a description of the moon can not impart the experience of the moon itself. Any description of reality, scriptural or otherwise, can only approximate reality. Those who rely on methods and ideologies to understand reality are those who take the finger (which points to the moon) as the moon.

The Zen emphasis on "going beyond method" (i.e., the established norm(s) of conceptualizing reality) is better understood within the historical context of the period of the introduction of Zen into China in 520 A.D. The Chinese Buddhists of that time mostly belonged to the Mahāyāna sect and were engaged in translating, interpreting, and commenting on the Mahāyāna texts (i.e., *Lankāvatāra Sūtra, Prājnā Pāramitā Sūtra,* etc.). Their philosophical discussions related to various doctrines of Buddhism expounded in the Mahāyāna scriptures, primarily aimed at the intellectual assimilation of Buddhism in China. The major motivation behind the study of the Buddhist texts was zeal for grasping logically, analytically and intellectually, the nature of enlightenment. However, as many scholars have correctly noted, the practical side of enlightenment, outside its doctrinal content (i.e. *dhyāna* 'meditation') was largely overlooked. It is in this context that Bodhidharma introduced Zen ideology in China.

## ***2.0 Zen Buddhism in China***

Bodhidharma had emphasized the experiential dimension which involves personal and intuitive knowledge of enlightenment, as opposed to its objective, analytical and intellectual understanding. Hui-neng (637–713 A.D.), the sixth patriarch after Bodhidharma, thus founded the Zen system of thought in China with a special emphasis on (a) the direct and personal approach to the experience of enlightenment, (b) *Ch'an* (the Chinese adaptation of the Sanskrit word *dhyāna* 'meditation') which identifies "looking inward" into one's own real nature as the way to enlightenment, and (c) abandonment of the fixed, established scriptural methods for direct insight, which according to Zen ideology was the essence of the Buddha's teachings. Thus Zen, without abandoning the objective and intellectual knowledge of enlightenment, harmonized it with its direct and personal intuitive experience.

There are many legends about Hui-neng—-specifically, about his deep understanding of the enlightenment. This, it is claimed, he received not through any established method, but rather, through reflection on his own nature. In fact, according to one of the legends, Hui-neng was originally a rice-pounder at master Hung-jen's house, It was only later, when Hung-jen realized Hui-neng's spiritual accomplishment, that he offered him the traditional robe of a patriarch.

It is believed that it was a learned pupil of the patriarch Hung-jen who interpreted the body to be like the Bodhi-tree (meditating under which Gautama Buddha had attained enlightenment, see also chapter 9, sections 2.7–8), and the mind to be like a mirror. According to this pupil, the message of religion is that one must keep the mirror clean (devoid of dust) to achieve understanding of the "true-nature." It is when the mirror is dusty that the "realization of the 'true-nature"' becomes hazy. In contrast to this, Hui-neng claimed that all of this description of the "true-nature" was wrong. If there was nothing (emptiness) to begin with, how can there be a tree of body and the mirror? If there is no duality, how can there be talk of a mirror and dust?

The patriarch Hung-jen realized that Hui-neng had understood the "true-nature" or Buddha-nature, which does not admit duality of any kind at any level—spiritual or physical.

Hui-neng thus opened up a new, fresh view of Buddhism in China, emphasizing "looking inward" as opposed to "looking outward" as the solution to the problem of understanding reality. After Hui- neng, various schools of Zen Buddhism were established in China.

## 2.1 Zen Buddhism in Japan

Now let us take a brief look at the establishment and development of Zen Buddhism in Japan. Zen was known in Japan centuries before the Kamakura period. Shotoku Taishi (574–662) wrote commentaries on Vimlakīrti's *Lotus Sūtra (*a treatise on Zen beliefs). Similarly, the Hossō and Kegon schools had already introduced Zen meditation in Japan during the Nara period (710–794 A.D.); however, these schools did not meet with much success. Myōan Eisai (1141–12 15) and Dōgen Kigen (1200–1253) were the two prominent personalities who were responsible for the foundation and propagation of Zen Buddhism in Japan during the Kamakura period. Eisai was ordained into Tendai Buddhism at Hieizan. However, wanting to grasp the original insights into the essentials of Buddhism, he was not satisfied with the knowledge he had received in Japan. For this reason, he planned to visit India and China. He studied *Ch'an* in China, specifically concentrating on *zazen* (physical and mental exercise, see section 5.0) and *koan* (riddles, see section 6.0). When his efforts to travel to India failed, he returned to Japan and decided to propagate Zen as a compromise between the Tendai Buddhism of Japan and Lin-chi (Rin-zai) Buddhism of China. He emphasized meditation as a crucial aspect of the Buddhist system but placed it within the Tendai structure in his well-known work *Kōzen gokokuron.*

Thus Eisai blended the doctrine of "direct looking into one's nature within oneself," with the esoteric (*mitsu*) practices of Tendai and Shingong Buddhism. The doctrine of "personal" and "intuitive" understanding of reality was enthusiastically welcomed in Japan, where other Buddhist sects stressed either faith (Pureland Buddhism) or complicated religious practices (Shingong and Tendai Buddhism). Eisai placed *koan* (riddles) in the center of his teachings.

Koans, according to Eisai, provided a "gateway" to enlightenment. Meditating on the koans and thereby losing himself, the seeker could achieve insight into reality. Finding an answer to a koan was an exercise of "cutting through the barriers of conditioning." The mind could reach the answer to the riddle only when it was totally free of the barriers of mental conditioning which obstruct reality. Once the seeker breaks through these, he no longer tries to conceptualize reality; rather, he has the sudden, direct experience of it. Thus, Eisai focused on the deconditioning of mind through meditation on *koans* and sudden enlightenment.

Dōgen, who introduced the Soto school of Zen into Japan in the early thirteenth century, had close contact with Eisai. However, he received his training under a Chinese Zen master of the Soto (*Ts'ao-tung* in Chinese) sect of Buddhism, which led him to enlightenment. The major contribution of Dōgen's system was his emphasis on *zazen* (seated meditation) as opposed to *koan*. Dōgen viewed enlightenment as a gradual and not a sudden process. He did not totally reject the authority of the scriptures (although he denied their primacy in the process of enlightenment); nor did he ignore the physical state of the body. If the body and mind are responsible for creating the barriers between the individual and reality, then, according to Dōgen, a proper training of body and mind is necessary to "drop off the body and mind." *Za* is the "proper posture" in *Zazen*, while *zen* is meditation. Thus meditation releases the mind, while *za* releases the body, and together they help the seeker go beyond body and mind. In order to attain enlightenment, one has to free oneself of I-ness (ego caused by the body) and also the thought (caused by the mind) of attaining enlightenment. *Zazen* is not the process of gaining anything; rather, it is the process of emptying oneself of the awareness of body and mind. It is neither a system nor an ideology; it is only practice—a continuous "emptying" without any goal of attaining anything—not even enlightenment. In the experience of *zazen*, similar to that of enlightenment, the individual goes beyond the body and mind and experiences emptiness as the essential Buddha-nature of all beings in the world. For Dōgen, koan is an intellectual exercise while *zazen* is an experience and an intuitive understanding devoid of any duality. There is no desire for enlightenment, there is no seeker of enlightenment. There is no distinction of time or space. Nor is there any difference between cause and effect. In *zazen*, there is an experience of emptiness.

In the following sections, some of the basic concepts of Zen (i.e. *Śūnyatā, Satori* and *koans*) along with the myths or stories that are used to illustrate those concepts are explained in detail.

## 3.0 Śūnyatā 'emptiness'—the ultimate reality

The following questions can be asked in this context: What is reality? What is the nature of reality? How (i.e. by which method/process) does one grasp/realize reality? How does one relate to reality (i.e. the relationship between reality and human beings)?

According to Zen, in accordance with the basic tenets of Buddhism, reality is emptiness (*Śūnyatā*), which encompasses the totality of all existence in the universe. This reality is generally illustrated by a circle. It is full as well as empty. It is full because it contains every existence; it is empty because it does not contain any particular form. Each existence (including humans, animals, plants) has its roots in this infinite *Śūnyatā*. Particular formal identities are transitory; they come and go. The ultimate reality is permanent.

*Śūnyatā* 'emptiness' is the central concept in all schools of Buddhism. In fact, as early as the 2nd century B.C., Buddhist teachers were known as *Śūnyatā*vadins 'those who believed in and taught the doctrine of emptiness'. While *Śūnyatā* is believed to be the nature of reality in every school of Buddhism, its interpretation varies from one school to another. While the Mādhyamika school of Mahāyāna Buddhism, led by Nāgārjuna, emphasized the emptiness of all existences (i.e. there is no self-existent existence), the Yogācāra school of Mahāyāna, led by Asanga, stressed the emptiness of consciousness. The Zen masters emphasize the realization of emptiness, which is the true-nature of reality, through the practice of meditation. *Zazen* releases the individual from the trap of concepts and ideas which create a barrier between the individual and reality. Once the barrier of concepts and forms is dropped, there remains only the realization of *Śūnyatā*. In Zen, *Śūnyatā* is described as 'Buddha-nature', true-nature', 'Buddha-mind', or 'reality' in Zen, these are all the same.

According to Zen, it is the ego, the I-ness, which separates one existence from all others (other human beings, animals, and plants and the inanimate world) as well as from *Śūnyatā*, the ultimate reality. If one detaches oneself from the form of ego, then one can realize one's identity with *Śūnyatā* as well as with other existences. Satori 'enlightenment', according to Zen, is this realization of one's identity, one's true nature, *Śūnyatā*.

The dynamic Śūnyatā is the substratum of all forms of existence. Nature, according to Zen, expresses the operation of *Śūnyatā*. New forms are created (trees for example); they sustain themselves and die and are replaced by other forms. The transitoriness is at the level of particular forms. At the ultimate level, there is no destruction, since the ultimate reality is devoid of forms.

Zen stresses the importance of the relationship of human beings with nature. Human beings must realize that, since they are one of the myriads of forms of nature, they are just as transitory as other forms of nature. Thus they are at once part of nature (and related to the other forms of nature) and to Śūnyatā 'emptiness', the ultimate reality.

## *4.0 Satori 'enlightenment'*

*Satori*, within the Zen system, is the state of consciousness which Gautama attained under the Bodhi-tree when he became Buddha 'the Enlightened one'. This state is variously described as *Nirvāṇa* (in Indian Buddhism), *Wu* (in Chinese Buddhism), and *Satori* (in Japanese Buddhism). Satori can be defined by looking at it from three perspectives: the way it is attained, the kind of state it is; and its impact on the 'Enlightened one'.

### *4.1 The method for attaining Satori*

When viewed from the first perspective, *Satori* is the understanding at which one intuitively arrives by looking directly into one's own nature. It is the direct realization of one's own nature, the nature of the world, and of the Buddha-nature, since according to Zen all three are the same. This understanding is not attained by any method—scriptural or other; nor is it attained through logical analysis of one's own nature and of that of the world. It transcends all methods of logical analysis. However, its experience is direct and unquestionable, similar to the experience of love which transcends empirical proof and/or analysis.

## *4.2 The nature of Satori*

When defined on the basis of the nature of its experience, *Satori* is the experience of *Śūnyatā* 'emptiness,' which, according to Zen, is the true nature of reality. It is the realization of the emptiness of all forms (including one's own) in the phenomenal world. It is the realization that individual forms do not have self-existence, i.e., they do not exist permanently, nor do they exist independently of other forms. The only self-existent (permanent and independent) reality *is Śūnyatā* 'emptiness'.

*Satori is* the awareness of the interrelatedness of all phenomena which emerge from emptiness and return to it. As long as one is "trapped" into the ego (I-ness) and divides the world into separate forms, one fails to see the interconnectedness. It is when one "drops" the ego (I-ness) through Zen meditation, that one sees their real, empty nature.

This state is often described as the merging of all dualities—I-ness and other forms, pleasure and pain, knower and knowledge, observer and the observed. The 'Enlightened one' does not crave anything, since there is nothing to crave (since everything is emptiness). He (he/his is used throughout in its generic meaning) is detached from the world of forms (including himself) but is connected with all forms, since he sees them as interconnected, rooted into emptiness. This is the realization of Buddha-nature (the real nature of all forms) which is *Śūnyatā* 'emptiness'.

## *4.3 The impact of Satori*

The impact of *Satori* 'enlightenment' is described variously in Zen literature. The 'Enlightened one' (realizing the essential emptiness of all forms) sees them all simply as forms; nothing more, nothing less. He does not treat them as separate self-existent entities; nor does he become attached to them. They are what they are—constantly changing, moving through *saṃsāra* (the cycle of life and death), manifestations of the nature of *Śūnyatā* 'emptiness.' He understands the life/existence of individual forms in a different perspective for what they really are (empty) and not what they appear to be (self-existent). This realization changes the attitude of the 'Enlightened one' toward life, events, and people. Each aspect of life is appreciated more, enjoyed more, because it is understood more. This change of perspective of the 'Enlightened one' toward the world of forms is vividly described in the Zen literature as follows:

(One Zen monk who "attained" enlightenment said the following:)

Before I became a monk
I saw mountains as mountains, rivers as rivers.

After I became a monk
I saw mountains as not mountains, rivers as not rivers.

Now I see
mountains as mountains still, rivers as rivers (again).

In the Zen system, the above can be explained as follows: before beginning the practice of Zen, one treats each existence (e.g. mountains, rivers, etc.) as a self-existent entity. Once one understands the "empty" nature of the individual existences (i.e. their impermanent and dependent nature), one treats them as nonexistent. However, once enlightened, one realizes that the forms (mountains, rivers, etc.) do exist, rooted into emptiness; they emerge from it and go back to it. One sees them for what they really are. The understanding of different forms before and after enlightenment appears to be similar, but it is so only superficially. Earlier, each form was viewed as self-existent, after enlightenment, it is viewed as "empty," reflecting the nature of all-pervasive emptiness (*Śūnyatā*).

The 'Enlightened one', according to the Zen system, is naturally compassionate toward the whole world. The compassion of the 'Enlightened one', according to the Zen system, is a natural consequence of the realization of his identity with emptiness and thereby with all existences in the world (including human beings)—their suffering, their ignorance, and the solution to their sufferings and ignorance. He identifies with all aspects of the world. His compassion does not emerge as a consequence of a sense of spiritual superiority or authority over the other ignorant people in pain, but rather, because of his very identity with them.

In summary, the Enlightened one (who is compassionate, who treats everyone alike, who craves for nothing) is viewed as the paragon of human (spiritual and ethical) values. He is the perfect human being because he has understood the true meaning of human life.

## 5.0 Zen realization and meditation

Zen realization (*Satori*) does not depend on any method, scriptures or teaching. According to Zen, a method can only be a pointer to reality. Meditation (*zazen*) helps the seeker undo, strip the garb of I-ness, the particular form, the ego, so that he can face the void, reality, directly. All methods stop there. A method is used in Zen to go beyond method itself! It only helps to wipe clean the mirror of the mind which, when cleared of the ego, will radiate the true nature. "Depending upon nothing, one finds one's own mind" is the essence of Zen.

In *zazen*, a student sits in a yogic posture and tries to calm the mind and set it free from every kind of conditioning. The student allows thoughts to float naturally in the mind. There is no effort involved. Gradually, the mind becomes still, calm, devoid of any concepts, ideas, or symbols. The zen pupil does not try to grasp anything intentionally. However, over a period of time a well-defined technique for the practice of *zazen* has been developed in Japan. This technique focuses on the training and the use of certain physical postures, breathing exercises, etc. This training is considered essential in *Satori*.

According to Dōgen, *zazen* is a necessary prelude to *Satori*; it is the "gateway to total freedom." For the mind to be enlightened, the proper sitting posture is crucial. Immobilization of the activities of the body contributes to the deep concentration of the mind. The legitimacy of *zazen* was strengthened by the belief that Buddha and his disciple Bodhidharma remained in the meditative posture for six and nine years respectively.

## 6.0 Koans

Koans are used as a technique in Zen for communication between the master and his pupil.

*Koans* are questions or riddles asked by Zen masters, along with the answers given by their students. The goal of *koans* is two-fold: (a) to free the conditioned mind of the student so that he can directly experience *Satori,* and (b) to examine the level of understanding (of the student) on the basis of how his answer is constructed.

*Koans* literally mean 'public records' *(ko* = public + *an* = records*)*. Most scholars believe that *koans* have two important features: (a) they do not merely express the private understanding of a person; rather, they are open to "public" interpretation; and (b) they are "case records" and therefore are authentic documents of dialogues between Zen masters and their pupils, whose experience /understanding is illustrated or "revealed" through koans.

*Koans* thus present a paradox: if *Satori is* a direct experience, and if words, language, logic, and reason only distort the nature of reality, how can *koans* be used to illustrate the experience? However, for Zen discipline, there is no paradox in the use of *koans* as long as the user understands that it is merely a device to measure/judge the level of understanding. For Zen, one's whole life is a *koan.* Once one has understood it's meaning, there is no longer a *koan.* A *koan is* a pointer *to* reality. It does not express reality; it suggests it. The one who is on "this" side of the *koan* (one who has not attained *Satori)* would answer the question differently from one who has attained *Satori.* Thus for the master and the student it provides a meeting point.

Some examples of the koans are the following: (a) Does the dog have a Buddha nature? (b) What is the sound of one hand clapping? (c) What was your face like before your birth? (d) If all existences go back to one, where does the one go?

Questions of the above type are presented to the student by the master. The student is expected to contemplate the *koan* "with his whole being" and find the answer. In the Zen system, an answer based only on intellectual analysis of the question is not acceptable, since that would only indicate that the student has not broken the barriers of "logic" or "reason" which restrict vision /understanding of the problem. The student is expected to find the intuitive answer to the problem by seeing directly through the problem by means of complete identification with the question. An answer should flash, burst out intuitively. Once the student becomes one with the problem, according to the Zen system, his answer will fit the question as naturally as the lid fits the box or as the boat floats smoothly on the waves. This intuitive or spontaneous understanding of the *koan* reflects the state of enlightenment. The *koan is* intended to shake up the student and make him strip his mind, which is generally engrossed in analyzing, calculating, and thereby missing direct contact with reality. In one sense, *koans* are the barriers raised by masters which the students must cross if they want to get to reality.

If the student's mind is still trapped within the conventional, established ways of analyzing the question, his answer will reflect that, and consequently, the master would have to fail him. For that would mean that he cannot transcend the trap of conventions which mediate between him and reality (the Buddha-nature).

In another sense, *koans* are pointers to reality. When the student sees the meaning directly, by becoming one with the question, he gets a sudden "flash" of understanding of the meaning, reality. He has to cross the barriers of words to get to the meaning. Then he understands that he must transcend all forms to get to reality. The medium through which reality is expressed consists of forms (words or existences). These forms often restrict the vision of reality, since the mind is focused on the medium, and the medium is thus perceived as reality. The understanding of reality necessitates a leap beyond the medium. This is the message conveyed by the *koan* exercise. *Koan* is a method to go beyond method in this sense. Seeing, hearing, and touching are only media. The Zen master encourages the student to understand what is being seen, heard, and touched. Once the mind is freed of all conditioning—whether it be of words, or senses or scriptures—reality will unfold to him as naturally as the blooming of the spring flower.

A good example of a *koan* is found in a conversation with master Seung Sahn. When he asked his student, "What is one plus two?" The student answered, "Three." Seung Sahn said, "You don't understand, one plus two is zero." "For when you give me one apple and I eat it, you give me two more and I eat them too. You see, one apple plus two apples become zero." This conversation confirms the assumption in Zen that the perception of reality (in this case, the student's answer, "One plus two equal three.") is determined by the conditioning of the mind and that a fresh unconditioned look presents a different view of reality.

It is claimed by one of the Korean Zen masters that a student must possess the following three things in order to be successful in his pursuit: (a) deep faith, (b) a strong determination and (c) a spirit of inquiry. If a student lacks one of the three, he is like a stool with only two legs. With all three, the student must approach a *koan*. He should constantly contemplate the *koan* to the extent that he becomes one with it. But this cannot be so until he is free of his ego, which divides the world into "I" vs. "not I," the *koan* vs. the seeker of truth, that he discovers the true meaning of the *koan*. Once the ego vanishes, he realizes that the true meaning of the *koan* is indeed beyond the words. The meaning flashes out from the *koan* and the student attains *Satori*–enlightenment.

## 7.0 Brief history of koans

*Koans* were used by Zen masters long before the 10th century. They provided an historical setting within which to present the Zen discipline.

In the 10th century, Lin-chi master Fen-yang Shan-chao systematically arranged the old *koans*, illustrated them with their purport, and added his own *koans*.

In the 12th century, Yuan-wu K'o-ch'in stressed the literary as well as the philosophical content of the *koans* and argued, "If you understand a single *koan* right now, you can understand all the teachings of the ancients, as well as of those of men of today." At this time, Ta-hui

Tsung-kao opposed the literary use of *koans* and pleaded that such teaching was against basic Zen practices. However, he accepted the value of the *koans* in *zazen* meditation. According to him, students should introspect on the meaning of *koans* while they concentrate on their true nature or reality.

However, there was a controversy between Ta-hui and Hing-Chih Cheng-chueh regarding the relative importance of *koans*. While Ta-hui advocated the importance of *koans* in *Satori*, the latter insisted on quiet meditation as a superior method of attaining *Satori* 'enlightenment'. Another master, Hakuin (18th century), added another dimension to *koans*. Like Ta-hui, he gave priority to *Satori* over *koans*. He subscribed to the view that, after *Satori*, *koans* served as a device for deepening the understanding of *Satori* itself.

There is a great deal of controversy regarding the usefulness of *koan* exercise after the student has attained enlightenment. According to some Zen masters, *koan* exercise is fruitless after enlightenment, while, according *to* others, it is necessary to deepen the student's understanding of *Satori*. Those who advocate the *koan* exercise after enlightenment claim that the sudden flash of enlightenment (which the student attains when he suddenly understands the true meaning of the *koan*) is a sudden glimpse into the true nature of reality.

However, the student is said to have attained *Satori*, in the real sense of the term, only when the enlightenment is not a mere glimpse; rather, it must be identical with the student's very being. By continuous practice of the exercise of *koan*, the student gradually reaches a state where his existence, as well as actions, naturally reflect his identity with the true-nature of reality *(Śūnyatā)*. What earlier was a glimpse now becomes his whole being.

Although the *koan* exercise was not intended to be an intellectual exercise, by the 10th century A.D. the standard examples of *koans* recorded in the monasteries were presented to students as part of their initiation into the study of Zen, and the students were often asked to look into the analyses provided by their predecessors. Therefore, Dōgen, who did not emphasize the use of *koan* in *zazen*, saw *koan* exercise as an intellectual analysis rather than an intuitive understanding.

In Dōgen's school, in each Zen monastary *koans* are part of the curriculum. A student is given a *koan* and is asked to write the purport of the *koan* in a sentence or two. If the answer satisfies the master, the student is given another *koan*. If the master is not satisfied, he gives the student a chore to do.

## 8.0 Myths, parables, and koans

Zen literature is rich in myths, parables, and *koans* which illustrate the major themes in Zen Buddhism, such as the nature of *Satori*, the meaning of life, dynamics of the activities of mind and body, the need, motivations, and nature of the quest for the knowledge of one's true nature, etc. In the following sections, some of the myths, parables, and koans are presented.

The parable of Enayadatta from the text of the *Śūrangama Sūtra* symbolizes human involvement in worldly affairs which prevent human beings from realizing their true Buddha-nature. It illustrates humans' disillusionment with the world of attachment, their intense need to find out their true nature, their futile efforts to find their true identity in the external world and their final realization that their true-nature /identity has always been within themselves, it was their preoccupation with the external world which had hampered this realization.

## 8.1 Enayadatta's head: lost and found

Every morning Enayadatta would get up and look into the mirror. "I am gifted with such unusual beauty!" she would exclaim to herself admiringly. She had every reason to admire herself because she was indeed blessed with unique charm.

One morning she looked into the mirror and was shocked to find her head missing! "Where is my head? Oh, I have lost my head! Who has taken my head?" she shouted in a state of shock. Enayadatta completely lost her poise and mental balance, for the head which was the source of her pride and continuous life-force was missing. In this turbulent state of mind, Enayadatta ran in a frenzy, asking everybody around, "Have you taken my head? Will somebody tell me where my head is?"

Her friends tried to calm her down, saying, "Your head, Enayadatta, is on your shoulders where it always has been. Stop being crazy. You have not lost your head. Stop running around looking for it, for it is where it should be and where it always has been. Foolish Enayadatta, don't torture yourself with this unfounded doubt." But Enayadatta was not convinced. She kept wandering around looking for her head, getting more and more exhausted. Finally, her friends restrained her physically and tied her to a post with a rope. At least Enayadatta's movements were stopped. She was physically immobilized so that her energy was no longer being wasted in aimless wanderings. However, Enayadatta's mind was not calm and peaceful; it was still filled with turbulence. "Where could my head be? Who could have taken my head?" Enayadatta's mind was occupied with myriads of thoughts like these. It was like a stormy ocean with millions of waves of thoughts. No one could convince her of the fact of her head being on her shoulders. All that she could tell herself was that perhaps her friends were right.

Suddenly, the friends thought of a solution. One of them picked up a wooden stick and hit Enayadatta hard on her head. An enormously strong blow it was! In the agony of unbearable pain Enayadatta cried, "I have my head! Oh, I do have my head!" It was a moment of *kensho*, the utmost exhilaration. Enayadatta's doubt had vanished. She was no longer an ignorant girl; she was the enlightened Enayadatta.

This story of Enayadatta from the *Śūrangama Sūtra*, elaborates the major principles of Zen. Enayadatta's admiration of her own beauty is suggestive of her indulgence in the world of forms and senses. The "head" symbolizes her true identity, the Buddha-nature, which is the true nature of all forms. Enayadatta's doubt regarding the existence of her head suggests that she could not identify herself with only her external form (which she had formerly taken to be her real identity). Now she thought that her true identity (head) was not there; she was looking for something real, more permanent, the very source of her existence. This, within the Zen system, symbolizes the first step toward enlightenment—doubt regarding the convictions which one pursues without ever questioning them. Moreover, her ardent desire to find her head suggests her faith in her true identity. She might not have found it yet, but she believed in it. She wanted to look for it.

Enayadatta's physical immobilization signifies the immobilization of the body in *zazen*, which, by restricting the movements of the body, prevents the body from decapitating its energy in fruitless endeavor. The entanglement of the body in the world of forms sways the mind away from concentrating on the true nature (one's own identity). Once her body stops moving, Enayadatta begins to half-way believe what friends try to tell her. However, it is the blow to her head causing sudden, severe pain, which shakes her off her conviction that the head is gone, since she immediately and spontaneously concentrates on the place where she has been hit with the stick. This, according to Zen is the awakening to the true-knowledge of one's nature from the deluge of the turbulent ocean of thoughts about the external world. The stick is viewed as a stroke of the master which accomplishes two tasks—the first of making the student get rid of his convictions and the second of awakening him to his true-nature. The true-nature (the head) was always there. Enayadatta neither "lost" it nor did she "find" it. It was due to her own ignorance that she thought she had lost it and later found it. A better description of her situation could be that she was unaware of her true-nature due to her insistence on identifying herself with her external form and ultimately it was due to her own realization of the true-nature that her doubt was removed.

Zen thus emphasizes the following: the existence of the true, Buddha-nature within every form in the world; human ignorance about this nature, the importance of *zazen* as a pointer to reality (one's true-nature); and, finally, enlightenment as the realization of one's true-nature, which is the same as the Buddha-nature or the nature of all forms in the world.

## 8.2 The ox-herding myth

The following "ox-herding" myth is translated from *The poems of Kuoan's Shih Niu Tu* ('Ten pictures of Ox' in the Chinese language). Like the parable of Enayadatta, this myth also emphasizes the major aspects of Zen Buddhism: (a) the loss of the true identity of human beings in the world of attachment, (b) their desperate need to find this identity, (c) their struggle to break away from the world of attachment, and (d) their realization of the true identity. The "ox" in the myth is a symbol of the "true identity or the Buddha-nature."

This myth illustrates the sharp contrast between the two states of mind of the man who has lost the ox, the first when he has lost the ox and the other when he has found it. In the first state, the man sees the world as divided into separate existences (including his own), and he tries to find his ox in the external world. When he finds the ox, he realizes that, in the absolute analysis, there is no separation of existences (they are all emptiness). He, his ox, and all other existences are essentially one; their true nature is emptiness.

### *Looking for the Ox*

Not knowing where to find it, I push aside the straw to pursue it in the vast thickets.
The water is wide, the mountain is far, and the path is far more indistinct.
I am exhausted and still find it nowhere.
I hear only the shrill sound of young cicadas on maple trees.

***Seeing Traces***

Near the water and in the woods are more traces.
Are they also seen under the scattered fragrant plants?
Even in the deeper site deep in the mountain,
How can it be hidden in a nostril as large as the sky?

***Seeing the Ox***

The oriole is singing in the tree.
The sun is warm, the wind is calm, and the willows on the banks are green.
There is no other place to hide.
In the luxuriant growth of plants horns are difficult to picture.

***Catching the Ox***

After devoting my energy to the fullest, I caught it.
Its strong will and powerful physical strength are difficult to get rid of after all.
Sometimes after we just arrive on the top of a plateau,
The next moment we come to a place deep in the mountain mist.

***Herding the Ox***

Whip and rope I never let go.
(Because) I am afraid it will freely walk away in the dust.
Together we then get along peacefully.
Without being tied by any string or chain, the ox voluntarily follows me.

***Riding the Ox to Go Home***

Riding the ox we meander home.
Every sound of flute bids farewell to the rosy clouds before sunset.
Every rhythm and every song have infinite meanings.
Close friends do not even need to move lips and teeth. (meaning: Close friends can understand each other without saying anything.)

***The Ox forgotten, Man Existing***

Riding the ox we arrived home on the mountain.
The ox is no more, and I am in a peaceful mood.
Although it is rather late in the morning, I am still dreaming.
Alone in the cottage lie the whip and the string.

***Both Man and Ox Forgotten***

The whip, the string, the man/I and the ox are all gone.
The blue sky is so vast that it is difficult to communicate /get through.

How can snow exist on the top of the flame of a heated stove?
It is only now that one can become one with the ancestors.

***Going back to one's Origin, Returning to Source***

It already took effort to go back to the origin and to return to the source.
Why not steadily reach the state of blindness and deafness?
Seeing nothing in front of the cottage while in the cottage.
The water is as vast as it is, and the flower is as red as it is.

***Entering the Market Place with Hands Hanging Down***

(meaning: entering the market place easily)
I come to the market place with bare chest and with bare feet.
I smear(ed) my face/body with dust and I am smiling all over.
There is no need for the real knack from an immortal.
One can on one's own make a withered plant blossom.

## *8.3 Koans*

In this section, four *koans* from the Zen tradition are illustrated. The major point to make about the *koans* is that these can be interpreted in different ways.

Some of the well-established interpretations are given following the *koans.*

### 8.3.1 *Mu*

"Does a dog have the Buddha-nature?" asked a monk of his master, Joshu.
Master Joshu replied "Mu."

*Interpretation:*

The word "Mu" literally means 'no'. The koan can be interpreted in various ways. For example, it could mean that the master said that a dog does not have Buddha-nature. Another interpretation could be that the question which requires a yes or no answer is itself wrong, since such a question is based on the concept of discrimination; i.e. a question, a dog, Buddha-nature, etc. The truth is that there is no essential difference among these. They are all one—the Buddha-nature. They are all emptiness, "Mu." Perhaps the koan meant to convey the point that everything is "Mu" (emptiness) and thereby assert that the dog does have the Buddha-nature. However, such logic is neither desirable, nor is it appropriate in a koan which aims at helping the student transcend such logical analyses.

The most likely interpretation then is that the master wanted to emphasize that the Buddha-nature transcends all discrimination.

### 8.3.2 *Hyakujō's fox*

Master Hyakujō used to deliver a sermon every day to his pupils. An old man used to attend it religiously. He listened to the sermons intently and left with the pupils. Once the master stopped him at the end of his sermon and asked, "Who are you?" The old man said, "I am not a human being. A long time ago, during the time of Kasha Buddha, I was the head of this place. I used to deliver the *teisho* (sermon) on Zen. One day one of my students asked me, does the enlightened one fall into causation?' and I answered, 'No, he does not.' As a result, I had to be reborn as a fox five hundred times. I have come to ask your advice. If you give me the appropriate answer to this question, I will be released from the form of a fox. Tell me, "Does the enlightened one fall into causation?" The master replied, "The enlightened one is not deluded by causation." At this point, the old man suddenly attained enlightenment. He was finally permanently freed from the form of the fox (which he had temporarily left behind in the mountain). The old man asked the master to conduct a funeral for the fox whose skin, he said, would be found behind the mountain. The master did accordingly. In the evening at the congregation, another pupil, Obuku, asked the master, "The old man became a fox because he gave an incorrect answer. If he had given the correct answer, what would he have become?" "Come here, I will tell you," said the master. Obuku got up and slapped his master. The master smiled and said, "I thought that a foreigner's beard is red, but I can see that a foreigner is with a red beard."

*Interpretation:*

There are several interpretations of this *koan.* According to some, the reason why the master's answer was viewed as right was that he accepted both—the transcendence of the enlightened one, (who is not caught in causation) and the reality of the law of causation in this world. He wants to stress the point that the enlightened one does not get attached to causation or deluded by it. He accepts it as it is.

According to another interpretation, the master conveys to the old man that falling into causation or being deluded by causation are both meaningless expressions. For the one who is enlightened, there is no causation in which to fall or by which he could be deluded, since he sees the Buddha-nature in everything.

The student Obuku slaps the master because the question, "If the old man had given the correct answer, what would he have become?" was truly incoherent. The enlightened one can not become anyone or anything and Obuku knew that. He knew that the master would have slapped him to shake him of his ignorance. Anticipating his master's reaction, he himself slapped the master to indicate his understanding of the situation.

### 8.3.3 *The sound of rain*

Once master Kyōsho asked a monk, "What is that noise outside?" "The sound of rain," answered the monk. Kyōsho said, "The people are in turmoil. They have lost themselves in the continuous search for worldly, material pleasures." The monk asked, "What about you, honorable sir? Do you understand your true nature?."

"Yes," said Kyōsho, "I know myself almost perfectly." The monk said, "Can you tell me exactly what you mean by 'understanding oneself'?" To this Kyōsho replied, "It is easy to be enlightened; it is difficult to explain it in words." In reply, the monk imitated the sound of rain, "Bisha, Bisha."

*Interpretation:*

The *koan* is powerful. It clearly conveys the point that the answer (i.e., the sound of rain) to Kyōsho's question (i.e., what is that noise outside) is correct; however, the sound of rain can not be conveyed through words. Words such as "Bisha, bisha" only resembles the sound of rain. One must remember that the word " rain" or "Bisha" is *not* actually *rain*. Similarly, any description of enlightenment is only the description of it and not enlightenment itself. The koan illustrates the inadequacy of words to explain the nature of enlightenment. As with the rain, one must directly experience enlightenment; there is no substitute for the direct experience of enlightenment.

### *8.3.4 A pitcher is a pitcher.*

Master Hyakujō wanted to choose one of his pupils to become the chief of a newly founded temple. In order to do so, he decided to test their ability to understand the true Buddha-nature. He asked the head of the monks to call all the pupils who he deemed qualified for the position. As all the qualified pupils gathered around Hyakujō, he placed a pitcher in front of them and asked them "If you were not permitted to call this a pitcher, what would you call it?" The head monk immediately answered, "You cannot call it a wooden stick." Hyakujō asked Isan the same question. Isan did not utter a word. He got up and kicked the pitcher, which broke into pieces, and walked away. Hyakujō smiled and said, "Isan has won; the head monk has lost." Isan was made the chief priest of the temple.

*Interpretation:*

This *koan* can be and has been interpreted in different ways. According to one interpretation, the pitcher could only be called "pitcher" and nothing else, which is what the head monk suggests when he eliminates other possibilities such as a wooden stick. By elminating other names, he is affirming the name "pitcher" However, his answer is too logical and self-conscious. It is not as spontaneous a response as Isan's, who, by breaking the pitcher (thus following a spontaneous action), conveys that a pitcher can only be called a pitcher as long as it exists as a pitcher.

According to another interpretation, the koan suggests that the process of affirmation, as well as negation (or elimination), operates at the level of the world of forms. A pitcher can be identified as a pitcher by the process of affirmation or by the process of elimination of its identity with other existences (i.e. it is not a wooden stick). The head priest thus operated perfectly well on the level of this world. However, for the enlightened one both processes are unnecessary. For him, a pitcher is a form which is in essence *Śūnyatā,* 'emptiness.' Isan's kicking of the pitcher, and breaking it, signifies his understanding of the ultimate truth, namely that all forms are essentially manifestations of *Śūnyatā,* 'emptiness.'

## 9.0 Influence of Zen on the arts and life

Zen provides an ideology which emphasizes the importance of the as-it-is-ness of reality, without any garb of artificiality. This very urge to capture the essence of life (reality) finds a unique expression in Zen art and in the life of the people.

In the art of painting, the Zen artist aggressively portrays natural phenomena as they are, without any garb of "subjective" interpretation, conceptualization, or impression. According to Zen ideology, the greatness of art lies in portraying the object as it is, naturally. A mountain is thus painted with all its ruggedness, unevenness and other natural peculiarities. No effort is made to suggest the existence or features of the mountain indirectly through its impressionistic or stylized presentation, such mediated presentation of the object takes away its real essence, its "as-it-isness," and reduces it to inferential /representational reality. The real nature of a mountain can only be expressed by a mountain itself. Therefore, Zen painters try to eliminate all possible distortions that are created by the use of symbols to convey the is-ness of objects.

Similar to the art of painting, Japanese Noh drama is rooted in the Zen philosophy of expressing a theme directly and naturally. Noh drama does not contain any speech; it is silent. The idea is to suggest rather than tell the story. There is no elaborate acting, nor make-up. The face of the actor is masked. Each movement of the actor is more eloquent than any sound, word, or speech. Each movement expresses the "inner emotion." The basic idea is to keep "artificiality" to a minimum, and let the movements of the actors "naturally" suggest the theme.

The widespread influence of Zen on Japanese culture is observed in the Japanese Zen tea ceremony and flower arrangement. The tea ceremony in Zen monastaries beautifully incorporates the spirit of Zen, which emphasizes simplicity (lack of artificiality) as the key to the understanding of reality. The tea ceremony is a simple ritual of preparing and serving tea in the peaceful atmosphere of a Zen monastery. The room has a simple decorum with no elaborate furniture—only a stove, a kettle and a few mats on which to sit. Tea is prepared in an informal atmosphere where people sit around the stove silently and listen to the sound of boiling water, which is otherwise not noticed over loud conversation. The tea is poured into a cup made of clay and is enjoyed by the people. The tea ceremony is thus understood and enjoyed as the tea ceremony (for what it is) and not as a token of celebration of any other event (i.e., birthday or graduation party). The tea ceremony is thus a simple ritual which strips off artificiality and emphasizes value of simplicity in Zen culture.

CHAPTER 13

# *Japanese Mythology: Shinto and Ainu*

## *1.0 Introduction*

The country of Japan consists of four major islands, plus 2000 small islands. The former are named Hokkaido, Honshu, Kyushu, and Shikoku. Although the islands have been permeated with diverse cultural traditions, over a period of time, the cultural traditions of the islands of Honshu and Kyushu have come to be recognized as dominant. The strong heritage of commonly shared mythology is the unifying bond among the diverse religious systems (i.e., Shintoism, Buddhism, Taoism, Confucianism, Christianity, folk religion, and the Ainu beliefs) included in the Japanese cultural tradition. The persistent undercurrent of mythological beliefs, largely pertaining to the Shinto system, has retained its vitality throughout the turbulent history of Japan. Perhaps this is because it expresses what is elemental to the Japanese mind.

It is very difficult to trace the ancient history of Japanese mythological traditions, since there is no clear mark separating mythical events from historical ones. While historical kings have been turned into mythical gods, the mythical sun goddess is depicted as the historical ancestor of the ancient Japanese race living in the Yamato region of the island of Honshu. The important point to note here is that Japanese cultural tradition is a uniquely homogenous blend of mythology and history—like the inseparable colors in a rainbow.

The earliest source of Japanese mythology are the two books named *Kojiki* 'Records of Ancient Matters' (7 12 A.D.) and *Nihongi* 'Chronicles of Japan' (7 2 0 A.D.). These books have primarily preserved the Shinto beliefs of the Yamato people. It is believed that their compilation in the 8th century was motivated by a desire to establish the divine ancestry of the Shinto kings.

*Kojiki* and *Nihongi* elaborate the Shinto system of beliefs, which deals with questions related to the origin of the world and human beings, the interrelationship of diverse levels of existence (e.g. human beings, animals, plants, etc.), and the relationship between life (creation), and death (destruction). Shinto 'the way of gods', is a system based primarily on belief in the all-pervading power of nature which is expressed in all phenomena—living and non-living—and on the belief that it is this power of nature which is responsible for the creation, sustenance and destruction of all that exists in the world.

The powers of nature revered most in Japanese mythology are the sun and the ocean. The very name of the Japanese island is "*Nippon,*" which in the Japanese language means 'the land of the rising sun'. Both *Kojiki* and *Nihongi* ascribe the origin of the Japanese people to Amaterasu, the Sun-goddess. According to myth, Amaterasu gave "three treasures" (sword, mirror, and jewels) to her grandson Ninigi, who descended from heaven to the southwest Pacific coast and gradually travelled eastward toward the central region of Yamato province. However, he did not reach Yamato. It was actually Ninigi's grandson Jimu Tenno who reached Yamato and became the founder of the Yamato royal dynasty. This myth is greatly cherished in the mythology, since it traces the divine origin of the royal lineage of the Yamato emperors in Japan.

There are several myths which describe the combats between the Yamato people (who allegedly arrived from the west) and the native inhabitants of Japan. Although there is controversy regarding the origin and cultural heritage of the people who inhabited Japan before the arrival of the Yamato people, it is clear from the historical evidence that they lived in the islands long before the arrival of the Yamato people. They included the "sea people" living on the coasts and the Ainu who lived by hunting in the central part of the islands. According to the myth, the Ainu were pushed northward and eastward by the Yamato people. The fact that several words, including the word for god (i.e. *kami* (Shinto) and *kamui* (Ainu)), are commonly shared by the two people (Yamato and Ainu), indicates a period of close interaction between the two.

The Shinto system itself was influenced by several other systems of beliefs, such as Buddhism (6th century A.D.), Confucianism, and Taoism (7th century A.D.). The Buddhist doctrines of the afterlife, rituals and monastic order were some of the features which became part of the Shinto system. Shinto gods (kamis) were given Buddhist names and were worshipped in Buddhist rites.

Similarly the Shinto laws of ethics were formulated according to Confucian thought. In addition, Taoist concepts related to the basic harmony of nature and the belief in the two apparently opposite elements (*yin* and *yang*) as the basis of the origin and the sustenance of the universe were also readily incorporated into the Shinto system of beliefs.

In 1868, during the period of the establishment of the Meiji Government, Shinto was accepted as the only national religion in Japan. An official document issued by the government excluded all religions other than Shinto from the category of national religion. Buddhist monks were expelled from Shinto shrines. According to the Japanese constitution in 1889, Shinto priests became government officials.

This elevation of Shinto over other religions continued until World War 11. In 1945, after the Allied occupation of Japan, Shinto was officially banned, since it was viewed as a religion which supported the military, headed by a monarch, whose authority was sanctioned by the Shinto mythology and religion.

Nevertheless, the Japanese people still revere Shinto beliefs and hold their emperor in high honor, with Shinto worship rituals and other practices being conducted in about 80,000 shrines even today. The conflict between the Buddhist and the Shintoist systems has once again disappeared, and Shinto and Buddhist priests may participate in each other's rituals. A Shinto kami can co-exist with a Buddhist altar in the same house, on the same shelf.

## 2.0 Shinto—"the way of gods" (shin = gods; tao = way)

Shinto is perhaps the oldest of the Japanese religions. It is Japan's native religion, and has existed as a persistent mild undercurrent throughout the turbulent sociopolitical history of Japan. Shinto represents an indigenous Japanese tradition of religious and mythological beliefs revolving around the nature of human existence and its relationship to the phenomenal world. The basis of these beliefs is the concept of *kami,* the supernatural, mysterious power which is not explicable in words but is "out there" and is to be experienced in all aspects of nature; e.g., tall mountains, continuously flowing rivers, trees, animals, human beings, etc. Crucial to Shinto beliefs is the world view which emphasizes the acceptance of this power of nature as a principle of harmony in the world, its all-encompassing nature, and its ability to control all aspects of the phenomenal world. Thus to understand Shinto one must understand this world-view. As with the Vedic or the Āryan system, there is no one founder of the Shinto system.

Shinto is not based on philosophical tradition; rather, its roots lie in the traditional rituals, ceremonies, and beliefs which have permeated the psyche of the common people. *Kojiki* and *Nihongi,* mentioned above, are not considered to be the "holy scriptures" of Shinto in the way the Bible functions in Christianity or the Vedas in Hinduism. There are no doctrinal/philosophical or theological laws which determine the Shinto identity; rather, it is the customs, rituals, and way of thinking which are believed to be the expression of the Shinto system forming the foundation of the people's behavior patterns. Through the various periods of its history, the Shinto system has undergone several changes in terms of standardization of the patterns of customs which gave rise to various kinds of Shinto organizations. Among these are: (a) shrine Shinto, which emphasized the worship of *kami* in a local shrine with various religious rituals (without any emphasis on a particular founder of the shrine or of the religious system); (b) Shinto groups organized by specific founders to revive and defend Shinto beliefs independently of other religious systems (around the 19th century); and (c) Shinto as a system, followed by the rural communities and the common people as the religion of their ancestors. This loosely formulated system incorporates rituals and customs, not only from ancient indigenous Shinto, but also those of Taoist, Buddhist, and Confucian origin. However, this diversification of the Shinto system did not violate its basic principle, namely, that *kami is* the all-pervasive controlling spirit of the cosmos and human beings can function happily only if they accept its authority.

## 3.0 The concept of kami in Shinto

Central to Shinto is the faith and worship of *kami.* Kami is generally translated into English as "god," since it encompasses various facets of religious experience; i.e., divine, powerful, etc. *Kami,* as already mentioned, is a mysterious power which is abstract and all-pervasive. The Shinto system claims that this power cannot be explained using mere words, since no explication of the power in words could express its "infinite" nature. Human capacity is limited, while the power of *kami* transcends any limit. Although it is impossible to describe *kami,* it may be experienced. The Shinto system claims that the *musubi,* 'the will' (the operation/function of *kami)* may be observed in the harmony which exists in nature. The divine *kami* expresses its will by regulating the phenomenal world, within which every creation is located and functions within the overall harmonious pattern of the cosmos.

Shinto *kamis* are of the following five types:

(a) personifications of the powers of fertility, growth, and production;
(b) natural phenomena such as the wind and thunder;
(c) natural objects such as the sun, mountains, rivers, trees, rocks, etc.
(d) animals;
(e) ancestral spirits.

It is immediately obvious that the concept of *kami* incorporates every facet of the universe, including both the animate and inanimate world. Nor does it exclude the abstract powers expressed in the animate and inanimate worlds (i.e., fertility, growth, etc.). There has been a great deal of controversy regarding the exact nature of *kami* and its role in human life. However, despite the differences in the interpretation of the term *kami* it is clear that Shinto acknowledges the importance/role of the diverse facets of nature. It does not establish any hierarchy of *kami;* i.e., the sun is no more important than animals, etc. Rather, Shinto emphasizes the diversity of roles of the *kamis.* Moreover, it stresses their cooperation. *All kamis,* according to Shinto, function in coordination with each other. This perfect harmony of the *kamis* is perhaps the most important aspect of Shinto.

It is a matter of controversy whether *kami* originally referred to many divine powers of nature which function in consonance with each other or to one single power which is expressed through diverse powers/concrete objects. Some scholars claim that the concept of *kami* may have originally been a polytheistic one and it was due to the influence of the Buddhist and the Taoist beliefs that it was interpreted as one (expressed in many) power. However, it is clear beyond any doubt that Shinto focuses on the interconnectedness of various facets of the universe. It argues for the need of human beings to recognize this fact and function harmoniously with the operation of the *kamis.*

## 4.0 The Structure of Shinto mythology

Shinto mythology emphasizes three major elements: (1) the creation of the world; (2) the sustenance of the world through opposite forces; and (3) the importance of rituals. These three elements are interrelated within the Shinto framework.

The Shinto creation myths relate to the time when the *kamis* functioned together. (This is viewed within Shinto mythology as the "Age of *kami.*")

Creation is viewed as the natural outcome of the blending of two *kamis* or two opposite forces, these being Izanagi and Izanami (the mate and female forces respectively). Sustenance of the world is depicted in Shinto mythology as a constant struggle between opposites, i.e., order vs. disorder at mythical, political, as well as social levels. This existence and struggle between opposites may be seen in the mythical background of the stories about Amaterasu, the sun goddess, who is seen as the goddess of order and her brother, Susano-o, the god of the thunderstorm, who constantly disrupts order. This prototype of the Shinto myths stresses the struggle between opposite forces in the world. However, it does not imply that the opposites necessarily are "good" or "evil" in nature. In other words, "good" and "evil" do not find expression in concrete elements such as the sun goddess or the god of the thunderstorm. These are merely opposite forces. "Good" is what is conducive to the creation, sustenance, and enrichment of the world. "Evil" is what threatens these things. This contrast and struggle between the forces and their relatively good and evil character are the essential elements in Shinto mythology.

Shinto rituals basically are oriented toward ordering (or reordering) the cosmos through human actions. Thus, the rituals involve the creation of order, a function which originally was performed by the *kami* in the "sacred time."

Purification and the communion with the *kami* are the two major aspects of Shinto rituals. Both of these have a mythical origin. According to myth, Izanagi the male creator of the world, purified himself after visiting the Land of the Dead. From this act of purification were created Amaterasu and Susano-o, and other *kamis* who consequently ordered the world. Therefore, it is assumed in Shinto that ritual purification (bathing in water, etc.) is a prerequisite to the ordering of the universe—or any event for that matter. Similarly, it is assumed that *kamis* are the forces which, when functioning in harmony, create order. It is assumed that they know the secrets of the universe and its order. Therefore, while performing the ritual, human beings must establish communion with the *kamis.*

According to Shinto, every event (birth, marriage, etc.) needs a ritual which establishes a link between that event and order in the universe and, secondly, between human beings and the *kamis.* Thus every event is seen as part of the whole structure of the universe, which, it is assumed, represents the harmonious operation of diverse forces.

## 5.0 Shinto shrines

Shinto is practiced at home or in shrines (Shrine Shinto). Shrines are equivalent to temples (Hindu and Buddhist), churches (Christian), and mosques (Islamic). Originally there were no shrines for Shinto worship, rather, natural settings such as the top or the foot of mountains, the banks of rivers or trees were viewed as sacred/pure places for carrying out the worship of the *kamis.* Later, shelters were built to protect the worshippers from bad weather. In the traditionally agricultural society of Japan, the *kamis* were invited to the shrine to participate in the harvest festival, thanksgiving festival, and the festival for timely rain, etc.

The shrines at Ise and Izumo are the most well-known in Japan. During the course of time, shrines were interpreted to be the permanent dwellings of the *kami* and not simply places they visited. Shrines are not viewed as places where Shinto *is preached;* rather, they are places where Shinto is *practiced* and harmony is recognized and reinforced among the diverse aspects of the phenomenal world. They are places where human beings recognize their participation in cosmic creation and harmony.

## *6.0 Divine symbols in the shrines*

Shinto shrines are sacred places where communion is established with one or more *kamis.* Shrines are marked by certain symbols which separate them from the profane/mundane world. These symbols are the *torii* "gateway," *gohei* "symbolic offerings," *harai gushi* "purification wand," mirrors, banners, sword, jewels, and the sacred rope.

a. *Torii-Torii* is the wooden gate at the entrance to the shrines which are themselves made of wood. *Torii* is the gateway into the world of the *kami.* The word literally means "bird." *Torii* separates the secular/mundane world from the world of *kami.* Although these gateways were formerly made of wood and were simple in structure, in modern times their structure has become more complex and metal has been substituted for wood.

b. *Gohei* "symbolic offering"—*Gohei* is a post around which strips of folded white paper are placed. At times, the number of strips of folded white paper signify offerings to the number of *kamis* present in the shrine. It is believed that this offering is a relic of the times when cloth was offered to the *kami* in the form of strips. *Gohei* is installed near the entrance doorway.

c. *Harai gushi* "purification wand"—This wand is important in the rituals of purification. Any wooden stick with long paper strips attached to it can serve as a wand. At times a branch of the Sakaki tree is used to perform the function of the wand.

d. Mirrors—Mirrors are sacred objects of worship in Shinto shrines. They have a special significance in Shinto mythology. The mirror symbolizes the impartiality of the divine will which treats all beings alike. In this sense, a mirror is like nature whose rules are equally applicable to everybody and everything in the world. A mirror is held to be sacred also because it symbolizes the honesty and sincerity of the *kami.* It simply reflects the nature of the object—good or bad—as it is, without any selfish motive. It also represents the sincerity and honesty of the devotee toward the *kami.* In this sense, a mirror is viewed as a symbol of the mind of the Shinto devotee, which, in order for him to receive the blessings of the *kami,* must always be kept pure. According to Shinto, a dusty mirror indicates impurity or insincerity of the mind. Therefore, 'polishing the mirror' is a symbolic act of 'purifying the mind.'

Another context in which the mirror has a special place is in the worship of Amaterasu, the sun goddess. According to myth, it is believed that the sun goddess came out of a cave when she saw her own reflection in a mirror which was held outside the cave. Thus, symbolically, the mirror is supposed to capture/reflect the spirit of the sun goddess in particular and of the *kamis* in general.

e. Banners—Banners bearing the symbols of the kamis, such as the sun, moon, etc., are present in the shrines to symbolize the presence of the kamis.

f. Sword and jewels—These are found in the shrines. Generally they are hung from the banners. There are several interpretations of the presence of these in the shrines. It is believed that they represent the qualities of courage, benevolence, and wisdom, which typically signify the nature of *kamis.*

g. Rope—The rope, similar to the torii, separates the divine/sacred places from the secular/mundane world.

## *7.0 Shinto creation myths*

### *7.1 The birth of the islands*

The history of the origin of the Japanese islands is shrouded in mystery. Kojiki, one of the major sources of Japanese mythology ascribes the creation of the concerns the creation of the Japanese islands is particularly interesting because it beautifully manifests the Shinto belief in the close affinity of nature and human beings.

According to this creation myth, in the beginning there was no land, no mountains, no trees, animals, or human beings. There was only the all-pervading endless ocean. The whole atmosphere was covered with mist which hovered over the ocean. The spirits in the heavens commanded two kamis, named Izanagi ' the male who invites' and Izanami 'the female who invites,' to descend down to the ocean to create a piece of floating land. The heavenly spirits gave a beautifully designed jewelled spear to the couple.

Seated on the arc of a rainbow which was floating in the mist, Izanagi and Izanami reached down and stirred the ocean with the celestial jewelled spear. They kept stirring it until the liquid started coagulating. "Earth, are you there?" asked Izanami. But there was no answer. As the couple lifted the spear out of the ocean, the drops of brine which fell off the spear's tip coagulated, and soon a patch of dry land began to float on the surface of the ocean. This was the island Onogoro, which means 'self-coagulating' island. Izanagi and Izanami descended to this island to fulfill the command to create the earth.

According to the ancient version of this myth, Izanagi and Izanami were brother and sister. It was after their descent to the "coagulated island" that they became lovers as the heavenly couple watched a pair of wagtail birds making love. (The myth emphasizes that this was their first encounter with conjugal love.)

The couple had erected a pillar on the island and had built a beautiful palace too. "We will circle around this pillar, then meet and make love," said Izanagi, and Izanami agreed to this proposition. Izanami walked around the pillar from the right, Izanagi walked around the pillar from the left. When they met, Izanami first said, "What a handsome young man!" Following her, Izanagi said, "What a beautiful maiden!" Izanagi and Izanami then declared themselves man and wife. The first child born to the couple was crippled. The couple decided to let it float away and promptly reported the matter to the deities in heaven. "A woman should not speak first in a marriage ceremony," said the divine spirits. "Izanami spoke first. Therefore, the child was not healthy. You should go back and say it again properly; let Izanagi precede you in taking his marriage vows." "I will do it," replied Izanami. Thus consoled, the couple descended once again and said their vows of marriage once more. Only this time Izanagi spoke first, saying, "What a beautiful young maiden!," and then Izanami followed him saying, "What a handsome young man!" Thereafter, Izanami gave birth to several healthy children—the eight islands of Japan, the waves, the mountains, rivers, forests, etc. Her last child was the god of fire who soon after his birth burnt Izanami to death. Izanagi, enraged by this act, cut his son to pieces with his sword.

After her death, Izanami went to the Land of Yomi, the lord of the dead. Izanagi could not bear the death of his wife, and helplessly followed her to the Land of the Dead. Little did he know that because Izanami had eaten the food in the 'land of the darkness', she had become a resident there.

Izanami, my beloved, come along with me. Let us go back to earth; I can not live without you," said Izanagi to his wife.

"How can I return with you? I have already eaten the food in the 'Land of Darkness'."

However, Izanagi would not leave without his wife. He kept insisting that she had to go back with him. At his unceasing insistence, Izanami finally said, "Go ahead; I will first seek permission of Yomi, the lord of the Land of the Dead, to return with you, and then I will join you."

"Very well," said Izanagi, delighted by her consent to return with him.

"Izanami then said, "There is a condition which you must first accept; do not try to look at me until I return to you."

"As you wish," said Izanagi.

But a long time had passed and Izanami had not returned. Izanagi became restless and impatient. "What is taking her so long?" he said to himself. "Let me go and find out for myself." Izanagi broke a tooth out of his comb and made a torch out of it and entered the palace of the lord of the dead. He was shocked to encounter the scene inside, His beautiful, slender wife Izanami was nowhere to be seen! Instead, he saw her corpse, covered with maggots, disintegrating and emanating a dreadfully disgusting smell. Eight thunder deities surrounded her, constantly exhaling flames from their mouths. Izanagi neither had the courage nor the desire to be there. He dropped the torch and ran away as fast he could.

Izanami suddenly awoke and was very sorry to see that her husband had broken his promise. "Why did you do this to me, my dear husband?" said Izanami. "Now there is no hope for me of returning to earth with you." Realzing that she was trapped in the Land of the Dead, Izanami became enraged. "I will not let you escape from the Land of the Dead without me," she cried. She then sent eight hideous female demons to stop her husband from running away.

In desperation Izanagi ran, trying hard to escape the attack of the female demons. But it was difficult, and they soon caught up with him. Izanagi then threw his hairdress down in front of them. As soon as it touched the ground, it changed into grapes. While the demons were distracted by this unusual treat of grapes, Izanagi made his escape. But once again they caught up with him. This time Izanagi dropped his comb in their path, and it became transformed into a bunch of bamboo shoots. While the demons ate the bamboo shoots, Izanagi ran away.

Izanami became enraged at this and shouted, "I will never let you escape." She sent the eight thunder deities and 1500 demon friends of Yomi to follow Izanagi. Izanagi kept running until he found a peach tree full of ripe peaches. These he threw at the demons who were following him. While the demons were confused by this sudden attack of peaches, Izanagi reached the exit to the earth. He quickly left the Land of the Dead and covered the pass with a huge rock, so that no one from the Land of the Dead could come out. Izanami, desperate and helpless, began striking the rock vehemently, screaming, "How could you do this, Izanagi, to your own Izanami whom you loved so tenderly? Why did you break your promise and leave me here in the Land of the Dead?" Izanagi could not bear this any longer. "You are not my wife anymore, nor am I your husband!"

"Oh Izanagi! For this I will kill 1,000 people on earth every day!" said Izanami, getting angrier by the moment.

"Well, I will cause 1500 to be born everyday," shouted Izanagi. "Goodbye!" Thus the lovers who had given birth to the eight islands were separated forever.

Izanagi was exhausted emotionally and physically. Because he wanted to purify himself of the pollution of the Land of the Dead, he stopped to bathe in the river which flowed at the exit to the earth. From his ritual bath of purification sprang multitudes of deities—some from the body, others from his garments—deities good and bad, benevolent and malevolent.

When Izanagi washed his left eye, Amaterasu the Sun goddess 'deity of heavenly light' came into existence. Amaterasu is the goddess of life, light, fertility, and prosperity in Japanese mythology. When Izanagi washed his nose, out came Susano-o 'the impetuous male', the god of thunder and lightning.

Amaterasu and Susano-o represent the opposite forces in the universe—light and darkness, life and death, woman and man, etc. It is important to note here that Shinto mythology, similar to Hindu mythology, ascribes the same origin (i.e. Izanagi in Japanese and *Eternal Waters* in Hindu) to the opposite forces. This myth of creation emphasizes the point that the creation of the universe necessarily involves creation of opposite forces.

Izanami's death after giving birth to her last child shows striking resemblance to Satī's death in Hindu mythology (see chapter 8) and to the death of *Hun-tun* and P'an ku in the creation myths of Chinese mythology (see chapter 11). The close affinity of life and death is symbolically represented in these mythologies in the myths alluded to above. Another point of similarity shared by these myths is the theme of renewal of life. In the Shinto myth, Izanami's death is followed by Izanagi's expedition to the Land of the Dead, which results in his return to earth for the continuity of creation. Recall the conversation between Izanagi and Izanami in which Izanami emphasizes her power, the power of death and destruction. "I will kill 1000 people every day," says Izanami. Izanagi, on the other hand, emphasizes the renewal and continuity of creation and life. "I will create 1500 people every day," Izanagi replies. This continuous cycle of life and death finds its expression in the re-creation of the world from the parts of Satī's dead body in Hindu mythology, and the dynamic operation of *Yin* and *Yang* in the Taoist Chinese mythology.

## *7.2 Amaterasu's retreat*

Another Japanese myth which beautifully portrays the belief in the close connection of human life and natural phenomena is the myth of Amaterasu the Sun goddess, whose disappearance causes darkness, famine, and death in the human world.

Amaterasu is the kindest goddess. Bountiful rice is her blessing. The rain clouds are filled with water because of her, and the forests grow thicker due to her bright lively glances. She is worshipped by every living creature, for she is the goddess of life. Her father Izanagi had given her a necklace made of dazzling jewels and had sent her to heaven to rule over the sky, and she obeyed his wishes.

Susano-o, her brother, the deity of the thunderstorm, who was entrusted the responsiblity of ruling over the Sea Plain, was a mischievous trickster. He never carried out his duties. Instead, he would dash through the rice fields to destroy them, suddenly circle Amaterasu, and cause the whole world to be covered with darkness.

Once when he was weeping and lamenting, Izanagi asked him, "What is wrong? Why are you weeping?"

"I want to see my dead mother. I want to go to the Land of the Dead!"

"Surely, this is a good idea," said Izanagi. "You are in any case not suitable for the job bestowed upon you. Go then!"

"Not yet!" said Susano-o. "I want to first go to heaven and bid farewell to my sister Amaterasu before I leave for the Land of the Dead!"

"So be it!" exclaimed Izanagi.

When Amaterasu learned about his forthcoming visit, she was frightened since she knew only too well that Susano-o's visit spelled destruction and trouble. She fully prepared herself for his visit. She tied a sharp-edged sword around her girdle, accompanied by a quiver full of 500 arrows, and built a fortified wall to protect herself from Susano-o. Her hair was knotted in strands with gems and resembled a serpent's hood. Susano-o was deeply hurt when he saw his sister's response to his visit. "My dear sister, I have not come here to fight, nor do I have any intention of bothering you. I ask only for your forgiveness for all of my past misdeeds. I have come to bid you farewell. Believe me, I have traveled this long way over the bridge of heaven only to see you before I vanish into the Land of the Dead. Do you not believe me?"

Standing on the banks of the heavenly river, the Milky Way, Amaterasu asked for proof of his good intentions. "My sister, let us share an oath to produce children. If the gods which are thus produced are all male, it will be the proof of my good intentions." Then Susano-o offered his sword to Amaterasu, who broke it into three pieces. As she chewed on these three pieces, from her mouth came three goddesses. She then offered her gem-necklace to Susano-o who chewed on the gems and produced male gods. Thus being assured of her brother's innocence and good intentions, Amaterasu welcomed him to her palace. But Susano-o's naturally mischievous disposition made itself evident before very long. Amaterasu soon noticed that he had started destroying the rice fields and creating havoc for all her kindly people. Susano-o's impetuous nature became intolerable to everyone around him. One day, while Amaterasu was weaving with her friends in the palace, Susano-o tore off the roof and threw a dead horse into the middle of the room. The women screamed. Amaterasu wounded herself. Able to bear the torture no more, she ran to a cave and hid from Susano-o.

The whole world suddenly lost its light- and life-force. The rice fields died, as did the forests. The flowers drooped and the darkness of night swept over all the world.

Thousands of deities of heaven received the news of Amaterasu's disappearance. They all gathered at the cave and begged Amaterasu to come out. "Without you,O goddess, we can not survive!" said the gods. But Amaterasu refused to come out. "I have been troubled enough! I shall never come out of this cave again," said Amaterasu.

The gods, knowing her disposition too well, realized that they would never be able to persuade her to come out unless they tricked her. "Let us play upon her curiosity," they decided. At sunrise, the gods created an artificial scene in front of the cave. They brought a densely branched tree from the heavenly mountain and placed it before the door of the cave, then they fetched some roosters and placed them on the branches of the tree. A beautifully designed mirror, decked with starlike jewels was placed on the branch closest to the door of the cave. If Amaterasu saw the tree, it would remind her of the time of the sunrise.

The gods then invited Uzume, the fat little goddess of dancing, singing and merry-making. They all began dancing and singing. The whole atmosphere was full of the joyous sounds of music and dancing.

Amaterasu became curious about what was going on outside the cave. She wondered how the world could be happy without her! She could not contain her curiosity when she heard the crowing of roosters! "Let me take a look and find out what is happening!" said Amaterasu to herself. She opened the door of the cave a little bit and asked, "Why do you laugh?"

"We have found a more beautiful Sun goddess, that's why," said the gods.

"I do not believe you," said Amaterasu.

"Then take a look," said the gods and held the mirror in front of her face. Amaterasu saw a beautiful goddess of light in the mirror. She was tricked! Surprised at the sight, Amaterasu came out a little further to take a close look at this "new" goddess, quickly the gods pulled her out of the cave. Suddenly the earth and the sky were filled with bright light again. The source of life had returned to the world and all was well again. Susano-o was punished by the gods, who expelled him from heaven for the safety of the whole world! Since that day, the Sun goddess has never left the world again!

## 8.0 Good and evil in Shinto: the eight-forked dragon

Shinto mythology describes natural phenomenon as it is; intrinsically neither good nor evil, but viewed as such depending upon its impact on human life. Susano-o, the god of thunder, who destroys the rice fields and covers up Amaterasu is viewed as evil, since his actions are detrimental to human life. But he is not evil all the time. The myth of the eight-forked dragon portrays the positive side of Susano-o's personality, when he kills the eight-forked dragon and saves the daughter of the old couple. The symbolism in this myth is vivid and suggestive, The eight-forked dragon symbolizes the stormy ocean which threatens to "swallow" the islands of Japan. The daughters of the old couple symbolize the islands. Susano-o pushes the tidal waves of the stormy ocean away from the shores of the islands and saves them.

When he was banished from heaven, Susano-o was depressed and lonely. He was wandering along the seashore when he met an old couple who were weeping pathetically. When asked by Susano-o the cause of their weeping, they informed him of their misfortune. They had eight daughters, young and beautiful. Each year the dreadful eight-forked dragon would come and take away one of their daughters. So strong was the dragon, that no earthly creature could possibly stop him. They had their last daughter with them, and they feared that the dragon would appear again and snatch away their only child—leaving them childless and helpless! Susano-o soon noticed their beautiful daughter standing by them and he was immediately attracted to her. I will save her, if you allow her to marry me," said Susano-o to the old couple. They then promised him their daughter in marriage if he would save her from the dragon. "But how will you save her?" asked the old man, "for no one so far has managed to stop him."

"Make eight vats of wine and place one tub of wine at each of the gates through which the dragon enters," said Susano-o. The old couple did everything as they were told. The wine was distilled and a vat was placed at each of the eight gates. Soon the presence of the dragon was felt in the air. The trees began to tremble. The hills began to swing in horror. The roaring sound of the dragon scared every creature. Susano-o could see the dragon's red eyes and his huge body. Susano-o hid behind the vats in such a way that he was not visible but his reflection was cast into the vats. Eagerly and impatiently the dragon moved toward the gates to devour the fair young woman. But Susano-o had transformed the maiden into a small comb which he had placed in his hair. The dragon saw the reflection of Susano-o in the vat. So hazy was his reflection, that the dragon mistook it for the maiden's and quickly jumped at it and swallowed the whole vat full of wine, thinking it was the beautiful girl whom he was swallowing! And there was still another vat and another reflection, another mistake, another gulp of wine! Gradually, the wine started producing its effect. Drowsily, the dragon moved from vat to vat, reflection to reflection, maiden to maiden—each time moving closer to intoxication and to loss of consciousness and strength. Susano-o had been waiting for this time. Noticing the drowsy state of the dragon, he quickly took out his sword and hacked off the dragon's heads. As Susano-o tried to chop off the tail, a shining sword suddenly emerged out of the tail which Susano-o recognized as a celestial weapon. He decided to give it to his sister Amaterasu.

Susano-o thus saved the maiden, who was attracted to him because of his brave feat. Susano-o restored her to her original form and she became a maiden again.

In the beautiful province of Izumi 'the rain clouds' Susano-o married the girl and lived happily with her for some time before going to the Land of the Dead to see his mother.

## *9.0 Search for happiness: Momotaro—the peach boy*

There was a time, before our time, when miracles took place as naturally as the flowers grow on the trees. It was then that a miracle happened. A boy came out of a peach!

A good old man and a good old woman lived in a village surrounded by rivers and mountains. The couple was childless. They were a kind couple. The good old man used to go to the mountain every day to fetch wood, and the good old woman used to go to the river to wash clothes.

One day, when the good old woman went to the river, she saw a big red peach floating toward her. It was a huge peach the size of a man, and it was fully ripe, radiating a peachy red hue from both sides. "What a beautiful peach! This must be my lucky day!" said the woman to herself. She brought the peach home and showed it to her husband. "Let us cut it open," she said. But before her knife touched it, the peach split open and out came a beautiful boy, healthy and charming. "Momotaro! Momotaro! (peach-boy! peach-boy!)," cried the good woman.

"What a wonderful gift," said the good old man. The couple was delighted to have the boy, treating him as their own son. With every bowl of rice he ate, Momotaro grew bigger. Soon he was a handsome young man.

One day, he declared to his foster parents that he had decided to undertake a long journey to Onigashima 'the island of devils' where the demon Akandoji had hidden precious treasures. Momotaro was determined to bring the 'three treasures' (the jewels, the sword, and the mirror) back to his foster parents. "I want to bring kibi-dango 'millet-dumplings' with me," said Momotaro. It was difficult for the couple to let their son go away but they had no choice. The good old woman prepared kibi-dango for him and bid him good-bye.

"Sayonara, dear son, and may all be well with you," said the couple to Momotaro. "Sayonara," said Momotaro to them.

On his way he met a monkey, a pheasant, and a dog who joined him one by one on his adventure in exchange for a kibi-dango each.

The four of them proceeded towards the island of Akandoji. When they reached Akandoji's palace, the pheasant flew over the door and pecked Akandoji on his head; the monkey pinched him, and the dog scared him with his fierce barking. After a day-long fight with Akandoji, Momotaro killed him and brought home the three treasures, which he shared with his friends and everybody. "Thanks, Momotaro," said everyone.

Momotaro's story is a very popular folktale of Japan, but there are no ancient records of the tale and no one knows its origin. Everyone in Japan believes Momotaro's story has always been a part of Japan and the Japanese mind.

The simple folklore depicts the age-old struggle of human beings to make at least a "livable life" for themselves in "this world." The three treasures suggest the three necessary ingredients of a happy life on earth; i.e., jewels (material pleasures), sword (physical protection) and mirror (spirituality /purity).

## *10.0 The concept of time: Urashima and the riddle of time*

A long time ago, there lived a fisherman of the Island Sea called Urashima. He used to go to the sea in the long hours of the night when the moon shone brightly and the pebbles on the seashore shimmered like dreams! Urashima would take his boat out on the green waters of the ocean and catch fish—big and small—for his family. When the mellow light of the moon would drift away from the horizon, Urashima would come back to land and sell his fish. Urashima was quite content with his life.

One day when Urashima had thrown his net in the water and begun to watch the rays of the moon dancing on the waves, he suddenly felt the net grow big and heavy. But it was not a fish inside the net, it was an old wrinkled turtle.

Urashima did not have the heart to bring the turtle home for dinner. "I will save you from all the dinners; I will let you go." The kindly Urashima let the creature slide back into the sea. From the splash of the turtle's jump into the sea there arose a stunningly beautiful girl. She said to Urashima, "You are a kind man Urashima. I am not really a turtle; in reality I am the dragon princess. I live in the palace of the dragon king at the bottom of the ocean, beneath the green waves. The long hands of time do not touch the palace. It is the land of no pain. I am thankful to you for saving my life. In return, I will take you to this wonderland. Come along with me Urashima, and I will take you beyond the limits of time."

"Very well," said Urashima, "but I must return to my home soon, since my old mother is waiting for me." The enchanting princess took Urashima to her palace, which was in the land of dreams where there was no end to the pleasures of life. It was eternal bliss.

Urashima and the dragon princess fell in love with each other and got married in the land of the dragon king. Living under the ocean and not constrained by the fetters of time, Urashima had found the eternal joy of freedom. Even though he was unaffected by the passage of time, time kept rolling on and after a while Urashima, even though he was happy, suddenly felt the intense urge within his heart to return to his own homeland. He could not wait to touch the seashore. He expressed to his wife his desire to return home. "I can not stop you from going if you wish to leave," said his wife "but remember that you may not be able to come back." She gave him a lacquer-box tied up with a silken sachet and cord. "Take this box and keep it with you, always. Do not open it ever! If you open it, you will not be able to return to me again!" said Urashima's wife. As much as it hurt her to see him leave, she could feel the intensity of her husband's yearning for his family, so peacefully and graciously she let him go.

As Urashima's boat touched the shores of the sea, he could not contain his joy, for this was the place where he led his life—a simple fisherman's life on these very shores. And he was back to live it once again.

He ran toward the village. But he was taken aback. The landmarks with which he was familiar were not there anymore. There were no familiar buildings, nor were there any faces which he could recognize. Everything looked so different and strange. Or was Urashima himself a stranger in the village? Everyone who passed by looked on him as a stranger. Finally, Urashima asked a passerby, "Do you know where Urashima's dwelling is?"

"Urashima?—I have never heard this name. You must be lost. There is no one by that name here."

Urashima stopped many more people but received the same answer from all of them. He had lost his home.

As an old man passed by, Urashima asked in final desperation, "Sir, have you heard of Urashima, and his family?"

"I don't know anyone by that name, but my great-grandfather used to tell us the story of a Urashima who was a fisherman and lived here a long time ago. Once he went fishing and was drowned. It must be 400 years ago that it happened. Everyone in his family died long ago. But I can't tell you where his house was or anything else."

Urashima realized that he had actually been away from his village for 400 years, even though to him it seemed only four years. In the land of the deep sea, there was no old age nor death. Urashima was as young now as he had been 400 years ago. But what good was that youth when everyone he cared for was gone, never to return again! In desperation and depression—and partly out of curiosity—Urashima opened the lacquer box given to him by his tortoise-wife. As soon as he opened it, all the years which had been sealed in the box wafted away in the form of misty smoke. With each cloud that came out of the box, Urashima grew older. His hair began to turn gray, and soon his face and gradually the whole of his body was covered with wrinkles. Urashima could feel the gradual disintegration of his body. In no time, time had caught up with him! The next day people found a very old man lying dead on the sandy banks of the ocean.

The myth of Urashima depicts the effort to unravel the mystery of the relationship of time with life and death. According to this myth, the process of beginning, sustenance, and end of life takes place only within the context of Time, and escape from aging and death is possible only when one escapes Time. Urashima's departure from the surface of the ocean to the Land in the deep is suggestive of his escape from Time and his freedom from aging and death.

In Japanese mythology the turtle is a symbol of longevity which implies escape from aging and death. When Urashima opens the box, Time catches up with him, and suddenly he ages and dies.

## *11.0 Ainu mythology*

Although the Ainu are recognized as the indigenous people of the Japanese islands, very little is actually known about their linguistic and cultural heritage. The Ainu (literally 'man') have no written language or history which could provide information about their past. It is believed that the original homeland of the Ainu was a part of the main Japanese islands Honshu (which they lost to the invaders) and Hokkaido, southern Sakhalin and the Kurile islands. Racially the Ainu are Caucasian and have much body hair, which distinguishes them from the Japanese, who are Mongolian who have little body hair.

The Ainu were traditionally hunters and food-gatherers who lived in different parts of the islands. Later on, the Ainu were displaced by the invading Japanese, and at present the Ainu communities are concentrated in the northern tips of the islands.

The Ainu system of beliefs varies from region to region. However, there are some common beliefs which they share, such as belief in the soul, *kamui,* and the bear festival.

*Kamui is* the term used by the Ainu for their deity. *Kamui* refers to animals such as bears, foxes, birds, sea animals such as fish, seals, etc., the sun, the moon, fire and water. Whether or not all forms of nature are deified in the Ainu system of beliefs is a matter of discussion. However, it is clear that those aspects of nature which directly or indirectly affect the life of human beings are viewed as *kamui.* Of all the deities, the bear is viewed as the supreme *kamui* who provides food and clothing for the Ainu.

The Ainu do not treat human life separately from the animals, birds and nature; rather they emphasize a constant interaction among humans, animals, and *kamui*. According to the Ainu the soul represents the intrinsic connection between *kamui* and the human world. Through these souls (abiding in bodies/forms) *kamui* regulate the world. Human beings should understand this truth and pay respect to all forms of nature and perform all actions which are in consonance with the order of *kamui*.

The concept which unifies the various forms of nature (including humans) is the soul. The soul is the divine aspect of the perishable body. The soul does not die; it leaves the body and goes to heaven. When a human being or an animal dies, the Ainu perform an elaborate funeral ritual for the departing soul, Death is the moment of freedom for the soul from the body. Therefore, the Ainu are extremely particular about the correct performance of funeral rites for the dead (especially to ensure peace for the soul in the world of the dead). It is believed that the improper treatment of a dead body results in the soul's turning into a demon, who consequently brings about illness and other disasters for the family of the dead in particular, and to the Ainu community in general. Several shamanic practices are followed during the funeral rites to indicate the devotion of the community to the dead and to the soul of the dead.

Central to the Ainu rituals is the ceremony of the bear. The ceremony involves a ritual killing of a bear. This ceremony is performed on a large scale and is attended by the community at large. A bear is viewed as a mountain deity who has taken the form of a bear to bless the Ainu people with meat and clothing. The ritual killing of the bear symbolizes the ritual of freeing the soul of the bear deity from its animal body so that it can go back to its abode and later return to the Ainu once again in the form of a bear to bless them with food and warm fur. Thus this ceremony is not viewed as the sacrifice of a living animal, but rather as a ritual release of a soul; and therefore it is a festival of joy and freedom. The ceremony is always accompanied by entertaining dances, music, and a big feast. A special bear cub is raised for two to three years before it is ritually "freed" from the bondage of its animal form.

Okikirumi Kamui was the son of a deity, who, the Ainu believe, came down to earth to teach them to till the land, build dwellings, and make their clothing. He also taught them how to make *sake* 'wine'. This deity is believed to be the destroyer of the demon who ruled over the world before his arrival. The Ainu believe that it was because they did not comply with Okikirumi's orders and rules that he left their land and went away to heaven. It is only if they behave properly, according to tradition, that the benevolent one will one day return to their land.

The Ainu tradition is largely maintained by oral transmission through generations. The oral literature primarily consists of songs, chants and long narratives. While the songs and chants are employed at religious as well as social ceremonies, the prose narratives are part of Ainu moral/ethical education. The souls of the ancestors, the origin of the world, and the significance and meaning of the rituals are the dominant themes of the stories narrated by story-tellers. The cultural heroes are generally deified in the stories and are generally held in high respect by the community.

### *11.1 Ainu creation myths: The wagtail bird and the creation of the world*

That mighty, all-pervasive round ball of water—the ocean—existed even when there was as yet no earth, no islands and no human beings. Above this vast endless ocean was heaven, where God lived. God decided to create the earth. He made a wag-tail bird and sent it to this ocean, which was an unordered chaos, full of slush. The wagtail fluttered its wings and stirred the ocean once, twice and many more times. The slush became muddier and thicker. As the wagtail kept fluttering its wings, there appeared on the surface of the ocean some dry patches of land; these were the floating islands. The word for 'world' in the Ainu language is moshiri "floating land."

This is the myth of the origin of the world (i.e., the Japanese islands) in the Ainu culture. The creation of the world is viewed here as the creation of order from chaos. Moreover, this myth, like other myths, assumes that creation is in some sense a result or an outcome of movement. The movement (the stirring of the ocean) here is caused by the wagtail bird.

### *11.2 Earth rests on a fish*

According to Ainu beliefs, the earth is round like a ball and not flat. It rests on a huge fish (trout) floating on the ocean. This fish is called the backbone fish of the world. As the fish moves, the earth trembles; when it exhales and inhales, the tides flow and ebb. Earthquakes, according to the Ainu, are caused by the shaking of the trout.

This fish can get violent and cause a great deal of trouble. There are gods who lay their hands on the fish to support it so that it does not lose its balance and the earth does not suffer from the resulting turmoil.

The Ainu believe that gods are the only creatures who are allowed to eat with one hand, since their other hand rests on the fish all the time. Consequently, all Ainu are supposed to eat with two hands; if a child forgets the custom of eating with two hands and eats with one hand, the mother asks the child, "Are you a god?"

### *11.3 From where did the Ainu come: the creation of the Ainu race*

Ainu beliefs vary on the issue of the origin of the human race. According to some, the bear is their ancestor. This belief is based on the fact that the Ainu are as hairy as the bear and also on the fact that the bear is the source of their life; i.e. it provides them food and warmth (Ainu eat bear-meat and wear warm clothing made of bear-fur). The bear festival is dedicated to the ancestor "bear."

According to another Ainu belief, the origin of the Ainu race is a goddess and a dog. In a place where the earth was not inhabited by gods or human beings, there came floating in a boat a heavenly goddess. She did not know how to adapt to the earthly dwelling. A male dog came from somewhere and stayed with her and showed her a rock cave where she lived. The dog helped her find fruit and food and protected her.

After they had lived together for a long time, according to Ainu myth, the goddess gave birth to two babies as hairy as the dog. Thus the Ainu trace the "heavenly" origin of their race.

# SELECTED READINGS

## Chapter 1: Mythology: Its Form and Function


Ausband, S. C. 1983. *Myth and Meaning, Myth and Order.* Georgia: Mercer University Press.

Campbell, J. 1959 (Reprint 1971. *The Masks of God: Oriental Mythology.* New York: The Viking Press.

———. 1988. *The Power of Myth (with Bill Moyers).* B. S. Flowers (ed.) New York: Doubleday.

Darian, S. G. 1978. *The Ganges in Myth and History.* Honolulu: University of Hawaii Press.

Eliade, M. 1958. *Patterns in Comparative Religion.* New York: Sheed and Ward.

———. 1960. *Myths, Dreams, and Mysteries.* New York: Harper and Brothers Publishers.

———. (translated from French by W. R. Trask) 1963. *Myth and Reality.* New York: Harper and Row.

Frazer, J. G. 1922. (Reprint 1942). *The Golden Bough: A Study in Magic and Religion.* New York: The Macmillan Company.

Girardot, N. J. 1988. *Myth and Meaning in Early Taoism: The Theme of Chaos (hun-tun).* Berkeley: University of California Press.

Hume, D. 1949. *Treatise on Human Nature.* L. A. Shelby-Bigge (ed.) Oxford: Clarendon Press.

Jung, C. 1917. *Collected Papers on a Science of Mythology.* New York: Moffat Yard.

Kitagawa, J. M. and C. H. Long. 1969. *Myths and Symbols.* Chicago: The University of Chicago Press.

Levi-Strauss, C. 1969. *The Raw and the Cooked: Introduction to a Science of Mythology.*

*Magic, Science, and Religion.* Malinowski, B. 1954. Garden City, NY: Doubleday.

Otto, R. 1929. (Reprinted 1958). *The Idea of the Holy.* London: Oxford.

Puhvel, J. 1987. *Comparative Mythology.* Baltimore: The John Hopkins University Press.

Zimmer, H. 1962. *Myths and Symbols in Indian Art and Civilization.* Bollingen Library 6. J. Campbell (ed.) New York: Harper and Row.

## Chapter 2: The Indus Valley Civilization

Basham, A. 1954. *The Wonder That Was India.* NY: Grove Press. Chapts. 1 and 2.

Fairservis, Jr. W. A. 1975. *The Roots of Ancient India.* 2nd Revised Edition. Chicago: University of Chicago Press.

Campbell, J. 1971. *The Masks of God: Oriental Mythology.* New York: The Viking Press.

Hopkins, T. J. 1971. *The Religious Life of Man: The Hindu Religious Tradition.* Dickenson: Encino, CA. (Chapt. 1)

James, E. O. 1959. *The Cult of the Mother Goddess: An Archaeological and Documentary Study.* London: Thames and Hudson.

Jayakar, P. 1980. *The Earthen Drum: An Introduction to the Ritual Arts of Rural India.* New Delhi: National Museum.

Mackay, E. 1938. *Further Excavations at Mohenjo-Daro.* 2 Vols. Delhi.

Marshall, J. H. 1931. *Mohenjo-daro and the Indus Civilization.* 3 vols. London: A. Probsthain.

Nagar, S. L. 1989. *The Universal Mother.* Delhi: Atmaram.

Possehl, G. L. (ed.) 1979. *Ancient Cities of the Indus.* New Delhi: Vikas.

Preston, J. J. (ed.) 1982. *Mother Worship: Theme and Variations.* Chapel Hill: North Carolina University Press.

Wheeler, M. 1968. *The Indus Civilization.* Cambridge: Cambridge University Press.

## Chapter 3: Mythology of the Vedas

Basham, A. L. 1954. *The Wonder That Was India.* NY: Grove Press.

Dandekar, R. N. 1979. *Vedic Mythological Tracts.* Delhi: Ajanta Publications.

———. 1979. *Insights into Hinduism.* Delhi: Ajanta Publications.

Das Gupta, S. N. 1922. (Reprint 1951). *A History of Indian Philosophy.* Cambridge: The University Press.

———. and S. K. De. 1947. (Reprint 1962). *History of Sanskrit Literature.* Vol. I. Calcutta: University of Calcutta.

De Bary, W. T., (ed.) 1958. *Sources of Indian Tradition.* New York: Columbia University Press.

Dimmitt, C. and J. A. B. Van Buitenen. 1978. *Classical Hindu Mythology: A Reader in the Sanskrit Purāṇas.* Philadelphia: Temple University Press.

Embree, A. T. 1966. *The Hindu Tradition.* New York: Modern Library.

Gonda, J. 1977. *Vedic Literature.* Wiesbaden: Harrassowitz.

Gupta, S. 1973. *Loves of Hindu Gods and Sages.* Bombay: Allied Publishers.

———. 1974. *Vishnu and His Incarnations.* New Delhi: Somaiya Publications.

Keith, A. B. 1920. Reprint 1961. *History of Sanskrit Literature.* Oxford: University Press.

———. 1947. *The Religion and Philosophy of the Vedas and Upaniṣads.* Cambridge: Harvard University Press.

Keith, A. B. and A. J. Carnoy. 1926. *Mythology of All Races.* Vol, VI, "Indian, Iranian." Boston: Marshall Jones Company.

Kosambi, D. D. 1965. *Ancient India: A History of its Culture and Civilization.* New York: Random House.

Lannoy, R. 1971. *The Speaking Tree: A Study of Indian Culture and Society.* London: Oxford University Press.

MacDonell, A. A. 1928. *History of Sanskrit Literature.* London: W. Heinmann.

MacDonell, A. A. 1963. *The Vedic Mythology.* Varanasi: Indological Book House.

Macfie, J. M. 1924. *Myths and Legends of India; An Introduction to the Study of Hinduism.* Edinburgh: T. and T. Clark.

Mandal, K. K. 1966. *A Comparative Study of the Concepts of Space and Time in Indian Thought.* Banaras: Chowkhamba.

Mandelbaum, D. G. 1964. Introduction: process and structure in South Asian religion. In Harper, Edward B., ed. *Religion in South Asia.* Seattle: University of Washington Press.

Martin, E. 0. 1972. *The Gods of India.* Delhi: Indological Book House.

Narayan, R. K. 1964. *Gods, Demons and Others.* New York: Viking.

Rādhākrishnan. 1953. *The Principal Upaniṣads.* New York: Harper and Row.

Ranade, R. D. 1954. *Pathway to God in Hindi Literature.* Sangli: Adhyatma Vidya Mandir.

Smith, D. 1981. *The Picturebook Rāmāyaṇa.* Maxwell: Syracuse, NY: School of Citizenship and Public Affairs.

Thomas, P. 1980. *Epics, Myths and Legends of India.* Bombay: Taraporevala Sons.

### Chapter 4: Mythology of the Epics: The Rāmāyaṇa

Aiyangar, K. V. R. S. 1952. *Some Aspects of the Hindu View of Life According to Dharma Sāstra.* Baroda: Oriental Institute.

Basham, A. L. 1959. *The Wonder That Was India.* New York: Grove Press. Chapter 9.

Brockington, J. L. 19,54. *Righteous Rama.* Bombay: Oxford University Press.

Buck, W. 1976. *Ramayana: King Rama's Way.* Berkeley: Universitiy of California.

Goldman, R. P. 1984. (trans.) The *Rāmāyaṇa* of Vālmīki. Vol. 1. *Bālakānda.* Princeton: Princeton University Press.

Gonda, J. 1965. Change *and Continuity in Indian Religion.* The Hague: Mouton.

Griffith, R. T. H. (tr.) 1895. The *Ramayana of Valmiki.* London: Trubner/Banares: E. J. Lazarus and Co.

———. *Hindu Literature*. 1900. New York: Colonial Press.

Iyer, 1. S. 1977. *The Concept of Tapas in Valmiki Ramayan*a. Madras: Samskrita Academy.

Kalghatgi, T. G. 1972. *Karma and Rebirth*. Ahlmadabad: D. Institute of Indology.

Kane, P. V. 1930–62. *(5 vols.) History of Dharmaśastr*a. Poona: handarkar Oriental Research Institute.

Khan, B. 1965. *The Concept of Dharma in Valmiki Ramayana*. Delhi: Munshiram Manoharlal.

Mees, G. H. 1935. Reprint 1960. *Dharma and Society.* Delhi: Scema Publications.

Moore, C. A. 1968 (ed.) *The Status of the Individual: East and West.* Honolulu: University of Hawaii Press.

O'Flaherty, W. D. 1975. *Hindu Myths*. Middlesex, England: Penguin Books.

———. 1976. *The Origins of Evil in Hindu Mythology*. Berkeley: University of California Press.

———. (ed.) 1980. *Karma and Rebirth in Classical Indian Traditions*. Berkeley: University of California Press.

———. and J. Duncan M. Derrett. 1978. *The Concept of Duty in South Asia*. New Delhi: Vikas Publishing House.

Raghavan, V. 1980. *The Ramayana Tradition in Asia*. Bombay: Sahitya Akademi.

Ragunathan, N. (tr.) 1981. *Srimad Valmiki Ramayanam*. Madras. Vighneswara.

Raychaudhuri, A. K. 1950. *The Doctrine of Māyā.* 2nd Revised Edition. Calcutta: DasGupta.

Reyna, R. 1962. *The Concept of Māyā from the Vedas to the Twentieth Century*. Bombay: Asia Publishing House.

*Sharma, R. 1971. A Socio-political Study of the Valmiki Ramayana*. Delhi: Motilal Banarsidass.

Shastri, H. P. (tr.) 1976 *The Ramayana of Valmiki.* London: Shanti Sadan, 3 volumes.

Smith, H. D. 1983. *Reading the Rāmāyaṇa: A Bibliographic Guide for Students and College Teachers.* New York: Syracuse University Press.

Thomas, P. 1980. *Epics, Myths and Legends of India.* Bombay: Taraporevala Sons.

Vyas, S. N. 1967. *India in the Ramayana Age.* Delhi: Atma Ram.

## Chapter 5: Mythology of the Epics: The Mahābhārata

Blair, J. 196 1. *Heat in the Rigveda and Atharvaveda.* New Haven. American Oriental Society.

Eliade, M. 1969. *Yoga, Immortality and Freedom.* 2nd Edition. Princeton: Princeton University Press.

———. 1978. *A History of Religious Ideas. Vol. 1.* Chicago: The University of Chicago Press.

Hazra, R. C. 1940. (Reprint 1975) *Studies in the Puranic Records on Hindu Rites and Customs.* Delhi: Motilal Banarsidass.

Hiltebeitel, A. 1976. *The Ritual of Battle. Krishna in the Mahabharata.* New York. Cornell University Press.

Hopkins, E. W. 1970 (2nd ed.). *The Religions* of *India. New* Delhi: Munshiram Manoharlal.

Jayal, S. 1966. *The Status of Women in the Epics.* Delhi: Motilal Banarsidass.

Knipe, D. M. 1975. *In the Image of Fire: Vedic Experiences of Heat.* Delhi: Motilal Banarsidass.

Narasiṃhan, C. V. 1965. *The Mahābhārata.* New Delhi: Oxford Book Company.

Patil, N. B. 1983. The *Folklore in the Mahabharata.* Delhi: Ajanta.

Pusalkar, A. D. 1955. *Studies in the Epics and Purāṇas.* Bombay: Bharatiya Vidya Bhavan.

Ganguli, K. M. (trans.) 1963. *The Mahābhārata of* Krishna Dwaipayana Vyāsa. 12 vols. Calcutta: Oriental Publishing Company.

Van Buitenen, J. A. B. 1973–1978. The *Mahābhārata. 3* vols. Chicago: The University of Chicago Press.

## Chapter 6: The Bhagavadgītā: "The Divine Song"

Barborka, G. A. 1967. *The Pearl of the Orient.* Wheaton, IL: The Theosophical Publishing House.

Bolle, K. 1979. *The Bhagavadgītā, A New Translation.* Berkeley and Los Angeles: University of California Press.

Dasgupta, S. N. 1924. (Reprint 1973). *Yoga as Philosophy* and *Religion.* Delhi: Motilal Banarsidass.

———. 1930. (Reprint 1974). *Yoga Philosophy in Relation to Other Systems of Thought.* Delhi: Motilal Banarsidass.

Edgerton, F. 1946. *The Bhagavadgītā, translated and interpreted.* 2 vols. Cambridge: Harvard University Press.

Feuerstein, G. 1980. *The Philosophy of Classical Yoga.* New York: St. Martin's Press.

Miller, B. S. 1986. *The Bhagavad-Gita: Krishna's Council in Time of War.* New York: Columbia University Press.

Minor, R. (ed.) 1986. *Modern Indian Interpreters of the Bhagavadgītā.* Albany: State University of New York Press.

Radhakrishnan, S. 1948. *The Bhagavadgītā.* London: George Allen and Unwin Ltd.

Tilak, B. G. 1935–36. *Gītārahasya.* (trans.) Poona: Tilak Brothers.

Van Buitenen, J.A.B. 1981. *The Bhagavadgītā in the Mahabharata.* Chicago: Chicago University Press.

Zaehner, R.C. 1969. *The Bhagavad-gitā. Oxford:* The Clarendon Press.

## Chapter 7: The Mythology of Kṛṣṇa: The Divine As Human

Archer, W.G. 1957. *The Loves of Krishna.* New York: Macmillan.

Banerjee, P. 1981. *The Blue God.* New Delhi: Lalit Kala Academy.

Dimock, E. C. Jr. and Denise Levertov, trans. 1964. *In Praise of Krishna: Songs from the Bengali.* Garden City, N.Y.: Doubleday.

Hawley, J. S. 1961. *At Play with Krishna: Pilgrimage Dramas from Brindavan.* Princeton: Princeton University Press.

———. 1983. *Krishna, The Butter Thief.* Princeton: Princeton University Press.

———. and D. M. Wulff (eds.) 1982. *The Divine Consort: Rādhā and the Goddesses of India.* Berkeley Religious Studies Series. Berkeley: University of California Press.

Hutchins, F. G. 1980. *Young Krishna* (translated from the Sanskrit *Harivamśa).* West Franklin, N.H.: Berkeley Religious Studies Series.

Jayadeva. *Love Song of the Dark Lord,* trans. by Barbara Stoller Miller. 1977. New York: Columbia University Press.

Kinsley, D. 1979. *The Divine Player: A Study of Kṛṣṇa Līlā.* Delhi: Motilal Banarsidass.

Lal, K. 1971. *The Religion of Love.* Delhi: Arts and Letters.

Miller, B.S. 1977. *Jayadeva Gitagovinda: Love Song of the Dark Lord (Eng. Trans.).* New York: Columbia University Press.

Sanyal, J. M. *The Shrimad-Bhagavatam of Krishna—Dwaipayana Vyasa.* Vol. 1. (translation). Calcutta: Oriental Publishing Company.

Singer, M., ed. 1966. Krishna: *Myths, Rites, and Attitudes.* Chicago: Chicago University Press.

## Chapter 8: The Mythology of Śiva: Destruction as Divine

Agarwala, V. S. 1965. *Shiva Mahadeva.* Varanasi: Vedi Academy.

Bhandarkar, R. G. 1965. *Vaisnavism Saivism and Minor Religious Systems.* Varanasi: Indological Book House.

Campbell, J. 1971. *The Masks of God: Oriental Mythology.* New York: Viking Press.

Coomaraswamy, A. 1952. *The Dance of Shiva.* Bombay: Asia Publishing House.

Courtright, P. B. 1985. *Gaṇeśa: Lord of Obstacles, Lord of Beginnings.* Oxford: University Press.

Danielou, A. 1964. *The Gods of India: Hindu Polytheism.* London. Rutledge and Kegan Paul.

Getty, A. 1936. (1971. 2nd edition) *Gaṇeśa: A Monograph on the Elephant-faced God.* New Delhi: Munshiram Manoharlal.

Gonda, J. 1970. *Viṣṇuism and Sivism.* London: The Athlone Press.

Gupta, S.M. 1979. *Legends Around Shiva.* Bombay: Somaiya Publications Pvt. Ltd.

Kramrisch, S. 1961. *The Presence of Śiva.* Princeton: Princeton University Press.

O'Flaherty, W. 1973. *Asceticism and Eroticism in the Mythology of Śiva.* New York: Oxford University Press.

———. 1975. *Hindu Myths: A Sourcebook Translated from Sanskrit.* Harmondsworth: Penguin Books Limited.

———. 1976. *The Origins of Evil in Hindu Mythology.* Berkeley: University of California Press.

———. 1981. *Śiva: The Erotic Ascetic.* Oxford: Oxford University Press.

Ramanujan, A. K. 1973. trans. *Speaking of Shiva.* Penguin Books.

Rao, T. A. G. 1916. *Elements of Hindu Iconography.* (Reprinted 1968). Delhi: Madras Law Printing House.

Thomas, P. 1980. *Epics, Myths, and Legends of India.* Bombay: D. B. Taraporewala Sons and Co. Private Ltd.

## Chapter 9: Buddhist Mythology and Thought

Boyd, J. W. 1975. *Satan and Māra: Christian and Buddhist Symbols of Evil.* Leiden: Brill.

Coomaraswamy, A. K. 1928. *Buddha and the Gospel of Buddhism.* London: Harrap.

Chang, G. C. C. 1971. *The Buddhist Teaching of Totality.* University Park, PA.: Pennsylvania State University.

Ch'en, K. S. 1964. *Buddhism in China: A Historical Survey.* Princeton: Princeton University Press.

Conze, E., trans. 1958. *Buddhist Wisdom Books,* containing "The Diamond Sutra" and "The Heart Sūtra". London: George Allen and Unwin, Ltd.

———. 1959. *Buddhism: Its Essence and Development.* Second edition. New York: Harper Torchbook.

———. trans. 1973. *The Perfection of Wisdom in Eight Thousand Lines and its Verse Summary.* Berkeley: Four Seasons Foundation.

———. 1967. *Buddhist Thought in India.* Ann Arbor: University of Michigan Press.

Cowell, E. B. (ed.) 1973. *The Jātaka, or Stories of the Buddha's Former Births.* London: Pāli Text Society.

Dayal, H. 1930. (Reprint 1970). *The Bodhisattva Doctrine in Buddhist Sanskrit Literature.* Delhi: Motilal Banarsidass.

DeBary, W. T., ed. 1969. *The Buddhist Tradition in India, China, and Japan.* New York: The Modern Library.

Eliot, C. 1921. (Reprint 1954). *Hinduism and Buddhism.* London: Routledge and Kegan Paul.

Horner, I. B. 1936. (Reprint 1979). *The Early Buddhist Theory of Man Perfected.* New Delhi: Oriental Books Reprint Corporation.

Katz, N. 1982. *Buddhist Images of Human Perfection: The Arhant of Suttapītaka compared with the Bodhisattva and the Mahāsīddhā.* Delhi: Motilal Banarsidass.

Kloetzli, W. R. 1983. *Buddhist Cosmology: from Single World System to Pureland: Science and Technology in the Images of Motion and Light.* Delhi: Motilal Banarsidass.

Ling, T. O. 1962. *Buddhism and the Mythology of Evil: A Study in Theravāda Buddhism.* London: George Allen and Unwin.

Murti, T. R. V. 1955. *The Central Philosophy of Buddhism: A Study of the Mādhyamika System.* 2nd Edition. London: George Allen and Unwin.

Percheron, M. 1960. *The Marvelous Life of the Buddha.* New York: St. Martin's Press.

Rāhula, W. 1962. *What the Buddha Taught.* New York: Evergreen Press.

Reynolds, F. E. 1981. *Guide to the Buddhist Religion.* Boston: Hall.

Rhys Davids, Mrs. C. AF, (ed.) *Buddhist Birth Stories.* London: Routledge and Kegan Perul.

Robinson, R. 1970. *The Buddhist Religion—A Historical Introduction.* Encino and Belmont (Calif.): Dickenson Pub. Co., Inc.

Stcherbatsky, T. 1956. *The Central Conception of Buddhism.* London: Royal Asiatic Society, 1923.

Streng, F. J. 1967. *Emptiness: A Study in Religious Meaning.* Nashville: Abingdon Press.

Suzuki, D. T. 1963. *Outlines* of *Mahāyāna Buddhism.* New York: Schocken Books.

Takakusu, J. 1947. *The Essentials of Buddhist Philosophy.* Honolulu: University of Hawaii Press.

Thomas, E. J. 1924. *The Life of the Buddha as Legend and History.* London: Routledge and Kegan Paul.

Welbon, G. R. 1968. *The Buddhist Nirvāṇa and Its Western Interpreters.* Chicago: University of Chicago Press.

Wright, A. F. 1959. *Buddhism in Chinese History.* Stanford: Stanford University Press.

## Chapter 10: Confucius: The Wisdom of Heaven

*The Analects: or the Conversations of Confucius with His Disciples.* 1937. London: Oxford University Press.

Chai, C., ed. 1965. *The Sacred Books of Confucius and Other Confucian Classics.* New York: University Press.

Chien, Mu. 1964. *Lun Yu Hsin Chien (New Interpretation of the Analects).* Hong Kong: Hsin Ya Yen Chiu Suo

Do-Dinh, P. 1969. *Confucius and Chinese Humanism.* New York: Funk and Wagnalls.

Fingarette, H. 1972. *Confucius—the Secular as Sacre*d. New York: Harper and Row.

Chen, Ivan. (trans.) 1920. *The Book of Filial Duty.* London: Murray.

Johnston, R. F. 1934. *Confucius and Modern Chin*a. London: V. Gollancz Ltd.

Kaplan, F., et. al. 1979. *Encyclopedia of China Today.* New York: Harper and Row.

Kramer, R. P. (trans.) 1950. *K'ung Tzu Chia Yu. The School Sayings of Confucius.* Leiden: Brill.

Lau, D. C. (trans.) 1979. *Confucius, The Analects (Lun yu).* Harmondsworth: Penguin.

*The Sayings of Confucius and a New Translation.* 1937. London: Murray.

## Chapter 11: The Way of Tao

Bodde, D. (Blanc, C. L. and Dorothy Barai, eds.) 1981. *Essays on Chinese Civilization.* Princeton: Princeton University Press.

Blofield, J. E. *Beyond the Gods: Taoist and Buddhist Mysticism.* London: Allen and Unwin.

Bonsall, B. 1934. *Confucianism and Taoism.* London: Epworth Press.

Chan, W-T. (trans.) 1963. *The Way of Lao Tzu.* New York: Bobbs-Merrill.

Chao, Shao-hsien. 1977. *Laotzu Yao Yi.* Taipei: Taiwan Chung Hua Shu Chiu.

Lao/Tao Teh Ching. 1961. New York: St. John's University Press.

Maspero, H. 1981. (trans. by Frank A. Kierman) *Taoism and Chinese Religion*. Amherst, Mass.: University of Massachusetts Press.

McNaughton, W. 1971. *The Taoist Vision*. Ann Arbor: University of Michigan.

Needham, J. 1956. *Science and Civilization in China. Vol. 2. History of Scientific Thought*. Cambridge, England: Cambridge University Press.

Overmyer, D. L. 1986. *Religions of China*. San Francisco: Harper and Row Publishers.

Thompson, L. G. 1989. *Chinese Religion*. Belmont, CA. Wadsworth Publishing Company.

Walls, V. and J. (eds. and trans.) 1984. *Classical Chinese Myths*. Hong Kong: Joint Publishing Company.

Watts, A. W. 1975: *Tao: The Watercourse Way*. New York: Pantheon Books.

Werner, E. T. C. 1922 (Reprint 1971). *Myths and Legends of China*. New York: Benjamin Blom.

## Chapter 12: Zen: Looking Inward

Bancroft, A. 1979. *Zen. Direct Pointing to Reality*. New York: Crossroad.

Cheng, Chao-hsiung. 1980. *Chung Kuo Chan Hsueh Ku Shih*. Hong Kong: Yu Chou Chu Pan She.

Eido, R. S. 1979. *Golden Wind. Zen Talks*. Tokyo: Japan Publications.

Hau, H. 1975. *The Sound of the One Hand: 28 Zen Koans with Answers*. New York: Basic Books.

Humphreys, C. 1968. *Zen: A Way* of *Life*. New York: Emerson Books.

Kapleau, R. P. 1980. *The Three Pillars of Zen*. New York: Anchor Press.

Kusano, E. 1962. *Stories Behind Noh and Kabuki Plays*. Tokyo: Tokyo News Service.

Leggett, T. 1978. *Zen and The* Ways. Boulder: Shambhalal.

Miura, 1. and R. Fuller Sasaki. 1965. *The Zen Koan. Its History and Use in Rinzai Zen*. New York: Harcourt, Brace and World.

Miura, I. and R. Fuller Sasaki. 1966. *Zen Dust: The History of the Koan and Koan Study in Rinzai (Lin-chih) Zen*. Kyoto: The First Zen Institute of America.

Reps, P. 1959. *Zen Telegrams: 81 Picture Poems*. Rutland, VT: C. E. Tuttle Co.

———. 1961. *Zen Flesh, Zen Bones: A Collection of Zen and pre-Zen Writings*. Garden City, New York: Anchor Books.

Ross, N. W. 1963. *Three Ways of Asian Wisdom: Hinduism, Buddhism, Zen and their Significance for the West*. New York: Simon and Schuster.

Suzuki, D. T. 1959. *Zen and* Japanese *Culture.* New York: Bollinjen Foundation.

Watts, A. W. 1957. *The Way of Zen*. New York: Vintage Books.

## Chapter 13: Japanese Mythology: Shinto and Ainu

Anesaki, M. 1931. *The History of Japanese Religion.* Reprint. 1963. Rutland, Vt.. Charles E. Tuttle.

Akiyama, A. 1936. *Shinto and Its Architecture.* Kyoto: Japan Welcome Society.

Aston, W. G. 1896. (Reprint 1956.) Nihongi, *Chronicles of Japan from the Earliest Times to A.D. 697.* London: Allen and Unwin

———. 1907. Shinto: The *Ancient Religion of Japan.* London: A. Constable and Company.

Earhart, H. B. 1984. *Religions of Japan: Many Traditions Within One Sacred Way.* San Francisco: Harper and Row Publishers.

Fujisawa, C. 1959. *Zen and Shinto: the Story of Japanese Philosophy.* New York: Philosophical Library.

Herbert, J. 1967. *Shinto: The Fountainhead of Japan.* London: Allen and Unwin.

Holtom, D. C. 1938. (Reprint 1965). *The National Faith of Japan. A Study in Modern Shinto.* New York: Paragon.

Huntly, H. 1910. *Kami-no-michi. The Way of the Gods in Japan,* London: Rebman.

Kageyama, H. 1976. *Shinto Arts: Nature, Gods and Man in Japan.* New York: Japan Society.

Kato, G. 1971. *A Study of Shinto: the Religion of the Japanese Nation.* London: Curzon.

Kitagawa, J. M. 1961. "Ainu Bear Festival (Iomante)." pp. 95–151. In *History of Religions I* (No. 1 Summer 1961).

———. 1966. *Religion in Japanese History.* New York: Columbia University Press.

———. 1987. *On Understanding Japanese Religion.* Princeton: Princeton University Press.

Miller, A. J. 1983. "Religions of China and Japan." *Religions of the World.* New York: St. Martin's Press.

Munro, N. G. 1962 . *Ainu Creed and Cult.* New York: Columbia University Press.

Muraoka, T. 1964. (trans. by Delmar M. Brown and James T. Araki). *Studies in Shinto Thought.* Tokyo: Japanese National Commission for UNESCO.

Ono, S. 1962. Shinto: *The Kami Way.* Tokyo: Charles E. Tuttle Company.

Philippi, D. L. (trans.) 1969. *Kojiki.* Princeton: Princeton University Press.

———. 1979. *Songs of Gods, Songs of Humans.* Princeton: Princeton University Press.

Piggott, J. 1969. *Japanese Mythology.* London: Paul Hamlyn.

Ross, F. 1965. *Shinto, the Way of Japan.* Boston: Beacon Press.

Saunders, D. 1961. "Japanese Mythology." *In Mythologies of the Ancient World.* S. N. Kramer (ed.) Anchor Books.

Wheeler, P. 1952. *The Sacred Scriptures of the Japanese.* New York: Henry Schumkan.

Yoshimura, T. 1935. *Shinto (the Way of the Gods).* Tokyo: The Japan Times and Mail.